Praise fo

"Tracy Clark-Flory is among the [...] to grow up in a digital world, an A[...] Her journey reveals possibilities, l[...] messages that present 'empowered [...] mance: being desirable rather than recognizing your desires; pleasing others rather than understanding your pleasure; being wanted rather than asking for what you want. This book is absolutely, crucially important to read in order to understand the world in which all girls, and boys, now come of age."

—Peggy Orenstein, *New York Times* bestselling author of *Girls & Sex*

"This book is about much more than sex—it's a candid and brave story about the collision of fantasies, ideals, and truths; it's a story about the search for self."

—Daniel Bergner, author of *What Do Women Want?: Adventures in the Science of Female Desire*

"I loved reading *Want Me*—its joys and sorrows, laughter and pain, all the memories and mysteries that resonate with women of all ages who wonder how we got here. A compelling, important read."

—Debby Herbenick, author of *Because It Feels Good*

"Tracy Clark-Flory is one of the best journalists of our generation writing about sexuality. When she turns her incisive lens on herself, the results are revelatory. The book is everything I want a memoir to be—a bracingly honest, messy, self-aware, inspiring road map to sexual selfhood."

—Tristan Taormino, sex educator and bestselling author of *Take Me There*

PENGUIN BOOKS

WANT ME

Tracy Clark-Flory is a senior staff writer at Jezebel. Her work has been published in *Cosmopolitan*, *Elle*, *Esquire*, *Marie Claire*, *Salon*, the *Guardian*, *Women's Health*, and the yearly *Best Sex Writing* anthology. She lives in the San Francisco Bay Area with her family.

Want Me

A SEX WRITER'S JOURNEY
INTO THE HEART OF DESIRE

Tracy Clark-Flory

PENGUIN BOOKS

PENGUIN BOOKS

An imprint of Penguin Random House LLC
penguinrandomhouse.com

Copyright © 2021 by Tracy Clark-Flory
Penguin supports copyright. Copyright fuels creativity,
encourages diverse voices, promotes free speech, and creates a vibrant culture.
Thank you for buying an authorized edition of this book and for complying with
copyright laws by not reproducing, scanning, or distributing any part of it in
any form without permission. You are supporting writers and allowing
Penguin to continue to publish books for every reader.

LIBRARY OF CONGRESS CATALOGING-IN-PUBLICATION DATA

Names: Clark-Flory, Tracy, author.
Title: Want me : a sex writer's journey into the heart
of desire / Tracy Clark-Flory.
Description: New York : Penguin Books, 2021. |
Includes bibliographical references. |
Identifiers: LCCN 2020045383 (print) | LCCN 2020045384 (ebook) |
ISBN 9780143134619 (paperback) | ISBN 9780525506423 (ebook)
Subjects: LCSH: Clark-Flory, Tracy. | Clark-Flory,
Tracy—Sexual behavior. | Journalists—United States—Biography. |
Self-realization in women.
Classification: LCC PN4874.C54 A3 2021 (print) |
LCC PN4874.C54 (ebook) | DDC 070.4/49306092 [B]—dc23
LC record available at https://lccn.loc.gov/2020045383
LC ebook record available at https://lccn.loc.gov/2020045384

Printed in the United States of America
3 5 7 9 10 8 6 4

Set in Adobe Caslon Pro
Designed by Cassandra Garruzzo

Some names and identifying characteristics have been changed to
protect the privacy of the individuals involved.

For Mom

Contents

I'm always interested to hear how a woman conceives of herself as a sexual person, because there is really no map for this, only a series of contradictory and shaming warnings. So whatever any of us comes up with is going to be wholly unique and perhaps a little monstrous—like a creature that has survived multiple attacks yet still walks, still desires.

Miranda July[1]

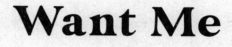

Want Me

"Girls These Days"

I'm in a warehouse in Los Angeles's San Fernando Valley anxiously scribbling in my reporter's notebook while waiting for a porn shoot to begin. Charles Dera, a performer with jet-black hair and a well-groomed beard to match, is crouched in front of me, stretching his calves. Tommy Gunn, a legendary performer named after his biceps, is sitting on the floor flipping through a release form. He hops to a stand and asks to borrow my pen.

We're in a fluorescent-lit office with paneled ceiling tiles and shuttered vertical blinds. A metal gurney and hospital privacy curtain are pushed into a corner alongside a rolling cart of textbooks and a plastic houseplant. Fake eyelashes and foundation in various shades of beige are spread out on a vintage wooden desk that practically purrs, "The principal will see you now." As a reporter writing about sex, I've been on porn sets more times than I can count, but this shoot is making me uncommonly nervous.

I started watching porn as a teenager in the late nineties

with a spotty dial-up connection. It seemed a vibrant human sexuality textbook next to lackluster sex-ed classes featuring black-and-white anatomy diagrams and condoms rolled onto bananas. When I started actually having sex, porn became my aspirational guide to seductive moans, gymnastic positions, and superior blow jobs. One person I saw receive lots of superior blow jobs was Tommy Gunn, who is now standing next to me, handing back my pen. That explains the anxious scribbles: I'm starstruck.

Then I hear something that yanks me from my distracted state: "Girls these days." *Girls. These. Days.* Three such innocuous words, until they are strung together in that particular order. I'm not even sure who said it, but I start taking notes—real ones underneath my scribbles. "Girls watch our porn, because it's free everywhere, and then they grow up thinking that's what sex is," says Dera. Gunn joins him in delivering the last four words such that they resound in stereo: *That's what sex is.* "They go and have sex with a normal dude," Dera continues, "and he's like—" He screws up his face in mock horror—the kind of face, actually, that women give in those tube site ads where they're surprised by a home intruder, snooping stepdad, or photoshopped monster cock.

This riff is a reversal of the usual media narrative: that boys spring pornographically inspired moves on unsuspecting young women. Nevertheless, Gunn nods knowingly. "When I have my private sex, I'm not trying to be like, '*Huh-huh-huh*,'" he says, theatrically grunting while aggressively humping the air. It's a parody of the work he's done for well over a decade.

They turn to me, a rapt audience of one with a notebook and digital recorder on my lap, and recount stories of the young women who send them naked selfies on Instagram and ask them to "fuck them like a porn star." That means choking, gagging, and face slapping, they explain. "Then *pay me*, because this is work now. I'm not enjoying this, I'm putting on a performance," says Dera, as if talking to one of these girls. "It's, like, not even my cup of tea. I want to go to dinner and have a fucking *nice meal* and take it from there. Where the *ladies* at anymore?" Gunn shakes his head and says, "It's a whole 'nother generation."

At this, I hear what I've already heard from conservative culture warriors, misogynistic internet trolls, and feminist critics alike: today's young women are sexually misguided, dreadfully warped. I'm brought back to the years I spent as a feminist blogger, attempting to defend against generational attacks on everything from hookups to "raunch culture." It's only on future listens to the audio on my recorder that I will recognize something other than familiar "girls these days" hand-wringing. These men are speaking to the way that they are conflated with their work, reduced to what they portray, and assumed to be sexually available. They are talking about the confusion of fantasy and reality, and how it impacts them as sex workers. But my vision is restricted, my focus folded inward. All I hear is: *You got it wrong, you did it wrong, you are wrong.*

Soon, Gunn throws up his square hands and tosses back his head as if doing Seinfeld-esque stand-up. "The new first date is anal," he says. Later, Gunn tests out another version of the punch line: "*Anal* is the new *handshake*." I'm laughing, like I'm in on the joke. The joke, as I narrowly understand it, being the absurdity of girls who think that porn is real, who want to be roughed up in the bedroom, who don't know what it means to go on a real date. But I was "girls these days." In many ways, I still am.

I grew up amid fizzy declarations of "girl power" and exhortations toward empowerment. It seemed to me women had every opportunity to break the glass ceiling. The same was true with sex, which was everywhere. The sexual revolution already happened, yes? Now I could do as men: watch porn, sleep around. Never mind the old double standards and dichotomies, which had persisted and expanded ever more confusingly with expectations of sexiness. Girls contended not only with the labels of "virgin" or "slut" but also with "prude."[1]

Against this backdrop, as a mostly-pretty-sure-I-was-straight girl, sexual empowerment seemed to mean being both like men and wanted by them. So, I tried to become an expert in both—mining tube sites, visiting strip clubs, embracing casual hookups, and delivering the kinds of bedroom performances that led one man to exclaim, "I feel like I'm a teenager discovering *Playboy* for the first time. No, make that *Penthouse*." Meanwhile, I faked nearly all of my orgasms.

In theory, my career as a journalist only furthered those ends of knowledge: reporting on peacocking pickup artists, interviewing guys about every never-before-told facet of their sex lives, reviewing virtual-reality porn shot from a man's point of view. Instead, it has complicated my assumptions, undercut my so-called expertise. Now, ironically, one of my unwitting, de facto teachers is saying that porn is an inaccurate representation of what many straight men want. In fact, his costar is suggesting that women like me horrify "normal" dudes.

It is far from the first time I've encountered these kinds of messages, but it is the most arresting. My ears pound with blood, like I've been hung upside down by my ankles. This isn't about porn. It's about the countless ways I've chased after a vision of straight men's desire only to watch it vanish right before me. I consider explaining all of this, inviting these men into this private moment of disenchantment. Instead, I keep laughing along like one of the guys at the specter of young women who treat anal like the new handshake. *Hahaha, girls these days.* I have to admit, there is something darkly funny about the possibility that I rerouted my desires in pursuit of a mirage.

Still laughing, I think: *The joke is on me, isn't it?*

CHAPTER 1

Perfect 10

I like to say that I was raised in Berkeley, California, by a pair of pot-smoking hippies. This is factually true, but it gives the wrong impression. Tie-dyed shirts, Birkenstocks, unwashed hair, co-ops, free love. Berkeley in the sixties, basically—the identity to which the city still so desperately clings. This creates an easy shorthand for a childhood lived outside the norm, but the abnormal aspects of my childhood can't be summarized by such a cliché.

We lived in a Craftsman in North Berkeley on a busy two-level street bisected by the Hayward fault line. You could walk a couple of blocks—down a secretive sun-dappled path, beyond the fence that neighborhood kids had, in a united act of delinquency, covered with discarded bits of bubble gum—to nearby Solano Avenue. There was a small movie theater with a vintage marquee, a progressive bookstore, and a wide array of "ethnic" restaurants, as some graying white hippies would imperiously call them.

It was small-town living in a not-so-small town. One that

trumpeted its liberal politics and famous history of war protests, and above all embraced the giddy spectacle of people doing their own thing—like Pink Man, a guy who donned a head-to-toe hot-pink bodysuit and silver cape and rode around town on a unicycle. "Berserkeley," I called it, smiling proudly. Across the sparkling blue-green bay was San Francisco, or the City, which I understood as a kid to be kooky in its own way. Although, all I really knew early on was Pier 39 with its kitschy souvenir shops and stinky, raucous sea lions—essentially, the opening credits to *Full House*.

Despite the setting, my childhood wasn't organic greens and whole grains. It was Lay's potato chips and party packs of Pepperidge Farm cookies (see: pot-smoking hippies). My mom had brought her Midwest roots with her to the crunchy Bay Area, so we didn't go to farmers markets, join a co-op, or grow vegetables in our garden. We didn't even compost. Instead, we bought Coca-Cola by the case and went to Disney on Ice. My parents rebelled in other ways, though, like the pot, and my last name: Clark *hyphen* Flory. It was what so many people did in their milieu at the time, which paved the way for plenty of jokes about a future Berkeley populace full of double and triple hyphenates. It's such a small thing, that hyphen, but it represented the kind of partnership that they wanted to have: emphatically, sometimes inconveniently equal.

My mom ran her own graphic design business in San Francisco and woke while it was still dark out in an attempt to beat traffic across the bridge. That meant my dad, a programmer at a Berkeley tech start-up, got me ready for school in the mornings when I was little. He supervised tooth brushing, poured my bowl of cereal, and combed out my long mass of hair. A "rat's nest," as he called it, often developed overnight, and he would take me out onto our sunlit porch so that he could delicately pick at it with a comb, whistling to himself while French-braiding my hair, a skill he had picked up from some moms on the playground during his paternity leave.

Even in our sensitive, liberal climate, my dad was unusual for a man. In my mom's circle of predominantly queer women friends, I would hear things like, "He's a special guy, your dad." He was stereotypically masculine—deep booming voice, copious body hair, towering stature—but quick to tear up at little things, like a thoughtful gesture or a dramatic movie scene. During college he had trained to become a peer counselor as an extracurricular activity and went through emotional workshops where, as he put it in his characteristically confident and unselfconscious way, "I got *really* good at crying."

Right on up until puberty, I spent every Sunday afternoon adventuring with him—rock climbing, windsurfing, skateboarding, hitting balls at the batting cages. It was our version of church, the objects of worship being nature, sun, and sweat. Sometimes he brought me to a sprawling park in the Berkeley hills, where we climbed through a creek looking for water skippers, threw whistling Frisbees on the grass, and picked blackberries from gnarled thickets. My tan scrawny legs were often caked in dried flecks of mud, my feet slipping and squishing in soaking wet Keds.

In those days, time with my dad always carried the thrill of possibility. We were going to go do things in the world. Things that made me burst through the front door with an exciting proclamation. *I threw a Frisbee! Look how many blackberries we got! I scraped my knee, but I'm okay!*

He never treated me like a princess, but then he did *build me a castle*—a large wooden structure that sat in our front yard, looming over our five-foot fence, with a drawbridge, stairs, and even a turret. He painted it gray to approximate the color of ancient stone and flew a rainbow-colored windsock at the top. But if I was a princess, he made sure that I was a roller-skating, creek-jumping princess who kissed banana slugs, and without any hope they would turn into a prince. Then again, I also was a princess who stopped using her castle when spiders moved in and spun pillowy nests of eggs in every corner. But he tried, really, he tried, to counteract every other message I might absorb about what it meant to be a girl.

My MOM WAS WHAT many men pointedly called a "strong woman." That's because, you know, she was smart and had opinions, but also because she made it clear she was not ever going to be stepped on, *especially* by any man. "Watch it, buster" was a signature line, said if my dad impishly overstepped even small bounds, like lightly teasing her about the trivial talk show she had on or stealing a bite off her plate. My mom had developed this defensive posture growing up with a 1950s caricature of a dad who worked too hard, drank too much whiskey, and, in her words, "ruled like a tyrant."

She was no tyrant with her "little bunny." From those early years, my mom lingers as a sense memory of safety and comfort: her hair-sprayed perm pressing against my cheek as she hugged me, the drip of wet washcloth held to my feverish forehead, the smell of Kraft singles melting onto a sizzling pan as she made me a grilled cheese. All the pain she experienced as a little girl and beyond? None of that for me. Maybe her daughter wouldn't have to be such a "strong woman."

My mom didn't exactly identify as a feminist—she preferred the term *humanist* in part because she felt there was something pleading and fragile about *feminism*—but the definition of the word described her fundamental belief: men and women are equal. That belief fueled her arm's-length relationship with feminine presentation. Her closet was filled with loose-fitting blouses, stretchy black cotton pants, and sensible flats with flexible rubber soles. She didn't own anything more than a modest kitten heel. During the workweek, she put her hair in curlers, unwrapped her flowy tops from the dry-cleaning plastic, and applied chalky makeup that dusted the top of her dresser, but she made a point of telling me that she *had* to do this to be "professional," not because she wanted to or believed in it. For my mom, makeup in particular was a drag, and a kind of drag.

She didn't work out or diet, either. My friends' moms owned pastel-colored dumbbells and aerobics VHS tapes, while mine proudly called herself a hedonist, stocking the freezer with Drumsticks. My mom thought it was silly for women to punish themselves for aesthetics, whether it was aggressively counting calories or wearing blister-causing high heels. When I asked in fourth grade to buy a razor to start shaving my legs, she told me, "Once you start, it's hard to stop," as though hair removal was a gateway drug.

Even absent any great feminine suffering, she made a value judgment about relying too heavily on your looks. After one of my dad's old college friends came for a visit with a busty girl-friend wearing a low-cut bodysuit, my mom remarked dryly, "She led with her chest." My mom led with her mind. That phrase "Beauty is pain"? The message I got from my mom was "Beauty is dumb."

My dad seemed to agree. One night, channel surfing across the Miss USA pageant, with its parade of women clad in neon swimsuits sashaying before a panel of judges, he tsk-tsked and shook his head. "Some people have such a limited idea of what makes a woman attractive," he said. "Your mom is the most beautiful woman I've ever met." At the time, I was twelve years old and entering puberty's hormonal assault. I had a thick mat of blunt-cut bangs that dusted the very tops of my eyelids—my awkward attempt at hiding the mountain-scape of zits on my forehead. I wore baggy T-shirts, wide-legged jeans, and skater shoes, feeling that it was safer to dress like a boy than to attempt to look pretty. My dad was trying to assure me that I didn't need to look like these women.

He was always finding these teachable moments, casting as-persions on titillating Victoria's Secret catalogs and emaciated Calvin Klein models. I would roll my eyes, as any young person does when cornered with one of their parents' life lessons, but it made me hopeful that the boys at school might see beyond my

not-so-secret pimples and tomboy style. It also gave me hope
about the adult world, the world of men, ahead of me.

I DON'T REMEMBER MANY specifics about what my parents told
me about sex. By sixth grade, it had become one of the topics I
cared about most—I was always sneaking off during family
trips to the bookstore to read snippets of *Our Bodies, Ourselves*—
but I didn't want to hear about it from them. The general message, though, was that sex was a beautiful and spiritual act that
took place between two loving and equal adults. Later, my dad
would describe it as "two star systems colliding in outer space."
That was the kind of vibe I got from them even as a middle
schooler. When done right, it was this ineffable, magical thing—
an idea that raised more questions than it answered.

At school, the message was presented differently. In sex-ed
class, I heard about the literal ins and outs of sex: here is the
urethra, here is the cervix, here's how babies are made. I wasn't
sure how to reconcile the abstract poetry of my parents' sex talks
with these antiseptic medical diagrams. Meanwhile, the culture
at large seemed to say that sex was something else entirely. It
wasn't a biological phenomenon *or* a spiritual experience. It was
college students during spring break gyrating in wet T-shirt
contests, taking tequila shots from pierced navels (I rued my
outie), or enacting things like the Triple Kiss (two girls and a
guy kissing at the same time).

Of course, I knew that none of this stuff was actually sex,
but it did seem to reveal something about what sex was, and

that something challenged everything I had heard at home and at school. Not only *did* looks matter, they were of the utmost importance. My dad could wax all he wanted about smarts and athleticism, but it wouldn't change the fact that perfume commercials featured naked supermodels, not women climbing Mount Everest or reciting pi. What was there to conclude, other than that the adults in my life were lying to me about sex? I set out to do some research.

Our household was equipped with two towering PCs connected to a modem that beeped, whirred, and dinged like a digital pinball machine. The dining room had recently been converted into "the computer room," as we called it, which tells you something about the size of these machines and just how much excitement our family had about this new technology. After school, while my mom watched *Oprah* in the neighboring kitchen, I would repeatedly swab my face with Stridex wipes and log on to AOL. I could have looked for other girls with similar interests to mine: art, animals, poetry. Instead, I looked for any chat room that seemed even vaguely adult. Eventually, I began looking for the boys, the men.

The first thing everyone wanted to know was "a/s/l?" At first, I told the truth ("12/f/California"), but soon I started lying ("21/f/Florida"). On one such occasion, I entered into a private chat with RedSoxxx72, or some such, who typed these words: "hey sweetheart." *Eek*. I pushed myself back from the computer desk, traveling a few feet in my roller chair before coming to a stop. Then I spun myself around a few times, as if to embrace the roiling of my stomach, and scooted back to the keyboard, summoning the women I'd seen in late-night phone sex commercials. "hey big boy," I wrote as goose pimples spread across my forearms.

We exchanged the stock self-descriptors of "tall, dark, handsome" and "brunette, tall, skinny." Then I added: "busty too." He asked for my bra size and I told him, "36DD." The truth: a training bra. Next came that ubiquitous question: "whatchu wearin?" I looked down at my Dr. Seuss T-shirt with a cartoon of Thing 1 and Thing 2 and wrote, "red lace stockings." He did not delay. "I'm taking those red stockings off right now and slowly licking up those long luscious legs." That was as far as I let it go before hammering out: "IM 12!!!!!!"

I used the same escape hatch whenever things got too intense during these online chats, inaccurately assuming the revelation of my age to be a universal mood killer. Then I would buckle over the keyboard snorting with laughter, but it was really more like relief. As much as I enjoyed a good prank—calling Jenny Craig was a favorite—these virtual stunts left me feeling disappointed. Were cup size, hair color, and perpetual nudity all men cared about? Some small part of me had been hoping that I would go undercover as an adult and find that I had something to look forward to. That sex was, I don't know, even slightly romantic.

That same year, I saw Baz Luhrmann's *Romeo + Juliet*, starring Claire Danes and Leonardo DiCaprio. Then I saw it again and again—nearly a dozen times in theaters, taping each ticket stub to my bedroom wall. I replayed the sex scene in my head many more times than that. Romeo sneaks through Juliet's window, soaked by the rain. She slowly peels off his shirt. He holds her face and softly kisses her. Juliet's fingertips brush over the soft hairs on the back of his neck. He takes her shirt off and they hold each other. *They hold each other.*

That's it, then it cuts. But it helped launch a Leonardo Di-Caprio infatuation. I started a website and daily email newsletter, which gained dozens, hundreds, and then over a thousand subscribers. Each of the four walls of my bedroom—and, eventually, even the ceiling—was papered with glossy images of Leo torn from *BB*, *Bop*, and *Teen Beat*. I downloaded audio clips from the *Romeo + Juliet* website and turned them into sound events on the family computer. Whenever an email appeared, Claire whispered, "Oh dearest Romeo, if thou dost love, pronounce it faithfully." When an error occurred, Leo howled, "I am fortune's foooollll!"

I talked my drama teacher into choosing *Romeo and Juliet* as that spring's school play and then landed the role of Juliet. I was thirteen years old, the same age as Shakespeare's pubescent heroine, and I'd never been kissed—by a boy, anyway. Less concerning than memorizing my lines was the question of how two faces could fit together without knocking noses. The night before we were set to practice the dreaded balcony scene at school, I hugged my mom good night and planted a kiss square on her lips. When I pulled back, my mom's eyes flickered with knowing. "Good night, honey," she said, smiling.

It was against this backdrop of obsessive, bumbling romanticism that I ramped up my cybersex explorations. Such could be the paradox of a young girl's coming of age in the nineties.

Studying Shakespeare by day, writing internet smut by night. Practice kissing your mom, fake virtual orgasms.

I started testing out various come-ons to see how men would react. "Wanna lick whipped cream off my naked body?" "I can tie a cherry stem with my tongue." "I'm double-jointed." "I have a pair of handcuffs." "My belly button is pierced." I crafted these enticements while taking excited sips of my after-school Coke. My chat partners' responses were sometimes half-formed and misspelled—the signature of an over-enthusiastic one-handed typist. Often enough, they snatched the narrative right back.

The things that boys and men detailed in turn were eminently more visceral. My novelty-store vision of sexiness gave way to one of sex as a physical ordeal. There was spreading and pulling and opening and bending and shoving and swallowing. None of the things they detailed sounded particularly good to me, except that many men seemed to like them. That fact alone gave them an electric charge. *I could learn to like these things*, I thought.

In the meantime, I faked it. No matter what my chat partner said, I would respond with a long, drawn-out, "mmmm" or "yessss." As the conversation proceeded, the additional *m*'s and *s*'s grew exponentially in number to the point where a single word could occupy the space of a paragraph. I was emphatic about the pleasure they were giving me, because I sensed it gave *them* pleasure. When the right moment arrived—invariably signaled by him asking some version of "u gonna cum?"—I would burst forth with a lengthy and unintelligible series of letters, numbers, and characters. It was my best digital approximation of the squealing women from the so-called scrambled channel.

I had never had an orgasm in real life. In fact, I had only just started to masturbate. The first time, I stuffed my comforter into my mouth, because I'd read that orgasms made you scream uncontrollably. I thought ecstasy would be that easy—putting my hand in between my legs and looking up at the constellation of Leo pin-ups taped to my ceiling. Instead, I laid there, moving my fingers one way and then another, staring into his narrowed blue eyes and wet mouth, and finding only a series of intriguing sensations that didn't amount to anything. It was building, searching, aching—for minutes, sometimes hours—without any resolution. Then my wrist would start to ache.

Eventually, I started slipping my hand down my pants during those cybersex sessions. What I wanted more than anything was to kiss a cute boy on the lips. Meanwhile, my chat partners made sex sound like an adult version of the gross-out Nickelodeon game shows of my recent childhood. I was both affronted and aroused.

CYBERSEX GAVE WAY TO *Real Sex*—not the literal act, but the late-night HBO show. It was a documentary series about sexual subcultures, from swinging to sex dolls, but I interpreted the name quite literally. One night while browsing TV listings, I came across that deeply unsubtle two-word title and hit the "select" button so firmly it stuck.

There was a strip club on the screen. Several blond women, a detail that made an impression on me as a brunette, strutted down a stage built like a runway. In a dizzying montage, they

flung themselves around a pole wearing rhinestone bikinis before eventually unveiling their nineties-era tan lines. When they
ripped off their bras—and they did *rip* them, as though undress-
ing was an act of aggression—their breasts defied gravity. Then
a panel of judges rated them on a numerical scale.

I clutched the remote, ready to change the channel if I heard
so much as a toe hit the floor upstairs. I knew the three digits to
key in for MTV and just how many beats it took before the
image on the screen actually changed. Then I was prepared to
quickly unmute the TV, because no one watched late-night
music videos without the sound. I had perfected this cautious
system after many hours watching the scrambled channel just to
catch the few split seconds when the static morphed into a pair
of boobs bouncing or a bare butt thrusting. But once we got
HBO, there was no need for that anymore.

I was less interested in the wild women on the screen than I
was in the men in the audience. They looked like America to
me, or the Bud Light version of it: bad mustaches and plaid
button-downs and wire-rim eyeglasses. There was even a cowboy hat or two. They looked to my eyes to be legitimate adults,
which is to say men who could be fathers to my friends. They
were the most average-looking guys I could imagine—not slea-
zeballs or creeps, just profoundly, impressively normal. Some
held their beers with flat expressions, as if to say, "Try harder."
Others smirked appraisingly, like experienced judges at a beauty
pageant. Then there were the bug-eyed ones wearing the crazed
look of men considering withdrawing another one hundred dollars from the ATM.

But one guy stood out in particular: he was sitting in the front row, alongside the narrow catwalk of the stage, when a dancer jumped into his lap and began riding him like a bull. The men around him leaned back with riotous "Can you believe this chick?" smiles. She flipped her bleached hair, bucked her hips, and shook her breasts in his face. Her movements to me seemed pulled straight from *The Exorcist*, a film that had not too long ago given me nightmares. But as he gazed up at this feral, seizing creature, the look on his face wasn't horror, but awe. He was absolutely dumbstruck.

Real Sex wasn't the first time I had seen men ogling women, of course. It wasn't even the first time I had seen women perform a lap dance or work a pole, because that stuff was everywhere at the time. A couple of years earlier, the movie *Striptease* had come out, and, though I hadn't seen it, the risqué movie poster and short clips that played during Demi Moore's promotional appearances were inescapable. The year before that, Elizabeth Berkley, whom I remembered watching as a kid in *Saved by the Bell*, starred in the NC-17-rated *Showgirls*. Then there was Aerosmith's "Crazy," a music video in which Steven Tyler's own daughter, Liv Tyler, twirls around a pole, strips down to her bra, and giddily collects wads of dollar bills.

But this was the first time I had seen stripping in such eyeball-arresting detail. Plus, this was *real*. I got that Hollywood sometimes presented an unrealistic and unattainable version of life, but this was a *documentary*. These were real men and real women. And as the name itself suggested, *this* was real sex—as opposed to the sex your parents told you about.

• • •

IN EIGHTH GRADE, I decided I didn't want to be a teenybopper anymore and started to privately refer to my newsletter subscribers as "punk-ass kids." I turned my Leo website into a shrine for AJ McLean, the Backstreet Boy with tattoos, questionable facial hair, and crotch-thrusting dance moves. My musical tastes were changing as well. The year before, the cool boys in our grade had worn skater shoes, ripped jeans, and Nirvana T-shirts. Now, suddenly, these privileged white boys were sporting loosely laced Timberland boots and baggy FUBU T-shirts, and listening to Tupac. My best friend, Meredith, and I followed the boys' sartorial lead, only we attempted to sex it up with tight jeans and lip gloss.

It was an unavoidable fact that Meredith was pretty—petite nose, full lips, clear skin—but she had a dash of endearing awkwardness. That awkwardness made it possible for me to be friends with her without overanalyzing each of her more desirable features. It was her braces—that helped—but also the way she, like me, let her nail polish chip and tended to collect stray bits of dog hair on her clothes. She was an unrepentant goofball who never held her hand over her mouth when she laughed.

Together, we used my family's handheld video camera to make puerile, unladylike movies—including our parody, *Tifartic*, which opened with a shot of a boat sailing across my bathtub as we blew wildly into our palms making fart noises off-screen. We were juvenile, inexperienced, and anxious to grow up.

Meredith started drawing manga-style comics in which

we were rendered as rap superstars, wearing Tommy Hilfiger everything—bra tops, boxers, and baggy jeans—à la the singer Aaliyah, along with a speech bubble with a line of verse. Only we didn't pull lyrical inspiration from Aaliyah, whose music was tame, or even Lil' Kim, who rapped raunchily about cunnilingus. Instead, our culturally appropriative cartoon alter egos sang about giving men pleasure, as in this memorable verse that we wrote together: "Ready to fuck, ready to suck / Hopin' for good luck / Ready to squirm, see guys get firm / Finally it was my turn / I was ready to lick, get some dick / Ready to kick, I was illin', sucking dick."

I was not even remotely tuned in to the historical fact of white people treating Black culture—and representations of Black sexuality, especially—as a form of rebellion. It would be many more years before I had any inkling of how white women in particular use hip-hop to cast off the strictures of "pure, chaste" femininity, as the author Brittney Cooper argues, and just how profoundly race and class factor into constructions of innocence. "The ability to take on and peel off the parts of Black culture that you like at will is exactly what is meant by the term 'white privilege,'" she writes.[1] I was focused on my own exceedingly narrow sense of oppression—which I then understood only as a vague notion of boys being mean—and failed to recognize how freely, and without real consequence, I was able to choose my sources of defiance.

In reality, Meredith and I weren't ready "to lick, get some dick," but we were wild about boys and men, and not just in a scrawling-hearts-in-notebooks kind of way. We talked about their bodies—the way a crush's biceps would flex when he shot hoops or the glimpse of pecs when he lifted his shirt to wipe away sweat. Occasionally, a fall on the basketball court would reveal a compelling view of pale upper thigh. Sometimes we imagined what their dicks were like, whispering about foot and hand size—we believed the myths—and studying the contours of their lightweight basketball shorts.

The next fall, when we started at Berkeley High School, I had two concerns. One was being pelted with eggs, stuffed into a trash can, and rolled down a hill as part of a tradition known as Freshman Friday. The second concern was both more pressing and enduring: Boys. *Boys, boys, boys, boys, boys.* Within the first month of school, Meredith and I had surveyed the vast student body of over three thousand and given nicknames to our crushes. Most notably, the "finest guy in school" was bequeathed the approximate acronym FIGIS.

Meredith continued drawing her manga-style comics, but now with our crushes as starring characters. She often sketched FIGIS with a box over his face that read, "CENSORED: TOO FINE." Our foul-mouthed lady-rapper personas were replaced by our everyday selves (just with bigger lashes and curves). Berkeley High was an open campus, meaning you could leave at lunch to grab food at neighboring cafés. So instead of such time-worn scenes as locker-side chats and passing a crush in the hallway, Meredith drew us walking down the streets surrounding Berkeley High and having run-ins with all the nicknamed boys.

Largely, these comics were faithful representations of the interactions—or, more often, noninteractions, mere adjacencies—that we'd already relentlessly cataloged with a rainbow's array of gel pens in notes passed during class. In one comic, she showed us simply standing in line near "Freddie," a Freddie Prinze Jr. look-alike, while waiting for our tuna salad sandwiches at Subway. In another, we stood in front of the YMCA and there came FIGIS, who made the simple act of walking down the street into an event on a level with a superhero brawl—sometimes there were even the attendant sound bubbles. WHAM! BOOM! ZING! Occasionally, she would imagine what the nicknamed boys had said after we left (e.g., "Damn, she's fine"). Eventually, upon my urging, the comics got more fantastical: she drew one in which I walked, uninvited, into the bedroom of my next-door neighbor, a senior soccer player, while winking and licking a lollipop.

Suffice to say, these storylines did not pass the Bechdel Test.

I STARTED PRIVATELY EXPLORING the explicit porn sites of the era, which were cheekily crude and ceaselessly alliterative. I discovered "HARDCORE PHOTO SETS" with descriptions reading, "Stacked blonde pornstar gets poked poolside" and "Jaded jizz junky begs for the big fix." Then I moved on to video clips—real, moving visuals of people having s-e-x. This was nothing like those hard-to-catch moments of intelligibility on the scrambled channel. This was graphic, educational, and arousing. I was fifteen, but still hadn't had my first real kiss.

That changed when I went to Hawaii with my parents during my sophomore year of high school. We stayed in a condo next to a series of sprawling hotels, all of which were connected by a single beachside path. One afternoon, as I wandered down that path, a guy around my age tapped my shoulder and invited me to a party on the beach that night. It felt like a scene from a teen movie, the kind where teens actually go to parties. I had never been to one. Instead, Friday nights had been spent with my small circle of friends hanging out at my house while watering down my parents' dusty bottle of tequila.

That night, just past dark, I willed myself to head toward the designated meeting spot: a circle of palm trees next to a mega hotel with a thundering waterfall in its lobby. If I wasn't brave, I told myself, the things Meredith drew would never happen for me. There I found a group of eight high-school-aged guys standing around smoking cigarettes. I walked up to them and said, "Hey, uh . . . I was invited to the party." Before long, I was sitting on a weathered wooden bench next to Brian ("or was it Ryan?!?" I later wrote in my journal) sharing a bottle of rum and a puckeringly sweet lemonade chaser.

I know that Brian wore a white Kangol visor, a plaid silk shirt, dark baggy denim, and Timberland boots, because I later drew a labeled diagram of his outfit, detailed right down to the Newport Lights tucked into his shirt pocket. We swigged and swigged, staring out at the white-sand beach, where a dozen or so other kids similarly swigged. Nearby, a girl around my age wearing a strappy tank top and short shorts was yelling while falling into some bushes of beach cabbage. The thick mass of waxy green leaves and bursting white flowers cushioned her tiny body before she bounced right back and then promptly fell again. Her words were slurred by booze and muted by the falls, but I got the impression she was yelling at me.

In response, Brian said, loud enough for all to hear: "Don't pay attention to her. That's just Trashy Ashley." I wasn't even sure of Brian's name in that moment, but all these years later, I still remember "Trashy Ashley" with the crystal clarity of the neighboring pool. Is it because I recognized her as the warning that she was? Did I realize the alliterative potential of my name, how easy it would be to become Trashy Tracy? Did it occur to me, as it does now, that Brian himself had hooked up with Trashy Ashley? If so, it didn't stop me from walking down the beach with him.

But first: I puked. Then I puked again. Brian, I wrote in my journal, "was so sweet about it." He told me I'd feel better once it was "out of my system" and walked me to a beach chair, where we proceeded to make out. "That shit was <u>SO amazing</u>," I wrote of this post-vomit tongue wrestling, my first real kiss. Then he suggested we try one of the cabanas by the pool, which had privacy curtains that could be closed completely. I'd just had my first kiss, but now came in quick succession: first fingering, first hand job, first blow job, first cunnilingus. Then, at his suggestion: first "titty fucking" and first "69."

All the while, I kept a vigilant eye on the curtains of the cabana, knowing that any of the nearby partiers could easily peek in, noting that the rum was making the edges of my vision blur, and understanding that "bad things" could happen to girls in moments like this. Brian suggested sex and I gave a firm no. About this, I felt "really good," I later wrote, feeling proud of standing up for myself. Now this makes me wonder whether I wanted to say no to any of what we did do, and if I even knew the answer at the time.

The developmental psychologist Deborah Tolman writes of how girls face a "dilemma of desire," which pits their "embodied knowledge and feelings, their sexual pleasure and connection to their own bodies and to others through their desire, against physical, social, material, and psychological dangers associated with their sexuality." Those perceived dangers vary by race and class, with privileged girls experiencing a greater sense of physical and material safety, and more "space for sexual curiosity."[2] Researchers also have suggested that the 1990s brought about a shift in perception in which negative judgments of young women's sexual behavior are moderated through the appearance of being self-interested and in control.[3]

In my journal, I concluded the Hawaii scene by writing, "He comes, yada yada yada." *Yada yada yada.* As though I'd ever done that before, as though it were already old hat. I was emphatic about my own enjoyment, though: "It was <u>fun</u>, & I'll be smiling & happy for the next week, <u>non-stop</u>," I wrote. "It was like an <u>AMAZING</u> in-my-dreams fantasy come to life." I went on to volunteer, "I don't feel demeaned or degraded or stupid or <u>anything</u>. He wasn't taking advantage of me, I did exactly what I wanted & got exactly what I wanted, same w/him." It was a lot of underscored text.

· · ·

My dad's hulking white computer sat on the far end of the former dining room with the screen facing a wall. I waited for a moment when my mom was in the garden pulling weeds and he was out kite-skateboarding at the Berkeley Marina—an activity that involved him dancing on his board while being pulled along by a traction kite, which had turned him into yet another amusing Berkeley oddity. I sat down in the rolling office chair, tapped the keyboard to wake the monitor from its slumber, and double-clicked on Internet Explorer. Glancing over my shoulder, I shook the mouse with a trembling hand and brought the arrow on the screen to hover over the word "History." I was fifteen years old and asking a question—about who my dad was, about who men were—and I was scared I wouldn't like the answer.

I wanted to click, I didn't want to click. I clicked.

The list of visited sites seemed innocuous at first—local news, weather reports, boring dad stuff—but then I saw it: Perfect10.com. I'd been holding my breath, but then I let it out in one big collapse of a sigh. I had never heard of this website before, but I instantly knew what it was all the same, and it made the room shift in an earthquake of disappointment. I'd found what I was looking for and what I hoped not to find.

There was a luminous blond woman in a see-through bathing suit lounging on a glossy expanse of sand as waves washed over her fingertips. Her back was arched, head tipped to the sky, as if in the throes of some inexplicable pleasure. *Click.* The same woman, lips parted, eyes squinting, like she was stepping into a slightly too warm hot tub. *Click*. She was naked now, ecstatically flipping her wet hair, sending ropes of water flying through the air. *Click*. Crouching in the ocean while staring off into the middle distance with great effort and determination.

As I kept clicking through his visited links, the women changed, and they didn't. It was a procession of blond young women with flowing mermaid hair, creamy unblemished skin, and *perfect freaking tits*. Thin noses, plump lips, delicate chins. Fake eyelashes, rouged cheeks, high heels. Reflected in the monitor, laid across these ideal women, was my teenage visage—brown frizzy "before" hair and middling B-cup boobs. Thin lips, big nose, square jawline. Perfect nothing.

These women represented everything that my dad had long told me didn't matter. *High heels are crippling. Makeup is unnecessary. Plastic surgery is unfortunate. Shaving your legs is silly. A woman's most attractive feature is her brain.* Is it, Dad?

When I look back to this moment of discovery, searching for the particulars of the scene, trying so hard to remember, here is what my brain conjures: a little cross-section of my teenage body, sliced down the center, like one of those cadavers from that *Bodies* exhibition, where human flesh is preserved for educational purposes. Only it's an imagined, cartoonish cross-section of my living self, a view of the internal drama of my body as I click through the images. My intestines scrunching up like a slug lightly poked with a stick. My heart contracting and then pumping at triple speed. Tears flowing like water through an unkinked garden hose. The physical experience of heartbreak.

Maybe that sounds melodramatic, but in a world that increasingly seemed to be full of questionable men, my dad had been a good one. He appreciated women for—I can picture my teenage self going all doe-eyed and placing a hand on my heart—*what was inside.* Can you sense how much I want to make fun of that little girl? How I have to distance myself from her because of how it hurts to think of the naivete?

Even at the age of fifteen, I must have unconsciously held on to that idea, the possibility that there were men out there like my dad. Men who weren't like what I encountered online or on HBO or in that cabana. Men who were swayed by biting intellect, a good sense of humor, and derring-do, not the batting of eyelashes and propping up of tits. Now even my dad had failed to meet that standard.

Lots of kids find their dad's porn. There is the archetypal story of a young boy discovering his dad's stash of *Playboy*s. He finds them in a dusty milk carton in the garage or hidden behind a cot in the basement. Whatever the particulars, it's almost always told as an exciting moment of sexual awakening—because, boobs. *Boobs.* It's a form of indirect intergenerational bonding, an affirmative masculine wink, an invitation into the intoxicating world of men's sexual secrets, a preview of what it is to be in possession of a dick. That is not what it was for me. Instead, it told me that my sexuality was a problem. I was a girl who liked men, and men—even the good ones—liked *this.*

Before logging off my dad's computer, I went searching through the site, beyond the photos that he had clicked on. Then I printed out some images. I chose photos of women who looked like me in the abstract: brown hair and eyes, small breasts, slightly olive skin. Then I slinked up to my bedroom, closed the door, and pulled my floral bedspread up to my chin. The pink-and-cream palette of the original images had been neutralized in the black-and-white of the laser jet. Sliding my hands under the covers, I unbuttoned my jeans and pulled a tangle of denim and lace Victoria's Secret panties to my ankles.

I held the stack of images up with my left hand like an actor reading off a script. After scanning the first image up and down several times, exhausting its every possible tingle and twinge, my hand surfaced from below to assist in switching to the next. I took in the puffy nipples, smooth skin, and arched backs, but I didn't picture kissing or caressing these women. I imagined myself in the images, posing against a desert landscape, narrowing my eyes at the camera, tossing my flowing hair around my shoulders. I thought about that man's open-mouthed awe at the strip club stage. The idea of being desired like those women caught my breath.

My dad would have been horrified if he knew: his porn membership, his daughter, and a blanket rippling between her legs. And in the future, when I looked back at this as an adult—after years studying feminist theory, interviewing sex researchers, writing about the porn industry, and living life as a heterosexual woman—my head would spin with various interpretations of the scene. What I felt in this moment, though, was that these women were going to teach me something. They would help me to learn just what men wanted, so that I could try to become it. And if I couldn't become it, at least I would understand it. That would be its own kind of power.

CHAPTER 2

Adult

Snow came from the East Coast. He blew into my sophomore year biology class a week after the semester had started and several minutes after the bell had rung. "I just moved here from New York," he said, handing a slip of paper to our incredulous teacher. "Sorry I'm so late." Snow had dark eyes, full lips, golden skin, and a dusting of stubble on his square chin. Massive headphones were slung around his neck with a cord trailing all the way down into his sagging pocket. He grinned affably at our balding, Oxford-clad teacher, who sighed and signed the piece of paper, waving him to an empty seat behind me.

It's on, I thought, and it was. I had barely spoken a word that whole first week of class, but when our teacher told us to pick a lab partner, I threw my arm over the back of my seat and asked Snow if he wanted to pair up. One of the sensitive bad-boy protagonists from my still secretly beloved Leonardo DiCaprio movies had materialized right in front of me. A boy from the East Coast with a charming smile and tender eyes that hinted he just might dabble in poetry (he did). I overheard Snow explain his name to a desk-mate with a shrug: "My parents named me after their coke dealer." I was done for.

Eventually, we were making out all over the place: BART, park benches, pool tables. Then we were fooling around for hours in my own bed, my parents preferring to let him sleep over rather than have me sneak around outside the house. One evening, Snow used a friend's computer to chat with me via AOL Instant Messenger and flirtatiously tell me about all the ways he planned to please me sexually. I pivoted to what most interested me:

> **me:** but the question is . . .
>
> **me:** what am *I* gonna do for *you*?
>
> **him:** what ever u like
>
> **me:** no . . . whatever u like
>
> **me:** seriously
>
> **me:** whatever u like
>
> **me:** tell me
>
> **me:** don't be shy
>
> **me:** haha
>
> **him:** hahaha
>
> **me:** no seriously
>
> **me:** I'm asking u up front . . . so be honest . . . what do
> *you* want
>
> **me:** ?
>
> **him:** I'll have to think about that
>
> **me:** no u don't

me: just tell me

me: NOW

me: haha

me: seriously . . . just tell me

me: straight forward

He relented and told me that getting a blow job with some ice cubes or crème de menthe would be "dope." I pressed on.

me: tell me what else

him: you

me: no really . . . what else do u want

me: say whatever else u want

him: i don't know

me: yea ya do . . .

me: u gotta have *some* ideas

him: i don't know im not all that picky

me: no c'mon!

me: just be straight forward with me

me: seriously

him: chill ill come up with something

me: man u gotta have some fantasy

me: or something

I printed out the entire seven-page conversation and stapled it into my journal, compiling my notes.

A year into our relationship, just past the turn of the millennium, we walked into a hotel room together as Snow toted a much too large convenience store bag that rustled absurdly with a tiny box of Trojans inside. On multiple occasions prior, I had tried to lose my virginity—to get him to just take it, already—but he insisted on a romantic setting. In this case, a mid-rate hotel in Santa Cruz made possible only because my parents booked the room; we both were underage. I had told my parents of our plans to stroll the nearby boardwalk, ride roller coasters, and eat cotton candy, but I omitted the main event: sex.

I responded to the romantic setting by enthusiastically urging us into a series of positions learned from porn as much as from the songs playing on loop in my Discman. Afterward, Snow—my loving, devoted boyfriend—softly told me, "That wasn't what I'd imagined, exactly." He must have imagined the missionary position, deep eye contact, and ceremonial crying—not me sitting astride him, a finger placed thoughtfully on my chin, while excitedly saying aloud, "What positions are left?" I cried silently in the buzzing, harshly lit hotel bathroom, feeling reprimanded for my enthusiasm.

I was wounded but undeterred. Using my meager salary from a part-time job at a greeting card shop, I subscribed to Vivid.com, the premier porn site of the time, and shared my login and password with Snow and my growing circle of guy friends, because I was cool like that. I worshiped the blow job skills of performers like Jenna Jameson, Savanna Samson, and Briana Banks, finding inspiration in these rising stars' ravenous enthusiasm, which seemed to turn men into puddles of desperation. No one was telling them, "That wasn't what I'd imagined."

• • •

COLLEGE HAD EXISTED IN my mind as wet T-shirts suctioned to perky breasts and shots slurped out of concave belly buttons. I spent years preparing for my entry into the bacchanal of late-night *Girls Gone Wild* infomercials in which partying collegiate women flashed their boobs with a howling "woo!" for roving camera crews. When the time came, however, I picked a school as far from that vision of coed debauchery as possible: Mills College, a progressive, feminist women's school with a quiet wooded campus in Oakland. The closest students got to a late-night infomercial was the annual Fetish Ball, a queer-run, kink-themed dance party featuring a profusion of leather, latex, and fishnets, which men were controversially allowed to attend.

"I chose it *despite* it being all women," I said of Mills with a wrinkled nose. "They have a great writing program is all." Feminism was a liability: even something as benign as challenging a joke about women being bad at math would make certain guy friends, some of the same ones with whom I'd shared my Vivid login, teasingly exclaim, "You're such a *feminist*." In response, I might punch them in the shoulder—and yet, there I was signing up for a class called Feminist Ethics.

Each night in the dimly lit dining hall of my turn-of-the-century dorm, I loaded up a plate with the carb du jour while scanning the room for a familiar face. My most frequent and harmonious dinner companion was a woman in her fifties with a practical blond pixie cut who was returning to school now that her kids were off to college. I twisted spaghetti on my fork while comfortably chatting with Lynn about the growing national battle over same-sex marriage and about reading Song of Songs, "the sexy part of the Bible," in class. This came naturally to me as an only child: making conversation with adults.

In my room before dinner I could practice a million different ways to approach a group of women my age: "*Hell*-oh. Hell-*ohhh*. Hi. Hiii. Hey, guys. Heyyy." Often, though, I sat alone in that lunchroom cliché, taking little comfort in its cultural ubiquity. "I just ate dinner all by myself—after eating lunch all by myself," I emailed Snow, who was newly an ex but still a trusted confidant. "I'm so tired of this. I just want a friend. One good friend would do for now."

I spent many lonely nights tucked into my twin bed with my fictional friends Jenna, Savanna, and Briana. The bacchanal was here, on my glowing laptop screen, and sometimes it seemed I might climb right in like the girl from *Poltergeist*. One evening, I posted to Craigslist's personals. "I'm stuck in my dorm room at a women's college, looking for a man to talk with on the phone." It read like a ludicrous porn scenario or a blackmailing setup, but it was true. Then I was emailing back and forth in rapid fire with a man in his twenties who lived in San Francisco.

When he called my dorm room phone late that night, the ring seemed to echo implicatingly through the silent hallways of the building. His voice was rough and glossy, a pine cone dripping with sap, and all too real. I slammed down the receiver, just like I'd hammered out "I'm 12!!!!!!" in AOL chat rooms. He called right back and I click-clicked the phone in its cradle. Then I disconnected it from the wall.

I swarmed with contradiction. Scattered across my dorm room floor were xeroxed essays and studies written by feminist scholars, papers covering topics like gender as a construct and the phallocentrism of Freud. At one point, there was the film theorist Laura Mulvey's paper on the "male gaze," which described the way Hollywood represented women as passive objects of straight men's desire.[1] (I did not yet fully appreciate that women, too, could see the world, and themselves, through such a gaze.) Stapled next to Mulvey's essay was the author bell hooks's piece on "the oppositional gaze," adopted by Black women who, encountering "a cinematic context that constructs our presence as absence," choose "not to identify with the film's imaginary subject."[2]

I highlighted these papers and scribbled double-drawn stars and triplets of exclamation points in the margins. Then again, I also enthusiastically annotated a copy of infamous anti-feminist Camille Paglia's *Vamps & Tramps*, in which she wrote, "Far from poisoning the mind, pornography shows the deepest truth about sexuality, stripped of romantic veneer." There was the textbook theory of feminism, and then there was the world that still awaited outside that gated wooded campus, and I believed in both. But it was women like Jenna, Savanna, and Briana who seemed best able to help me prepare for the latter. In fact, Jenna was now a *New York Times* bestselling author, thanks to her autobiographical *How to Make Love like a Porn Star*. The book's subtitle: "A Cautionary Tale."

It wasn't long before the subject of pornography seemingly leapt off my laptop screen and went streaking across campus. Larry Flynt's *Hustler* magazine published a detailed first-person account of "crashing" Mills's Fetish Ball. The article, which was framed as an exposé, sparked righteous outrage on campus, not least because the author had written offensively of "hairy dykes" and "slutty go-go dancers." I was a staff writer at the school newspaper, which responded by publishing a series of articles exploring feminism and sexuality, including my piece with the simply adorable headline "Porn: Not Just a Black and White Issue." One afternoon, I passed in the hall a respected English professor, who leaned in and told me with an enigmatic grin, "You're certainly making a reputation for yourself."

Despite all the feminist texts on my dorm room floor, I had only a vague historical sense of what I was walking into. The feminist "sex wars" of the late seventies and early eighties existed in my mind as a polarized caricature of pro- and anti-porn positions—essentially, yea or nay to smut. In truth, members of the "pro-porn" camp were to varying degrees enthusiastic about and critical of porn (not to mention deeply engaged with discussing the broader politics of sex). Journalist Ellen Willis lambasted the "generalized, demagogic moral outrage" of anti-porn activists, while at the same time writing, "For obvious political and cultural reasons nearly all porn is sexist in that it is the product of a male imagination aimed at a male market." Most of what I heard in college, though, were the arguments of the sex war's losers: the censorship-favoring anti-porn camp.

In 1983, Andrea Dworkin and Catharine MacKinnon's

infamous draft legislation posed pornography as a civil rights violation against women. The draft, a version of which passed in Indianapolis before being declared unconstitutional, deemed it "sex discrimination to produce, sell, exhibit, or distribute pornography." The legislation had been supported by Women Against Pornography, a New York feminist group known for leading gawking tours of Times Square's sex shops and that, without reliable evidence, linked adult material to violence using the slogan "Pornography is the theory, rape is the practice."

In this simplistic historical view, the sex wars were reduced to a clear-cut battle over censorship, effectively erasing the reams of brilliant writing from the "pro-porn camp" on sexual moralism, politically incorrect fantasies, and the opposition's then-popular argument that women who enjoyed porn were experiencing "false consciousness."

It's a shame, as otherwise I might have been better prepared to grapple with the brash title suddenly featured at the campus bookstore at the beginning of my senior year: Ariel Levy's *Female Chauvinist Pigs: Women and the Rise of Raunch Culture*. The book took aim at a moment in which women were "making sex objects of other women—and of themselves" amid the "frat party of pop culture." Some of the presented evidence: the popularity of thongs, implants, bikini waxes, and *Girls Gone Wild*. Levy dedicated several paragraphs to Jameson's bestselling memoir. "Female chauvinist pigs," she argued, had responded to decades of feminist advancement by endeavoring to "be one of the guys" and act "like a man." American women "don't want to be excluded from anything anymore: not the board meeting or the cigar that follows it or, lately, even the trip to the strip club that follows that," she wrote. Women were subscribing to a vision of sexuality that was "less about connection than consumption."

I flinched whenever passing *Female Chauvinist Pigs'* hot-pink cover. It wasn't that I intellectually disagreed with the general assessment; it just felt at times that Levy was arguing against a caricature, like the one-dimensional mud flap girl leaning against the title on the book's cover. She led with political outrage verging on mockery and polemic, but where was her freaking empathy? I felt I was just trying to navigate the world in which I lived, rather than holing up until a suitable feminist utopia arrived. Levy, in her early thirties, was a decade older than I was. How easy, I thought, to critique these sexual trenches from such a safe vantage. Still, when she came to town for a reading, I sat in the audience, glowering most intensely at her strongest points. She was right, there was no denying: I wanted in on the frat party.

After graduation, I moved across the bay into a shoebox of an apartment in San Francisco's Hayes Valley and brought along the gender studies readers, the inflammatory Paglia rhetoric, and all my favorite women porn stars.

I STILL COULDN'T QUITE believe that I was an "adult." If I ever said, "I'm an adult," the final word always came with ironic air quotes. At the age of twenty-three, I was an "adult" who lived in a dingy studio apartment with a sink perpetually full of dirty dishes. I was an "adult" who made herself dinners of Kraft mac and cheese with a side of single-serve Mott's applesauce, always pulling back the aluminum cover and eating it right out of the plastic container. I was an "adult" who routinely paired those Kraft dinners with cheap chardonnay followed by a solo dance party to Britney Spears or Justin Timberlake, which seemed only slightly less embarrassing at the time.

I took the Muni Metro, San Francisco's underground light-rail system, to work alongside the city's finance and tech workers, feeling alien among ladies with nude tights and commuter sneakers. Then I blogged about feminism all day. An unpaid college internship at the online magazine *Salon* had segued into a low-paid job. As an intern, I had written for *Salon*'s feminist blog *Broadsheet* whenever I wasn't making fact-checking calls or fetching coffees for board meetings. Then, at just the right moment, some money was freed up to hire me on as a blogger who still, occasionally, fetched coffees.

The feminist blogosphere had just exploded as a cultural force, and my workdays were spent hammering out pithy thoughts on things like burkinis, the pay gap, and pole-dancing classes for tweens. It was real adult life, but not at all.

Often, my nighttime solo dance parties turned very quickly into strip routines. I had been stripping in my bedroom for nearly a decade, ever since those pubescent evenings with *Real Sex*. I would close the door and enter a parallel universe in which I was someone else entirely: a sexy someone. Throughout high school, I fashioned outfits out of discarded clothing, cutting ripped jeans into booty shorts and turning black fishnets from a Halloween costume into a see-through tube top. Then I would turn on the pop song of the moment—usually Britney, Christina, or P!nk—and position myself in front of the long mirror on the back of my closet door.

This routine continued into my college dorm room, and into my first adult apartment. Same moves, different mirrors. It always began with the hip-swaying sashay, which was something like a supermodel stomping down a runway. Then I would turn to the side, spread my legs apart, and fold over to touch the floor while arching my back. Wiggle of the butt. Then I'd rest my hands above either knee and flip my hair back like I was starring in my own Pantene Pro V ad. I might even grab at an imaginary pole and twirl around it—an awkward trick that I had perfected over the years—all while watching myself reflected in that mirror. Laura Mulvey grounded her theory of the "male gaze" in Jacques Lacan's theory of the "mirror stage," in which a child recognizes its reflected image as superior to its own bodily experience and "projects this body outside itself as an ideal ego." I idealized that writhing reflection, but I also limited its expression.

The mirror, in all its forms, was any number of men I had encountered in the world: friends, crushes, strangers. Sometimes while dancing, I imagined I was on a strip club stage, as though I'd been invited up as part of an amateur competition. The daydream was never that I was choosing to strip as a job, as some of my college classmates had, only that I was talked into it for fun, as a larky dare. I was privately pantomiming the work of stripping while maintaining a privileged remove. That was an aspect of "female chauvinism" that went unexamined in Levy's analysis, which referred to "most employees of the sex industry" as "sexually damaged" and decreed that strippers and porn performers "*aren't even people*" but rather "erotic dollies from the land of make-believe." A safe distance can be kept in both worship and scorn.

That distance is by design, as Jill Nagle wrote in the essay collection *Whores and Other Feminists*, which would soon find its way onto my shelf. She described the paradigm in which women are forced "to choose, or at least negotiate between" the categories of good girl and bad girl, the latter of which applies to sex workers. She dubbed this "compulsory virtue" in reference to Adrienne Rich's concept of "compulsory heterosexuality," through which "women's choice of women" has been "crushed, invalidated, forced into hiding and disguise." Nagle explained, "Whores, too, are something that women are not only supposed to not *be*, but also, not be *mistaken* for." The societal edict is to time and again "demonstrate our affiliation with the privileged half of the good girl/bad girl binary."[3]

Outside my bedroom, that sexy, reflected image in the mirror strutted through my imagination whenever I listened to the crappy pop song of the moment. Whether I was driving in my car with the volume dial spun to the right or commuting to work with earbuds in, the music summoned to my mind's eye a miniature hair-flipping woman, like a pole-dancing Tinkerbell trapped within the confines of my skull. I'd be sitting stone still on a Muni bucket seat, wearing a turtleneck and tasseled loafers, while a faceless woman visible only in outline was projected on the walls of my private fantasy. I thought of her as "the dancing woman," as though she was an other and not a fractured, disembodied part of myself.

AFTER NEARLY A DECADE of dancing in my room and in my own head, I decided to take a pole-dancing class. My gym in downtown San Francisco attracted suited businesspeople who rushed in, brows already sweating. That the building also had a whispered-about windowless room equipped with four different glinting poles seemed only slightly incongruous.

It was the mid-2000s and stripping had been sanitized for the mainstream. Mostly, in the popular consciousness, it didn't actually involve any stripping. Several years earlier, the *Washington Post* had declared that "everybody wants to be a stripper," pointing to the release of Carmen Electra's aerobic striptease DVD series and Oprah learning the "stripper walk" on daytime TV.[4] Since then we had entered the era of Paris Hilton's leaked sex tape and Britney Spears flashing her waxed nethers for paparazzi. Now gyms routinely offered pole-dancing classes as a way to access your inner sex goddess and tone your abs.

In the locker room beforehand, I watched out of the corner of my eye as a middle-aged woman blow-dried her hair while fully naked. She rose from the fluffy white towel folded under her butt, stood to bend at the waist, and unselfconsciously flipped her head upside down for added oomph. Another woman of the older-than-me variety padded by in wet flip-flops with a towel wrapped around her waist and her glistening chest displayed like it was nothing at all. Just breasts. *Mammary glands*, you might even say.

Meanwhile, I was sitting in the corner of the locker room doing that thing where you put on a new shirt while still wearing the old one. It's the kind of move that adolescent girls pull during gym class. In one fell swoop, and with very little skin exposure, the turtleneck I'd worn earlier to work was replaced by my baggy workout T-shirt. I didn't bother to change into a sports bra, because there was no modest workaround there. I couldn't fathom displaying my body so casually. I was afraid to get naked in front of strangers, and yet there I was about to take a pole-dancing class.

Inside the windowless classroom, I found two walls of mirrors and a series of purple-hued fluorescent overhead lights. The teacher, dressed in an electric pink crop top and psychedelic yoga pants, fiddled with the sound system while chatting with a woman strapping herself into a pair of Lucite platform heels. There were regulars, the ones pairing their workout gear with high heels; and then there were the newbies, like me, wearing clunky running shoes with double-knotted laces.

We took turns on the poles, trying out isolated moves with names like the Fireman Spin and the Carousel. I executed each like I might a push-up, pull-up, or any other effortful physical feat. But then, near the end of the class, the teacher dimmed the lights and turned on a pink lava lamp in the corner of the room. She divided us into three groups and announced that we would be dancing for each other, taking all the individual moves that we'd learned and improvising them into a routine, right there on the spot.

When it was my group's turn, I dropped and arched and crawled as though rigidly executing boot camp exercises. The whole while, my face contorted itself even more than my body. I pursed my lips, puckered them to the side, pulled them into a cringing grin. The teacher floated nearby and slowly ran her palms over her capacious curves before whipping her dirty-blond hair around her head. "*Let out* the sexy lioness inside," she said, and I was pretty sure she was talking to me. One pole over, a woman in booty shorts hooked her leg around the pole and swung with blow-dried hair tossed back and an arm raised victoriously in the air. The teacher proudly clapped. "Yes, girl! You are a goddess!"

I clutched the pole with sweaty hands and leapt into the air, tucking my feet under my butt like Tarzan clad in athleisure. I made it halfway around and landed with the squeal of my running shoes against the buffed wood floor.

IT WAS NOT TOO LONG AFTER that pole-dancing class that I was sitting in a strip club at one a.m. eating chicken tenders with a side of ranch. My greasy fingers reflected the Hustler Club's fluorescent-pink overhead lights as I dipped a hunk of meat into the creamy dressing. I washed each fried bite down with a sip of a vodka soda, perhaps my fifth or sixth, or *who really knows* drink of the night. I would tell you about the particular friends who accompanied me, if only I could remember. What I do know is that it was my idea to go to the strip club, because it was always my idea—usually after a few drinks out with a coed group of friends and with a frat-bro-like declaration on my part of, "Strrriiiiiip clllluuub!"

A woman in a green Day-Glo bikini crawled along the edge of the mirrored stage, pausing intermittently to lift up her G-string so that men could tuck crisp dollar bills along her hip. A handful of other women circulated the room in platform heels, placing manicured hands on the backs of plush leather chairs as they offered up lap dances and smiled gamely while guys peeked in their wallets. "Best fried chicken in the city," I told my table of friends while holding a chicken finger aloft. "It's actually *so good*, you guys."

Here I was, armed with a quickly diminishing wad of dollar bills in the heart of San Francisco's North Beach neighborhood, where stories-high vintage neon signs advertised "topless entertainment." Those marquees outside were dated, but I felt, quite earnestly, like a new kind of woman. When it came to strip clubs, I was more experienced than my guy friends and, if my body language was to be trusted, more comfortable: they sat on their hands while I leaned forward toward the tip rail. By day, I was a feminist blogger. By night—some nights, at least—I found myself reveling in moments like this one that felt pleasingly contradictory: the feminist sitting at the strip club stage. I hoisted this supposed dichotomy up in the air like a gleaming trophy.

These moments seemed part of a larger conversation about young women and sex that was gaining mainstream traction. Everywhere I turned there were finger waggers fretting about the rise of casual hookups, pornography, binge-drinking, girl-on-girl make-outs, and strip aerobics classes. They worried about girls like me.

As manifested in the media, the young woman of concern was often specifically white, middle class, and heterosexual. The very concept of the "girl gone wild" implies a passage from "good" to "bad." Historically, women of color have been portrayed through racist stereotypes as inherently wild. The sociologist Lorena Garcia wrote, "African American women have been depicted as sexually aggressive and uncontrollable, Latinas as sexually provocative and hyper sexual, and Asian women as sexually submissive, 'dragon ladies,' or a combination of the two."[5] Black women, in particular, are assigned by default to the category of "bad" girl, as the professor Patricia Hill Collins has explained.[6] The same is true of queer women. To be granted movement within that dichotomy, to raucously reject the constraints of "goodness," is a privilege, and one I took for granted.

At this point, I'd lost count of my strip club visits. There was the time on my twenty-first birthday, a spur-of-the-moment several-drinks-deep suggestion by my friend, who used to strip, and whose ex co-owned some clubs in San Francisco. She got half a dozen of us into the VIP section for free, where she paid for a "double lap dance" in which two bikinied women straddled my lap and made small talk. "I just had my birthday, actually," one of the women told me, before squeezing her breasts. "These are my birthday present to myself."

It was during the subsequent visits that my tally climbed. I was taking a class self-seriously titled "Urban Constructions of Gender and Sexuality," which required a dozen hours of fieldwork observing "gendered interactions." I chose a strip club as my site of study, because of course I did. It seemed to me a literal manifestation of the figurative boys' club, what with the bachelor parties and after-hours business meetings. Various friends took turns keeping me company on my visits while I scrawled notes on cocktail napkins featuring a cartoon beaver wearing a top hat. A manager had approved my request for access on the grounds that I not do anything to announce myself as an observer.

I can't recall the notes I took, but I know that my observations of "gendered interactions" failed to account for a man brokering my own access to the space. I wasn't clued into the power imbalances between dancers and management, which have played out in labor battles over everything from wage theft to racist business practices to customers being allowed to nonconsensually film dancers and post the resulting videos online.[7]

After that college assignment, I kept returning. I liked the boys' club, it turned out. It was exhilarating to be on the inside. I would sit at the stage, my stomach flipping, while feeling something like, *I'm here, I'm here, I'm here.* A drink or two later, I would be leaning back in my chair, smiling dumbly at the woman snaking her body above me, while thinking: Yes, girl, you are a goddess. A few more drinks and I might order those chicken tenders.

While it is true that they were good, ordering them was about more than just my genuine, enduring love of fried foods and dipping sauces. They were about taking up space with my unladylike behavior. They were meant as a bit of a "fuck you" to the men in attendance. Eating in a strip club would have been a statement, but ordering a mound of deep-fried comfort food was, I felt, a battle cry. As I told my guy friends, "I like invading male spaces."

It wasn't a "male space," though: it was a workplace. I hadn't considered how my "battle cry" was impacting the dancers and their ability to make a living. I hadn't thought of my own privilege to tipsily teeter in there, having withdrawn one hundred dollars from the ATM, and turn their labor into my own political symbol. In truth, I wasn't an "invader," but a customer. During an earlier visit sitting at the tip rail with a group of women friends, a dancer had crawled toward us and whispered conspiratorially, "I'm so glad you ladies are here." After this sisterly nod of solidarity, the suggestion of relief at our presence, we showered dollar bills onto the stage. We had paid for the fulfillment of our own fantasies—about the meaning of this space and our place within it.

Judith Butler's famed anti-essentialist essay, "Performative Acts and Gender Constitution," describes "the mundane way in which bodily gestures, movements, and enactments of various kinds constitute the illusion of *an abiding gendered self*." I believed stripping literalized that performance on a stage, which seemed potentially subversive. Meanwhile, I saw myself as "performing" counter to gendered expectations. What I didn't appreciate was that Butler wrote of gender not just as performance but as *performative*, meaning that "it constitutes as an effect the very subject it appears to express."[8] She argued these "acts" were "compelled by social sanction and taboo" and "never fully self-styled." Using the metaphor of theater, she wrote, "Actors are always already on the stage, within the terms of the performance."[9]

Sometimes, when the status of my wallet coincided favorably with the right degree of intoxication, I would pay for a lap dance. This night, following the spectacle of the chicken fingers, was one such occasion. I bashfully flagged down a woman in a silver bikini that wrapped multiple times around her perfectly flat torso and said, almost apologetically, "I'd like a lap dance?" She smelled of baby powder and peach body spray. Her skin was unfathomably soft as she slid over me, brushing against my bare arms. She was a woman and I was a woman—and yet it seemed to me that she was vastly better at it.

"You're so cute," she said, leaning into my ear. "What are you doing here?"

I hadn't known until she said it, sending a wave of warmth through my body, how much I'd wanted to hear that, or something to its effect. I wanted someone to notice that I was *here, here, here* and to wonder why. I wanted to be told that *I* belonged up on that stage. I knew so many women who lived their lives like they were waiting to be noticed by the right man, but it's like I was just waiting for an invitation up to the pole. I stammered something in response, I'm sure, but she prodded further.

"Do you like girls?" she wanted to know.

My god, what did I actually say in that moment—something unbearable like, "I appreciate the female form," or even worse, "I like female sexual power"? In college, I'd tentatively fooled around partially clothed with a woman classmate while Snow joined in. In a couple of years, I would grab drinks with a new writer friend only to end up unexpectedly making out with her in the Montgomery Street BART station, all while filtering the experience through the eyes of the suited businessman watching from nearby. When we went back to my place, the man followed in my mind. My moments of attraction to women felt inextricably linked to men. There was always a hard dick involved, defining what was sexy, validating arousal.

"You know, you're allowed to touch my legs and arms," the dancer told me.

I didn't dare, nor did I particularly want to in that moment. What I wanted, more than anything, was to have her brush off on me, to absorb her right through my skin. Just beneath my fantasy of sisterly solidarity and defiance in the face of gendered expectation was this other, aching one: being wanted by the men in the room.

If it had been as simple as "liking girls," I would have gone next door to the Lusty Lady, the famously unionized peep-show cooperative. The one that had played host to sex educators, radical thinkers, and feminist porn performers. But I didn't want to sit in a private booth by myself and watch women dance. What would be the point? I might have talked about worshipping the dancers' sexual power, leaning over to my friends as a woman performed a gymnastic inversion on the pole and whispering, "Do you know *how hard* it is to do that?" I might have given dancers the sort of head-nodding slow clap that you would see now in a well-circulated GIF.

Ultimately, though, I was there for the men.

• • •

Far more often than visiting strip clubs, I would crawl into bed with my laptop and navigate to YouJizz.com. The site's logo was similar to YouTube's, only it dripped with an illustration of ejaculate, as though some cartoon brute had just wandered by and busted a prolific nut. I had transitioned from the high-end production values of Vivid to the Wild West of tube sites, which were suddenly emerging as a free alternative to pay sites.

Many of the videos were pirated from mainstream porn companies, but some were filmed by shaky-handed amateurs. The women in these clips ran the gamut from busty blonde to flat-chested brunette. There was an array of categories, everything from "voyeur" to "swingers," "hairy" to "squirt." I was introduced to a whole new X-rated lexicon: "creampies," "bukkake," "gang bangs," "double penetration." I learned some head-scratching abbreviations: DP, BBW, MMF, ATM. These sites, I believed, were the male id laid bare.

I jokingly mentioned YouJizz to a guy friend and his eyes grew wide. "How do *you* know about that?" he practically whispered. It was clear that *he* knew about it but couldn't fathom that a woman had managed or would even want to infiltrate this cum-covered terrain. It was true that tube sites might as well have had a "no girls allowed" sign tacked on their clubhouse door, but that was precisely what had drawn me in. Of course, tube sites were actually filled with "girls," or rather content made by women who either uploaded footage themselves or, too often, had it stolen.

I always navigated right to the "Top Rated" and "Most Viewed" sections of these sites. I hadn't even paused to think of what my turn-ons or fetishes might be. I wanted to watch what *men* wanted to watch, which I assumed—despite my own presence on the site—to be reflected in the most popular videos. This meant opening tab after tab of videos of women gagging on dicks until they teared up, their mascara smearing like that of horror movie heroines. It meant saliva—so much of it, frothy and thick—desperately spit out amid gasping breaths or escaping from the sides of women's mouths. It meant this unforgettable, instantly recognizable sound—a *glug-glug-glug*—not unlike that of a plunger in a toilet. It meant "throat fucking" videos.

It sometimes turned my stomach to watch these clips, but I persisted. The same was true for the frequently accompanying "slut, whore, bitch" dialogue, which seemed in blatant opposition to my feminist beliefs. At the time, I interpreted pornographic fantasy as a candid, if exaggerated, reflection of what one believes and desires. These videos were the simple truth about men.

I took that truth in, again and again, with my hand between my legs. I could masturbate like that for hours, pursuing my elusive orgasm—until I soaked my sheets with sweat, until my wrist seized up in protest. It was, perhaps, a feat of empathy: trying to get off on men's pleasure. Or maybe I was hoping to catch a form of Stockholm syndrome, to inculcate myself with the contours of men's fantasy. I massaged it in, literally. I made it feel okay—and then I made it feel kind of good, actually.

At least, that is what I told myself. It's one version of the truth. Then I arrived at another: those videos turned me on from the start. My stomach had occasionally turned at the implications of my own arousal. Watching Top Rated and Most Viewed clips and insisting it was what men wanted was a creatively engineered way to feel comfortable with being sexual, to abdicate my drive. The psychotherapist Michael J. Bader argues that fantasies are unconsciously designed to make us feel safe enough to experience our desire, often by removing feelings of shame, guilt, inhibition, and worry.[10] How could my own wanting be too much while imaging someone else's desire being shoved down my throat?

Maybe this was my erotic feint: men's desires were being done to me, and what better representation than choking on a hard dick?

I SPENT A LOT more time watching men, in strip clubs and on my laptop, than actually interacting with them in any kind of romantic or sexual way. Yes, sure, there had been the frat boy who worked at Abercrombie, the tattooed Starbucks barista who looked like Jake Gyllenhaal, and the coast guard member with a physique built for pulling water-weighted bodies from the ocean. But those few hookups, all of which happened while I was still in college, were short-lived and relatively unremarkable.

Then, that spring, my friend Katherine invited me to go salsa dancing with her and her friend Kiley at a place called Cafe Cocomo. We were standing at the bar—fresh off a beginner's class held before the place turned into a salsa free-for-all—when a man in an iridescent red dress shirt unbuttoned to mid-chest strode right up to Katherine and Kiley. He said something I couldn't hear over the live congas and horns, but it must have been funny because they tossed back their heads with laughter. It must have been brazen, too, because Katherine put her hand on her hip and spun toward him with a defiant grin. Katherine was a few years older than me and worked in TV, writing the promos that made people tune in to the ten o'clock news. Even outside of work, she was a captivating and confident storyteller, gesticulating wildly while peppering in outrageous laugh lines. *I'll let her handle this*, I thought.

Vinh, as I learned was his name, had a friendly face with warm brown eyes and a dimpled smile. I couldn't get past the flashy button-down, though. He also looked to be in his midthirties, which seemed far too old to me. As I sucked at my straw, though, I noticed that he appeared to be entirely unaware of my existence. I edged in closer. He was asking what we—but, really, what *they*—were doing there. Was it our—*their*—first time salsa dancing? He didn't look at me once. I edged in a bit more. He was a lawyer, he owned a house in the Oakland hills, and he had been salsa dancing for years. Vinh managed to seamlessly slip all of this information into the span of just a couple minutes.

"Well, wanna dance?" he asked Kiley, while confidently taking her hand. *I guess he likes blondes* is what I thought, defensively. But several songs later, after I spied him confidently working the room, he passed by and tapped Katherine's shoulder for a dance. *So, he likes brunettes, too.* My internal monologue turned adolescent: *Why isn't he giving me attention? What's wrong with me?* Several more songs passed and he finally asked me to dance—and it felt like a gift. In a fraction of an hour, I had gone from disinterested to silently begging for a crumb of attention.

Toward the end of the night, he passed by once again. "My friend, he's a doctor, he has a house in the hills with a pool over-looking the bay," he said, once again focusing on my friends. "He throws an epic party every year and invites all the best dancers in the salsa community. If you're into dancing, you should come." Vinh was still looking only at them, as he suggested that they put their numbers in his phone so that he could invite them. But once Katherine and then Kiley entered their numbers, he handed his cell phone to me. *Well, that's nice*, I thought. *He's doesn't want me to feel left out.*

Then a couple of days later, he called me and left a message. "Hi Tracy, it's Vinh from Cocomo. I wanted to see if you'd be interested in going dancing this weekend." By the end of his smooth, well-rehearsed message, I was shaking my head, impressed. He had *wanted* me to feel left out. Still, I called him back.

Vinh picked me up for our date in his black Mercedes SUV. When he led me to the car and I saw the silver hood ornament, my stomach turned. It was the kind of conspicuous show of wealth that struck me as pathetic, but it also felt disturbingly far from my own "adult" reality, what with my beat-up Honda Accord that I had inherited from my dad. Vinh owned a home and a fancy car. He was an adult, without the air quotes. I learned that he was thirty-four—and yet here he was with me, a woman more than a decade his junior.

When he discovered my age that night, his eyes bulged. "Twenty-three, twenty-three, twenty-three," he said, astonished. After that date—at another salsa club, where he spun me and dipped me and fought my propensity to lead—there was another date and then another. At random moments together, he would look at me and say: *Twenty-three, twenty-three, twenty-three.* He continued to feign surprise, but I could tell he liked the sound of it.

Our dynamic quickly presented itself: Me, plucky twenty-something feminist unwilling to genuflect to his gender, profession, or age. Him, thirtysomething lawyer mightily impressed with his own rhetorical skill but amused at my unflagging persistence. We argued for fun, mostly about insubstantial things, like how many days away Saturday is from Thursday (one or two). "Congratulations," he told me at the end of one of these debates. "You have worn out a litigator." He held progressive political beliefs but liked to antagonize me about my feminism, especially when I interrupted traditional habits of courtship by, say, insisting on a split bill.

Soon, I developed a better understanding of why. On one of those early dates, after dancing at Cocomo, the same salsa club where we had met, we went into the courtyard to cool off. Sitting on a love seat set against a scattering of tropical plants wrapped with white Christmas lights, we talked about a recent blog post of mine. It must have been something to do with gender roles and modern dating, because he used it as an opportunity to tell me about his friends who were in the "seduction community."

Vinh smiled at my cocked eyebrow and then excitedly spilled. He told me about "pickup artists" who ran high-priced seminars on "seducing" women and formed secretive members-only clubs— "lairs," they called them. These "PUAs" purportedly taught men to manipulate women into finding them attractive and, ultimately, wanting to have sex. He explained jargon like "peacocking," which essentially meant wearing flashy clothing to draw attention, and "negging," a way to subtly insult a woman in order to inspire insecurity. The biggest pickup artist of all, Vinh told me, was Mystery, a man who had written a book bearing the title *The Mystery Method: How to Get Beautiful Women into Bed.*

I would later learn that Vinh had a copy of the book, and that said copy was dog-eared and highlighted throughout. I'd find out that he had also read the *New York Times* bestseller *The Game*, a book written by journalist Neil Strauss about the PUA scene, in which Mystery alarmingly advocates "blasting through" women's "last minute resistance" to sex. But in that moment, all I knew was that the techniques Vinh described sounded cynical and manipulative. They didn't value women as equals or individuals. I told him as much, almost rising to stand in my outrage.

He paused and pursed his lips. Then he said, with a smile, "What if I told you that I used it on you?"

• • •

I WOULD LIKE TO SAY that I broke things off in that moment, but I did not. We kept dating for several more weeks. I understood that the scheme of acting disinterested at Cocomo had "worked" in that it had successfully triggered my insecurity, which simulated something like attraction. But I also understood that I would have gone out with him even without the elaborate charade. So many of the things that had perplexed me during our short relationship—from refusing to go out to dinner for our first few dates to the overly familiar way that he engaged with my friends—seemed to have been his attempts at following the "Mystery Method." I liked him *despite* these things. I had seen the kind and vulnerable person underneath all the posturing.

In fact, sex with him was something different from most of what I'd experienced before. He was slow and steady and focused almost entirely on me. It wasn't particularly intense or passionate, but it was pleasurable. There was none of the amorous antagonism that defined our interactions outside the bedroom.

Not too long after breaking up with him, I pitched a Q&A to an editor at *Salon*: an interview with Mystery, who was about to get his own VH1 reality TV show. It was a phone interview, so I was left to only imagine him on the other line. From photos, I knew he favored kohl eyeliner and an oversize fuzzy top hat that he sometimes curiously paired with goggles worn around the crown. He also had a tattoo of a pair of bright red lips on his neck. These were all obvious attempts at "peacocking." By then, I had read both *The Game* and *The Mystery Method*, so when Mystery tried to "neg" me—responding to a tough question with, "Wow. Did you write that?"—I sighed directly into the phone.

I was disturbed by the rise of pickup artistry, and not just because I kept running into men in bars who would launch into conversational gambits that I recognized from *The Game*. Beyond the goggles and fuzzy top hats, past the deceptively amusing exterior, was a burbling well of entitlement and resentment, one that was destined to violently explode. In bestselling PUA texts and online message boards alike, there was the evident conviction that men had been disempowered by decades of feminist advancement, which had made women less dependent on men. Where I saw an incomplete revolution, many PUA acolytes saw a movement that had cheated men of sexual access. They responded by approaching love and sex as if it were a game to be won, but then, so did I.

Case in point: Nate—or "the Pilot," as I called him with friends. It seemed almost like a setup: I was lugging my suitcase down a perilous set of BART station stairs when a man materialized next to me. "You headed to the airport, too?" he asked. I looked up to find a classically handsome young guy in a pilot's uniform carrying his own, much smaller suitcase. He had light brown eyes, closely cropped hair, and the perfectly proportioned face of a Hollywood actor. The uniform pushed the scenario into the absurd. Surely someone had sent me a strip-o-gram. I was inclined to look over my shoulder for hidden cameras.

We rode BART to the airport together, standing in the aisle and laughing as our suitcases rolled this and that way. Much like Vinh, he seamlessly peppered in some intriguing facts about himself: he did MMA, wrote poetry, and liked to shoot guns for fun. Well, now, a sensitive tough guy—just my type. My mom had recently told me, "Many women confuse fear with attraction." I suspected at the time that she was pointedly saying this because of what she had observed in my own attractions. Perhaps it was my giddiness over the Rock, who was then still more of a flexing, roaring, eyebrow-wiggling WWE wrestler than a leading man.

True to type, Nate confidently, and casually, asked for my number by the end of the BART ride. Within a week, we had scheduled a date—although he didn't call it that—for the next time his flight schedule would permit an overnight in San Francisco. It was a Thursday night and it was unclear where, exactly, he would be sleeping, but I was hoping my bed would be the answer.

He buzzed at the front door of my apartment building, having come straight from the airport and still wearing his pilot uniform. We went upstairs so that he could store his luggage and change into street clothes. Nate surveyed the room, peeking out my bay window at the auto body shop across the street with a big yellow sign reading DISCOUNT MUFFLER & BRAKE, and then started to unbutton his shirt. I sat on my bed, facing him. "You gonna watch?" he asked confidently, with a laugh.

Nate shrugged the crisp white shirt off his sculpted shoulders and slowly folded it, biceps flexing overmuch. Then it was off with his white tank top. His body was the dedicated project of someone who spent most evenings in the gyms of airport hotels scattered across his flight paths. It was the kind of torso I

had never seen before in person: a rigidly drawn desert landscape of sunbaked pectorals and abdominals. Nate started to
undo his belt, smirking at me, daring me to look away.

I didn't look away, but I did start laughing, and uncontrollably. It was as though he and his body were a fantastic and
outrageous joke. I doubled over against my thighs and tried to
breathe my way out of the laughter—and it was decidedly *laughter*, not demure giggling. He paused, his hands on the button of
his pants. His cocky confidence was replaced by a look of irritation. The power dynamic had shifted. "A little privacy?" he
asked, as though I were a Peeping Tom and not that he, a near-
stranger, had waltzed right into my bedroom and begun casually taking off his clothes. When Nate was done, he said gruffly,
"You done being a little girl? Let's go."

Looking back at this moment, I can't help but think of that
line often attributed to Margaret Atwood: "Men are afraid that
women will laugh at them. Women are afraid that men will kill
them." Sometimes women laugh because they are afraid. There
was something calculated and sexually intrusive about his display. There was something subtly threatening about it, too—not
murderously so, but still. Laughter, I told myself afterward, was
just the right way to neutralize it. *Good job.*

At the time, I clung to the appealing idea that with the right
savvy and command, as opposed to sheer luck, I could avoid "a
bad experience" with a man. I held tight to that belief even as I
intellectually understood it to be a victim-blaming myth, even
as I could recite the statistics on the prevalence of sexual violence against women. When I took men home, my enthusiasm

often served as its own defensive posture: *I'm down for whatever, so nothing can be done against my will.*

We headed to a neighborhood tiki bar that served big bowls of booze accented with paper umbrellas and oversize straws, and that had a thundering waterfall that fell two stories and made my hair frizz out. My laughter earlier, followed by his prickly response, had set a combative tone for the night. But after a few drinks, I softened to his bluster. "You make me feel like such a *woman*," I told him with amused annoyance. Nate responded, "That's okay, babe, you *are* a woman."

By the time we walked the few blocks back to my place—our bodies lightly, and unintentionally, bumping into each other— we were wasted. We were so wasted, in fact, that we had already made out at the utterly empty bar, right in front of the bartender. If drunken memory serves, the kiss was the result of him instructing me, out of nowhere, "So, kiss me." This was shortly after it came up in conversation that he, too, had read *The Game*. To which I thought, *Men. Men! What are you gonna do*—a statement, rather than a question. I already knew what I was gonna do—about them, and about him.

Teeth hitting teeth. Flesh slapping flesh. The memory of his biceps, my squeezing them with an unrepentant "mmm." My hair wrapped tight in his fist, and the open-mouthed smile I gave in response. Mutual pushing and pulling and tumbling. Sensations that were not unpleasant at all, but that were not necessarily pleasurable. Then I was on top of him.

With most of the men I had slept with, it would reach this moment. I would decide to scrunch up my face and begin panting unevenly. I always drew it out, never letting it happen too quickly. That would be unrealistic. It wasn't a consistently steady rise, either. It built and then fell and then built up more, until it exploded into a burst of desperate air-sucking followed by a cresting, emphatic moan. I might grab at their skin or my hair or let my mouth twitch in an unattractive fashion. A simulacrum of losing myself.

In those moments, I felt like all of the women I had ever watched on that laptop screen, moaning and writhing and trembling. A million different images that all looked so much the same. This wasn't the divine union of two people, I felt, but of me with my heroes. I was Jenna, Savanna, and Briana—and all the nameless women from YouJizz. I was the pole-dancing teacher. I was those women on the strip club stage. I was, *Yes, girl, you are a goddess*. I was a woman being watched by a man or many men or all straight men in existence.

I was, I felt, a woman in control.

CHAPTER 3

Cautionary

After a rendezvous at an airport hotel and some half-hearted attempts to hang out, Nate stopped calling. All of those faked orgasms, although Oscar-worthy, had not been enough to keep him around. If anything, they had only made him more confident to move on. My willingness to do whatever he wanted—impromptu anal without lube, heroically gagging on his ejaculate—didn't keep him around either. I gave him everything he wanted, with my studied enthusiasm and non-surprise, but I didn't get any high fives. I got the freaking door.

This was painful in its own right, but more exquisitely so because it seemed to validate the broader cultural moment. The critique of "hookup culture" had exploded and, to my mind, it seemed both to be coming from and geared toward sexless moms in sweater sets. Recently, Laura Sessions Stepp had published *Unhooked: How Young Women Pursue Sex, Delay Love, and Lose at Both*. It was an extensive journalistic project that raised reasonable questions about the impact of a changing sexual landscape on young women, but it also was prone to stunningly old-fashioned declarations, like "having sex with lots of men might limit [one's] ability to sustain a long-term commitment." (That isn't to mention such bromides as "Admit it, the bar scene is a guy thing" and "Guys will do anything for homemade baked goods.")

Stepp and her ilk seemed to be telling young women that they couldn't engage in sexual exploration without damaging themselves and their future romantic prospects. I wanted to prove them wrong, but these boys were not exactly cooperating.

Then I met John. My friend Sarah invited me to go out with her, her British boyfriend, Jack, who charmingly pronounced her name Say-ruh, and his friend who was visiting from Canada. We all met at my neighborhood bar, a place where San Francisco's older society folk, "the gray-hairs," went before going to the opera or ballet. I was delicately sipping a suitably snobby cocktail that I could not afford, when the three of them walked through the front door together. I shot a look toward Sarah, who was pursing her lips in a "gotcha." She had failed to mention that Jack's friend vaguely looked like Prince William, only hotter and with more hair. Even across the dimly lit bar, John's light blue eyes sent me hurtling back in time. I was fourteen years old again and mesmerized by glossy pin-ups of Leonardo DiCaprio ripped from *Teen Beat* magazine.

More important, the tilt of his head and the kneading together of his eyebrows telegraphed warmth and softness. He seemed unlike Nate and Vinh, with their particular styles of masculine swagger, which had felt at the time like an intriguing challenge. John instantly seemed a kindred spirit—not like a contentious other, but a close friend. And yet I couldn't bring myself to say anything directly to him. The four of us stood in that packed bar, shifting from foot to foot, trying not to spill our overpriced drinks, as they shouted over the crowd and I was rendered speechless.

When we all grabbed a cab to New Wave night at the DNA Lounge, a former leather bar in the South of Market District, I sat in the back next to Sarah and impotently watched as the city, and conversation, flew by. It was one thing to combatively parry with a man like Nate or Vinh. I was good at lobbing skeptical glances and feminist quips toward men like that. But engaging with a sensitive softie of a guy like John meant revealing that I was a sensitive softie of a girl. It meant shrugging off my suit of armor, which I was willing to do, but not without grabbing at a shield of another kind. I convinced the group to do shots and then, with a declaration of "woo, shots," yet more. Suddenly, I was sitting on John's lap as Morrissey crooned his multisyllabic "whys" and Sarah and Jack snapped and hopped around the dance floor in that enthusiastically dorky way required by New Wave music. I even slung my arm around John's shoulders as though we had been dating for years, and not like his presence had stitched my mouth shut just a couple of hours earlier.

Before long, the two of us were back at my place. I made him wait at the front door while I kicked my dirty laundry into the closet and haphazardly made the bed, just so that we could aggressively unmake it. What followed was entirely unlike the push-pull of sex with Nate. There was frequent pausing to talk or laugh or make smiling eye contact. In those moments, John asked me questions about myself—what questions, I can't recall, but I do know that I called them "shrewd" in an email I wrote to him the following week. "I keep having flashes of moments from this weekend. Like, lying on top of you, sweaty and out of breath and just . . . talking," I later wrote in amazement. "There's something honest and real about you—I feel like most people build up so many defenses just in dealing with the world that they lose the ability to tell their true self and the facade apart."

I spoke of what I knew. Despite all the meaningful eye contact, I had faked my orgasms with him, too. I wanted intimacy, but only so much.

The next day, we went to a movie, during which we tentatively touched fingertips and then held hands. After he flew home, we started emailing back and forth. He began his first message to me, "Dearest Mademoiselle Clark-Flory," but then he made a joke about sending me a dick pic. This seemed promising. We signed each message with things like "Bittersweetly Preoccupied," "Distance Sucks," and "Toiling Away On An Experimental Transporter (Because When All Is Said And Done, It'll Be Cheaper Than Plane Tickets)." Within a week, we had exchanged nearly a hundred emails.

There were hours-long phone calls, but mostly we wrote and wrote, every single day. As the weeks and then months passed, we started emailing video diaries in which we detailed the mundane events of our days. Sometimes we would send time-lapse videos of our nights at home by ourselves—dinner eaten, a glass of wine sipped, or a *New Yorker* read in fast-forward.

Here was a relationship that existed squarely in my comfort zone: the mediated realm of the internet. I could share some of my most vulnerable thoughts in carefully composed emails that made me feel smarter and funnier than I was in real time. It was my truest self, alongside my aspirational self, the self that might actually be able to speak without first running her thoughts by a panel of interior judges who invariably held up low scorecards. When I finally flew from San Francisco to visit him in the so-called Texas of Canada—"home to the *largest shopping mall in North America*," I wryly enthused to friends—I was without the intoxicating power of the keyboard.

In person, it took me a few days to drop my defenses with him, but I did. As John introduced me to friends and family, though, I smiled and laughed at people's jokes, while struggling once again to open my mouth to actually speak. A few times I caught him looking at me as though I'd catfished him, and maybe I had: I was one person at a distance and another person up close. At the end of the trip, as John stiffly walked me to airport security, it all came pouring out, along with the tears. *Where had I gone? Where was the smart, warm, funny, confident woman that he had fallen in love with?* When I got home, we emailed it out. I explained my shyness, no longer feeling shy—and finding that I had returned, he softened. It continued that way, visit after visit.

Then, a year into our long-distance relationship, as we started talking about him getting a job in the States, there was a sudden flood of books with titles such as *Sexless in the City* and *The Purity Code*. There was even *Hooked: New Science on How Casual Sex Is Affecting Our Children*. All of these books, to varying degrees, emphasized the merits of abstaining from sex. My editor at *Salon* thought the broader conversation could use a dispatch from someone actually belonging to the demographic under discussion, so I wrote a personal essay breezily recounting my own experiences. We ran the piece with the headline "In Defense of Casual Sex" and a photo of a pair of jeans being unzipped. "I'm a 24-year-old member of the hookup generation . . . and, like innumerable 20-somethings before me, I've found that casual sex can be healthy and normal and lead to better adult relationships," I wrote.

I now read that essay with a big, fat grin. There's my pluck and sincerity. There's the omission of my faked orgasms and the depths of my hurt feelings. And there's my all-too-cooperative adoption of the "hookup generation" label, as though my parents hadn't been doing the same thing in Berkeley in the seventies, just with a lot more naked hot-tubbing involved. This was a point my editor raised before publishing, and I dutifully revised the piece to at least concede that my generation didn't invent sex. For the most part, though, I had willingly accepted the terms of the broader cultural debate, because my perceived opponents spoke to one of my worst fears: ending up unwanted and alone.

My piece concluded with what seemed my strongest defense: After all my hooking up—and in truth there hadn't been that much, but, again, I understood the terms of the debate—I had found a committed relationship. The final line of the essay: "Oh, and we had sex the first night we met."

Take that, sweater-set moms.

IT WAS TRUE THAT I had found a meaningful emotional connection with John, but in the Goldilocks fashion of early-twenties dating, I soon started to feel that something was missing. Without his asking, I regularly sent him videos and photos of me stripping to Britney, posing in a new pair of lacy lingerie, or, you know, casually spreading my labia apart for the camera. I found these performances arousing as I anticipated how much they would turn *him* on. John might email me back something like "hott photos" or "this greatly improved my night," but, to my mind, his reaction was never sufficiently enthusiastic. Was this not *exactly* what guys wanted? What was wrong with him-slash-men? Again and again, I sent a sexy something, he gave a lukewarm response, and I pouted.

After one of these perceived slights, I hit "Send" on one of my characteristically overwritten emails. "It just doesn't feel right to me that sex isn't a part of our relationship unless we're in the same physical space," I wrote. "We're incredibly emotionally intimate, but sexual intimacy, in my mind, is also a critically important component of romantic intimacy, and it isn't limited to the actual act of doing it." I was looking for validation of my digital come-ons, of course, but I also longed for sexual connection. John explained that he was made uncomfortable by "performed" intimacy to the same degree that I felt it essential.

Around this time, I finally read Naomi Wolf's 1991 book, *The Beauty Myth*. Wolf argued that "images of female beauty" were used "as a political weapon against women's advancement." These images manifested everywhere from perfume ads to pornography, she argued, and functioned to keep women in check and maintain the patriarchal status quo. The book, often considered a classic feminist text, neglected the fundamental role of race: Recently, the author Tressie McMillan Cottom powerfully revisited Wolf's argument and highlighted how Black women are excluded from idealized mainstream representations, writing that "beauty is for white women."[1] *The Beauty Myth* also has been irreparably tarnished by Wolf's recent factual inaccuracies, rape apology, and conspiracy theories, among many other issues.

At the time, though, the book admittedly resonated with me, especially the chapter devoted to the subject of sex. She memorably wrote, "The sexual urge is shaped by society"—and society, she pointed out, was full of images of heterosexual men's desire. As a result, little girls learned "not the desire for the other, but the desire to be desired." Wolf wrote of a woman's sexual coming of age: "Left to herself in the dark, she has very little choice: She must absorb the dominant culture's fantasies as her own." I finished that chapter and promptly sent John an email announcing that I wanted to "find an authentic sexual self." I told him I was interested in tossing "aside the porn script" and that I wanted to have sex like "two people having sex," instead of "Man having sex with Woman." I told him, "I'd also like to focus more on my own desire, rather than the desire to be desired." I told him there was "a lot of cultural pressure put on women to satisfy and perform, go through the script, instead of engaging in an open, equal, vulnerable and authentic exchange."

I was unknowingly referencing what sociologists call "sexual scripts," which we adapt from cultural messages conveyed everywhere from TV sitcoms to church sermons to tube sites. These scripts influence how a hookup unfolds (kissing then tongue then hand under the shirt) as much as its ultimate aim (oh, say, ejaculation). A traditional sexual script for women dictates "being desired but not desiring sex."[2] As for an "authentic sexual self," sociologists have suggested that *everything* in social life is a performance. In the 1950s, Erving Goffman argued that people constantly gauge others' reactions and tailor behavior to manage impressions, all while limited by cultural norms. The "self" comes about only through these unending performances.[3] Similarly, Judith Butler argued that performativity creates the illusion of a gendered self, and that there is no "subject who might be said to preexist the deed."

I was confused enough as it was, even without the awareness of decades of theory capable of inciting an existential crisis. One minute I was emailing John videos of me whipping my hair while stomping around in my underwear, the next I was writing missives about "vulnerable and authentic exchange." I wanted to be wanted, and I wanted to want *more* than to be wanted. I didn't expect him to solve that riddle for me, but I did want to be able to talk with him about it. Due to some combination of his discomfort with talking about sex and my hunger for a sexual outlet, though, that isn't what happened. What happened is that I turned to my old friend YouJizz, as well as the broader crop of emerging free tube sites.

You might say, then, that I turned to the "porn script" that I was trying to escape. But YouJizz, as with similar sites, didn't have a predictable aesthetic or narrative in the way people usually imagine when shaking their fist at porn. There were pirated videos of mainstream adult content that sometimes fit the cliché, but there were many more videos featuring an encyclopedic compendium of niche interests. It was a sprawling sexual theme park designed specifically for men, the ultimate aim of which was explicitly, laughably, spelled out right in the title: *You. Jizz.* But as much as it was not designed for me—as much as it seemed designed, in fact, to repel women—I absorbed some of men's sexual entitlement while walking those grounds. It stuck to my shoe like a piece of gum.

I STARTED EXPLORING PORN sites of the indie, feminist, queer, and kinky variety. Some of these sites, like NoFauxxx, CrashPadSeries, and Kink, were even based in San Francisco, which lent their films an air of accessibility and relatability. I found women performers who portrayed sex as a weird, messy, and sometimes deeply unpretty affair. They lost themselves in a flurry of sweat and saliva. Hair frizzed and makeup smeared amid guttural moans of ecstasy. Whether that pleasure was acted, experienced, or some combination, no matter: I felt it.

These performances made me believe that giving a blow

job could be an erotic, instead of obligatory, experience—and that a man could feel the same about going down on a woman. They gave me a model for what mutually enthusiastic sex might look like. But these women also played with power dynamics— pegging a man in one scene, getting face-fucked in the next—in what felt like cathartic drama. Sex could be creative, fun, and theatrical, it turned out. It recalled the possibility proposed by Butler of making "gender trouble" through "the mobilization, subversive confusion, and proliferation of precisely those constitutive categories that seek to keep gender in its place."[4]

Gay porn provided another outlet, one in which men's bodies were luxuriously eroticized and in which I didn't automatically, complicatedly project myself into the film. It meant being a true sexual spectator—and what a relief, that. In her book *Girls Who Like Boys Who Like Boys: Women and Gay Male Pornography and Erotica*, researcher Lucy Neville surveyed hundreds of women about their interest in porn and erotica featuring what she calls "m/m pairings." One of the most common explanations she received from participants about their interest in gay porn in particular was that they simply "find men attractive, and therefore like looking at them, particularly without their clothes on." As one participant responded when asked why she liked gay porn, "Well, cocks!"

Neville also reported that "many respondents state they enjoy m/m porn because it is marketed to a target audience they feel they have more in common with (gay men as opposed to heterosexual men), and invites them to adopt a point of view that is more in keeping with their own sexual preferences and desires where 'men are the objects of sexual attraction, instead of the women.'" That is, gay porn allowed them to experience something other than the omnipresent heterosexual "male gaze."

It goes without saying: As I was growing up, no one had talked to me about the sexual politics of power, performance, and perspective. No one—not my parents, not my sex ed classes, not the writers of glossy magazine sex advice—had bothered to go beyond basic mechanics and technique. Yet sex was more than just nerve endings, blood flow, and muscle contractions. It was more than angles, friction, and rhythm. The physical and psychological experiences of sex were inseparable. Every act was embedded with social and political meaning, and porn let me explore that meaning from a comfortable distance.

On YouJizz, I stopped navigating right to the Most Viewed and Top Rated tabs; browsing further, I found a host of idiosyncratic fictionalized scenarios that made my insides move: masseurs who unexpectedly slipped their oiled-up hands between women's legs, golden-haired frat boys sucking one another's dicks in initiation rituals, and beer-bellied men posing as Hollywood directors to trick women into casting-couch sex. Many of these fictionalized videos eroticized coercion and abuse of power. Men and their desires had been the focus of my amused, and occasionally horrified, attention, but now I was riveted by my own.

How many different doors could I walk through? What dusty, dimly lit rooms might I discover? I'd taken the master key and was eager to unlock every hidden corner. In the process, I was getting to know my body: the precise route to summon what was at that point a minor, skin-prickling wave of curious sensation. More than anything, though, I was becoming familiar with my own mind.

I walked the few blocks from my apartment to the stately San Francisco Public Library and checked out Lisa Palac's memoir, *The Edge of the Bed: How Dirty Pictures Changed My Life*. Palac wrote of being horrified by the discovery of her college boyfriend's collection of hard-core porn, only to confront her own enjoyment of the medium. "Now I understood the power of sexual fantasy and realized that my own sexual satisfaction was a state of mind that existed independently from a lover's touch or the perfect romantic moment," she wrote. "For the first time in my life, I felt sexually autonomous."[5]

I also read journalist Sallie Tisdale's phenomenal *Talk Dirty to Me: An Intimate Philosophy of Sex*, in which she argues that "fantasies are waking dreams" where images and scenarios—the archetypes of "one's psychological environment"—sprout "from the soil of the subconscious."[6] To what extent were these my own images, though? I especially wondered about those casting couch videos, which eroticized real-world abuses of power. Had I absorbed men's sexual entitlement or, as Wolf had suggested, their fantasies? These things felt impossibly intertwined. It was hard to tell where one ended and the other began. Again, the question of authenticity.

I didn't fully appreciate that I was stumbling upon some of the same dilemmas endlessly debated during the second wave. Amid the feminist "sex wars," some activists suggested that women who enjoyed pornography had been brainwashed under patriarchy. But there also emerged feminist thinking—much of

it from the landmark 1982 Barnard Conference on Sexuality—
that sought to examine the politics of everything from porn to
BDSM to butch-femme relationships, while also acknowledging, even celebrating, that the realm of sexual fantasy rarely ca-
pitulated to such critical analysis. The personal was political,
and yet sexual fantasies didn't necessarily have to answer to
feminism—and certainly not at the expense of pleasure.

Surely, many feminist thinkers argued, women's sexuality
was influenced by our culture, but these things could not be
easily disentangled. As feminist anthropologist Carole S. Vance
rhetorically asked in the 1984 anthology *Pleasure and Danger:
Exploring Female Sexuality*, "Do we distrust out passion, thinking it perhaps not our own but the construction of patriarchal
culture? . . . Must our passion await expression for a safer time?
When will the time come? Will any of us remember what her
passion was?"[7] The year before, Jessica Benjamin, a feminist
psychoanalyst, wrote, "A politics that . . . tries to sanitize or
rationalize the erotic, fantastic component of human life will
not defeat domination, but only vacate the field."[8]

I was still many years away from finding these words, which
would feel like overdue validation and permission. At *this*
moment, though, I felt that as a feminist, especially, I wasn't
supposed to like these coercive pornographic scenarios. It seemed
I wasn't supposed to like these things as a woman, either. A year
earlier, in 2007, the gift book *Porn for Women* had been released,
featuring photos of handsome men doing household chores. It
was supposed to be humorous, but it made my face flush red
with anger when a promotional copy arrived at the *Salon* office.

This book seemed to cheerily reflect the popular wisdom that women's sexuality was practical, domesticated, and not having much to do with sex itself.

I saw the same accepted wisdom reflected in the bachelorette-party phenomenon of men dancing in tear-away pants and banana hammocks. They had none of the beckoning sensuality of women strippers—it was all crotch-thrusts right in your face. Then there were romance novels—I had never actually read one, but I despised their existence all the same. Why did men get hard-core fuckfests while we got floor humping and Fabio? Of course, the cultural bromide is that men are more "visual creatures."

The scientific literature does reveal evidence of sex differences in subjective reports of arousal in response to what academics call "visual sexual stimuli." Researchers have pointed to a variety of potential explanations, from the role of testosterone to the influence of societal expectation. (To the latter point, one paper speculated, "The social teachings experienced by men and women throughout their lives may mediate their subjective feelings of sexual arousal in response to sexual stimuli."[9]) It also appears that the content and context of porn is influential in responses: Women report higher levels of arousal to films made by women—and even films selected by women researchers.[10]

In this period, I sent John a video in which I recounted having spent a couple of hours idly masturbating while watching porn. "Nights like this definitely make me feel like I'm . . . abnormal," I said wryly. What I meant was "abnormal for a woman"—because I masturbated and watched porn, but also because I liked these fantastically fucked-up scenarios. "Normal" women took bubble baths and read romance novels while sipping a large glass of chardonnay. Next to that cliché, I felt like a visitor from outer space, but one who was, if I was honest, much more highly evolved.

Never mind that romance novels—*bodice rippers*, for crying out loud—often were filled with coercion if not outright rape. I was on such a superiority trip about other women not watching porn, not *wading into the muck* like me, that I dismissed these other mediums outright and failed to find any kind of thematic connection to my own fantasies. That is despite the movie *Twilight* having just come out, following the international fanfare over Stephenie Meyer's teenage vampire series. A friend of a friend had passed along a thrice-read copy of the book, but it sat unopened on my bookshelf. If I had deigned to crack open that dusty tome, I would have found themes around the threat of men's desire, as well as the erotic thrill of being desperately, and dangerously, wanted. It wasn't all that unlike a "most-watched" video of a woman gagging on a dick.

Instead, the connection I recognized was of mine to men. I was like *them*. I, too, was a pervert—and it felt like I was increasingly coming out as one.

I NEVER IMAGINED MYSELF standing in front of a wall of gem-colored vibrators while reading about the intimate details of my sex life as my parents and their closest friends looked on, but life is funny that way. My hookup essay had been chosen for the

Best Sex Writing anthology, which led to a series of local readings, and the Good Vibrations not too far from my parents' house was on the itinerary. When I laughingly told them about it, my mom excitedly asked for permission to attend, and then to invite some friends. "What a hoot," she said, eyes shining. "How *fun*."

Now there they were in the front row: my parents, flanked by the crew of earthy Berkeley women they had known since their naked hot-tubbing days in the seventies. These ladies were full of meaningful eye contact and lingering hugs, but also trenchant political commentary delivered alongside the occasional well-timed expletive. They were my first models of the possibilities of womanhood: soft and sharp, brilliant and profane.

Two of them had been a couple back when and had a son together. One of my earliest memories is placing my hand on Margie's pregnant belly and feeling the thump of a foot against my palm. Later, amid the rabid anti-gay rhetoric of the nineties, it became clear to me that some of the most important women in my life existed well outside of the prescribed box—not just for womanhood, but also sexuality, relationships, and family.

Afterward, my parents and their friends surrounded me in the conversational equivalent of a hug. "I am so proud of you," Margie said, before turning to my mom. "She did so great, didn't she?" My mom responded, breathing deeply, "Yes, she survived." But it was more like *she* had. Beforehand, I had been nervous, but my mom had seemed even more so, quickly knocking back a margarita at the bar next door as though it were her doing the reading, as though she went to bars, as though she drank margaritas. Later, at a vaguely celebratory dinner out with just my parents, I silently fiddled with my silverware, and pushed and pulled at my empty plate. Had I only just *survived*? There was an awkward silence and then I looked up with tears in my eyes.

"Did you not think I did a good job, Mom?"

"No, honey, you were great," she said, her voice strained. "I was expressing my own relief, my own nervousness. I worry for you, sometimes." She paused and sighed, pinching the stem of her wineglass. "You're so much braver than I was."

At those last words I took a sudden breath, one of those half yawns of discovery. I thought back to the nervous emails my mom sometimes sent me after reading comments on *Salon*. *Broadsheet* was haunted by anti-feminist trolls, but in the wake of that hookup essay, the comments on my articles had gotten worse. The trolls started calling me fun things like "slut," "whore," and "cum dumpster." I had printed out and posted the worst of these remarks on my fridge—finding them laughable or willing myself to—but my mom found them threatening. What I only started to understand in that post-reading moment was that my mom worried for me because she knew firsthand how a woman could be punished for her sexuality. She knew and she could not forget.

In high school, shortly after I got together with Snow and went on birth control, my parents sat me down at the kitchen table for a talk. "When I was eighteen—" my mom started and then stopped. Her eyes wide, face draining to white. It seemed she was warning me that I had the power to annihilate her with my response. "I had sex and I got pregnant," she continued. "It was an accident, and I decided to go through with the pregnancy." My mom stopped, tilting her head in the way she often did while feeling my forehead when I was home sick. Her terror was giving way to concern for me. "I had the baby, a girl, and I gave her up for adoption," she said.

I flashed to the many nights I had spent as a little kid lying in bed at night concocting a fantastical story about a secret sibling who lived in the guest room down the hall. *If only I hold my breath long enough, I might be able to hear her breathe.* Sometimes I imagined my secret sibling similarly lying in bed and holding her breath in search of mine. *We'll never find each other that way,* I thought. The news of my half sister created a sudden, disorienting fissure in my world—and yet it revealed something I had seemingly already known for a long time.

Over the years, I learned more, but not much: my mom, who had grown up in conservative Indiana, was sent away by her father to a camp for "unwed mothers," as she put it. These camps had emerged in the 1940s, in the decades before *Roe v. Wade* made abortion legal, as a means of protecting families from the shame of these out-of-wedlock pregnancies. Girls and young women were told that they could go away for a few months, give birth, sign the adoption papers, and return to their lives as though nothing had ever happened. Of course, that is rarely how it played out. As Ann Fessler wrote in *The Girls Who Went Away: The Hidden History of Women Who Surrendered Children for Adoption in the Decades Before Roe v. Wade*, "moving on and forgetting proved impossible."[11]

My mom did not like to talk about her time at the camp, nor did she seem to remember much beyond the vague sketch of a night when a young pregnant girl left a trail of blood across the floor. She recalled unbearable screaming and staff members' indifference to the girl's pain. After the adoption, my mom went off to college, but she was followed by it all—the pregnancy, the camp, and her baby, whom she had never even gotten to hold. Then, in her overwhelming grief, she sought out a therapist, who committed her to a mental institution, believing that she was a danger to herself. It would take several more months for this last detail to emerge, and only as my mom and I idly watched HGTV one afternoon and I bizarrely, possibly knowingly remarked, "That garden looks like it belongs at a mental institution. Have you ever been to a mental institution?" My mom then muted the television with a heavy, "Well, honey."

She had spent weeks or months in the institution—she couldn't remember—resolving to get herself out of "the loony bin" so that she could repair her life. And she did: completing her undergrad, getting her masters, and moving to San Francisco, where she worked in an art gallery in the Fairmont hotel. The hotel was set atop a hill, where the regular clanging of cable cars reminded her that she was thousands of miles from the suburban flats of Indiana—and also from her daughter, whom she thought about every single day.

For my teenage mom, sex had been a rebellion against her tyrant of a dad. It had also been her undoing. That didn't stop her from enthusiastically sleeping around during her twenties in San Francisco, and then Berkeley, in the seventies. But, despite the era and her liberal milieu, she felt at the time—and even in her contemporary retelling—that her enthusiasm for sex made her "unusual for a woman." That is in no small part because of what her early experiences had told her about the liability of her sexuality. Later, my dad would tell me of her first pregnancy, "Your mother felt that she was marked with a scarlet letter for the rest of her life."

Now my mom had a daughter who was writing publicly about her sex life. I was making the scarlet letter into my career.

I FOUND IT ODDLY freeing to have people say the worst imaginable things about me on the internet. *Slutwhorecumdumster* was attached forever more to my Google-able name, which felt like a permission slip. It drained the power from the same slurs that have been used to control women's sexual behavior since time immemorial. For me, it meant I could venture further into writing about sex with little worry about what people would say or think. But I was having a harder time directly asking for what I wanted in my relationship. One night, amid an hours-long phone conversation with John, as I sat in my bay window and watched the slow creep of red taillights in the street below, I told him, "I'm worried I'm going to do something bad." John asked what that meant and I told him, haltingly, "I dunno. I might kiss someone?" The line went silent for a few cuticle-nibbling seconds. He was remarkably calm when he spoke. "I would . . . rather you not," he said. What I didn't say was that I already knew the who of this "might."

We had been dating long-distance for over two years. For weeks, I had been telling John things like, "I wanna cut loose" and "I'm sexually frustrated." I said these things in emails, phone calls, and those interminable video blogs, which were now filled with sniffling and puffy eyes. In those clips, my once-beloved forest-green ficus is visible in the background—its unwatered leaves withering, drying, and then falling to the ground, where they sat gnarled and untouched. I was in decay, too. I wasn't just weepy in my videos to John. I was weepy as I lathered my hair in the morning and late at night as I stared blankly at my reflection while brushing my teeth and leaving my therapist's office for the wind tunnel of Market Street and on the way to my fluorescent-lit neighborhood pharmacy to fill my new prescription of antidepressants.

There were many things to blame. The recession had decimated *Salon*'s San Francisco office through two rounds of layoffs, leaving the rest of us overworked and anxious in a sea of empty cubicles. One of my parents' good friends—Harold, a constant and beloved figure from my childhood—had suddenly died from cancer. Then, of course, there was the fact of my boyfriend living thousands of miles away. As I'd told John in a recent video blog, "Sometimes it feels like our relationship is kind of . . . abstract."

I was also coming up against the fact of our sexual mismatch. He was the kind of man I imagined marrying: moral, kind, romantic, intelligent, and emotionally expressive. We shared political and religious—or irreligious, as it were—beliefs. He would be an *excellent* dad. I cared deeply about these things, but

I also cared about sex—and being able to talk about it openly and excitedly and pervertedly. It seemed unwise, though, to give up on all the good for, what, some dirty talk and maybe dick pics delivered with slightly greater enthusiasm? Even still, I was consumed by this feeling of *I'm not done yet*. I still needed to sow my wild oats, like folks routinely say about young men, and rarely ever say about young women.

At this point, though, oat sowing seemed a threat to my desire for eventual motherhood. I was not yet cooing at babies on the street, but I had long channeled my parental impulses into other living creatures. In my early teens, I swaddled my overweight beagle in a blanket and carried her around like a very large baby, whispering to her about what a sweet "dog-onality" she had. In my early twenties, I purchased a dog statue from Target, which I clothed with a sweater, referred to as Douglass, and placed in the entryway of my studio apartment. Then came the plants, which spilled and sprawled and sprang from every surface and corner, and which were bequeathed with names like Benjamina (for the scientific *Ficus benjamina*).

I wanted to one day turn that nurturing impulse away from houseplants and dog statues, and the deadline for fulfilling that hypothetical eventuality seemed to be approaching fast. I had just turned twenty-six, and, not too many years earlier, I'd imagined twenty-eight as the perfect age for marrying. That way I could settle into a marriage and start trying to have kids at the age of thirty, which would give me enough time to have two well-spaced kids before I entered the official category of "advanced maternal age" (or, as some doctors still called it, "geriatric pregnancy"). I was, after all, highly acquainted with the constant stream of articles about age-related fertility decline. *Ticking clocks! Dying eggs! Ovarian reserves!*

Not unrelated was the topic of settling. The journalist Lori Gottlieb had recently published a wave-making *Atlantic* article arguing "the case for settling for Mr. Good Enough"—her belief being that you shouldn't strive for a perfect partner. If you did, you might end up like Gottlieb: a fortysomething woman pregnant by donor sperm and very publicly regretting her past decisions. "My advice is this: Settle! That's right. Don't worry about passion or intense connection," she wrote. "Because if you want to have the infrastructure in place to have a family, settling is the way to go." Gottlieb's thesis catapulted her onto the national stage not because it was particularly trenchant or wise, but because it played so well to women's fears, just as the hookup handwringers had. Collectively, it seemed these cultural commentators were telling young women to police men's sexuality, hedge their romantic bets, and not take too seriously their own desire for passion, adventure, or experience. This latter bit especially contradicted what I had heard growing up from my mom, who had once unforgettably told me, "Sex is one of the most fundamental ingredients of a marriage."

I was too scared to break up with John, but I was too scared to stay. So, I kept warning him that I might "do something bad" or "make a mistake."

My coworker Eric became that "mistake." If I was a hipster in training, with my Etsy-purchased jewelry and collection of terrariums in vintage cloches, he was a professional: fixie bike, skinny jeans, facial hair, keys on a carabiner, and a scattering of random forearm tattoos. On his foot was the result of a lost bet: a tattoo of a dinosaur surfing on a piece of bacon while throwing up a "shaka." He had man bangs, drank cans of Tecate, and played in a punk band. He was such a hipster that a photo of him floating around the internet had ended up *illustrating* a listicle detailing all of the most annoying things about hipsters.

It's easy to paint a retrospective caricature with these absurdist details, but the truth is that he was also funny, smart, and kind with a charming gap-toothed smile. He was popular with women, too—something I knew because I had eyes, but also because he often came to me for a woman's perspective on his romantic entanglements. We were buddies, the only two remaining post-layoffs of what had been a friendly crew of younger staffers. A handful of us would grab lunch from a Financial District burrito truck and then sprawl out on a lawn next to the glistening bay. Nearby sat an oversize sculpture of Cupid's bow and arrow, which was partially lodged in the ground, as if it had been flung there in resignation. Less a monument to love, it seemed an abandonment of it, but maybe I'm projecting.

As often happens in the presence of guilt, my memory blurs around specifics. What I know is that there were some flirty texts and then Eric invited me out drinking at a grungy Mission District bar in the bottom of an otherwise picturesque two-story Victorian. It was graffiti and security bars on the bottom and crown molding flourishes up top. At last call, Eric invited me back to his apartment just a few blocks away, and when we got to the front door, he turned, smiled, and slowly went in for a kiss—so slowly that it necessitated my meeting him halfway. Eric knew I had a boyfriend, so this was only fair: he was making me do some of the work of destroying my relationship. My lips hit his and it was like: finally. And also: *fuck*. Also: yes. Then: fuck it.

The next morning, I climbed into bed with my laptop and started composing a message. "Babe, this is a serious e-mail," I wrote. "There is no good way to put this, there is just the truth: I cheated." I kept the details of the night brief—I didn't even use the word *sex*, lamely favoring the euphemistic *slept with*—but I went long on my emotions. "I don't know what I'm doing or what my life IS. It's all so abstract. My job is virtual, my relationship is virtual," I wrote. "Nothing feels real anymore." I had cheated on him, but apparently felt he owed me a therapy session about it. I never sent that email, which still sits in my drafts folder in Gmail. Instead, I called him, perhaps starting to understand that there was nothing abstract about any of this. The relationship had been real, the cheating had been real, and the consequences would be real.

In that Gottlieb article that had so lodged in my brain, she wrote, "Our culture tells us to keep our eyes on the prize (while our mothers, who know better, tell us not to be so picky)." That is emphatically *not* what my mother, who knew better, told me when I informed her a couple of days later that I had cheated. Sitting on my couch—the same one where I had filmed my evenings in time-lapse and composed thousands of emails to John—I called her, heart pounding.

When she didn't answer, I poured a glass of screw-top wine,

prepared a rough ball of toilet paper, and began to write an email. I wrote about cheating and shame and the pain I had caused. I told her about having wanted more sexually from my relationship and feeling like I hadn't done enough "exploring" yet, and I admitted to feeling like a "weirdo" on both counts. I wrote nearly a thousand words—tears streaming the entire time, the wad of toilet paper melting into a sodden knot.

Then, with a visible cringe, I hit "Send."

My mom soon wrote back. "It clearly wasn't a thoughtless thing you did. You are not thoughtless. It means something," she said. "Somewhere in you is the answer to what is right for you." Then, a few minutes later, she followed up with another message: "I just want to say that you are not a weirdo." It was what I wanted to hear, but all those cautionary outside voices still lingered—the Stepps, the Gottliebs, and, more important, the cultural forces that had paved the way for their individual platforms. I wrote back with my hyperbolized worst fear: "If things don't work out with John, then will I end up as some lonely cat lady regretting my past decisions and writing books about how young gals should snag the first good guy they find?"

At the risk of a spoiler: This is not that book.

THE BLUE HOUSE ON Eighteenth Street felt like a life reboot. It was a two-story Victorian less than a block from Dolores Park, a sunny pocket amid San Francisco's thick blanket of fog, where it seemed half the city gathered on weekends to lounge on ratty picnic blankets, crush cans of PBR, and carefully nibble at gourmet edibles of unpredictable strength. The top-floor apartment was filled with original built-ins and ornate crown molding but decorated in the decidedly contemporary style of twenty-something millennials living on their own for the first time. The living room walls were the color of eggplant and the coffee table appeared to be a stoner craft project involving puffy paint.

Just as it had become clear that John and I were going to break up, I got an email about an open room in this four-bedroom flat. Finally, I would have roommates who were not plants. There was Jess, a raspy redheaded waitress at the gourmet pizzeria down the street, and Shane, a tech guy who left his body hair all over the bathroom floor. But, most important, there was Elissa, a fellow writer, and the one who emailed me about the house.

We had met a few months earlier when she judged Literary Death Match, a competition held at a local bar involving a traditional reading followed by an absurd activity, like a potato sack race. I made it past the first round with an essay about masturbating to my dad's porn, and then won the competition with a game of beer pong. My mastery of men's worlds had paid off—not because of the chintzy dollar-store medal I was given as my prize, but because that night's reading made Elissa, as she would later put it, "fall in friendship love" with me.

That friendship love was almost instantly and intensely reciprocated. Elissa had cat-eye glasses and wild curly hair that she dyed with streaks of the hottest pink. When doing a reading, she would often wear retro dresses and patent-leather red high heels.

I, on the other hand, went shopping at J.Crew, favoring cotton boatnecks, stripes, and ballet flats. "You dress like you're on a yacht," she told me with endearment. I bought a sleek wood dresser off Craigslist, which Elissa remarked looked like it was from Pottery Barn, so I took a piece of sandpaper to the dresser's corners in a futile attempt to model it after the charmingly beat-up secondhand furniture in her room.

She was not quite the Rayanne Graff to my pre-dye-job Angela Chase, but on the way there. Despite all my sex writing, I was pretty buttoned up. Elissa was completely unbuttoned, often as a form of inappropriate comedy. As we both typed away in our respective rooms, she would Gchat me things like, "I put 20 gumballs in my mouth and am topless." Then she would follow up with, "Shall we not work together in the living room? I will put on a robe." At times it felt like I was falling in actual love, not *friend* love, with her. I had never before met another woman who was so similarly interested in talking about sex and feminism and books and writing. She could go dark, too, joking about depression and SSRIs and suicidal ideation. With Elissa, anything could be said or done, all was destined for the light of day, and everything was funny. So I could say: *I am heartbroken and depressed and afraid I will end up alone forever.* And she might say: *Let's go eat a wheel of brie.* Often enough, we would go dancing at the gay club a few blocks away in the Castro.

Whenever I handed my ID to the bouncer sitting on a barstool in front of Badlands, I felt an electric jolt not unlike the one I got waiting outside the Hustler Club. It was the thrill of entering a "male space." The circular dance floor had hot pink backlighting and flat-screen TVs playing music videos synced with the blasting music. It was Beyoncé, Gaga, and Rihanna. In other words: heaven. A disco ball spun in the center, reflecting a mass of hands extended skyward, a multiarmed amoeba of joy. At Badlands, we danced like Elissa always danced—freely, wildly—and like I rarely ever did, even in the privacy of my own bedroom. I never would have danced like that in front of straight men, because there was always the worry of being watched, of how I was seen.

At the time, I didn't appreciate the absurdity of being a heartbroken straight girl—one distraught at the thought of potentially missing her ticket into the institution of marriage—going to a gay bar to find a sense of freedom in dancing among a bunch of men who at that point couldn't legally marry. I was absorbed in my own escape from the straight "male gaze," not appreciating that gay bars can provide queer people harbor from the "heterosexual gaze," as Miz Cracker would later argue in an article about the "straight lady invasion of gay bars."[12] Elissa and I often spilled onto the street at closing and headed for the neighborhood 7-Eleven to get a carton of milk and a sleeve of powdered doughnuts (we called them "white bagels"). Who needed men—straight ones, anyway—when there were good friends and fried dough?

But that brand of intoxicated empowerment tends to slip through your fingers like a shot poured straight into your hand. By the time we got home on one of those otherwise indistinguishable Badlands nights, it seemed a great idea to have Elissa leave a rambling voice mail telling John how wonderful he was and how desperately I missed him. I could only distract myself with these rollicking girls' nights for so long. I was consumed by grief over my failed relationship, which seems darkly comical considering what came knocking on my door next.

CHAPTER 4

Rough

I'm afraid it's bad news, honey." Then there was a collection of other words: CT scan, tumor, metastasis, bones. There was the street underneath my feet, something literally concrete amid this abstract but devastating news. I could see the signature sparkle of the Mission District sidewalk, and I could also see myself—or, really, some other girl—standing there clutching her cell phone and staring at the ground.

I had been headed toward the Make Out Room to watch Elissa do a reading, when my bag started to vibrate. Then my dad was telling me that my mom was dying. "Six months to a year," was a phrase that came out of his mouth and into my ear and heart and everything. It was a feeling of sudden illness, a convulsive physical state as blinkering and all-consuming as food poisoning.

I know, as a distant fact, that I traveled the several blocks back to my apartment while sobbing and hyperventilating. Surely, I passed many other living, breathing human beings on this walk, in this moment of internal demolition, but I don't remember a single face or expression. There was just my cell phone pressed tightly against my ear, like I might be able to escape into it, and my dad saying things like, "Oh, honey" and "I love you, sweetheart" and "I am so sorry" and "Try to breathe slowly" and "Are you near your apartment yet?"

When I got into my apartment and off the phone, I buckled onto the moss-green Ikea carpet in my bedroom, which my mom had bought for me several years earlier. Tears slipped down my face, silent but streaming, and I watched detachedly as carpet pile turned to boggy marsh. It was like my basic emotional and physical infrastructure had suddenly cracked and flooded. Sticking my finger into the swampy carpet, the *squish* of it seemed a representation of how I felt.

I texted Elissa an SOS: "Bad news. Can't come." Then I held up my iPhone and took a series of selfies. This I do not remember, but I know, somewhat regrettably, that it happened, because I still have the time-stamped photos. They show a woman who looks to be having a severe allergic reaction: eyes, nose, and cheeks puffed and grotesquely distorted. The photos also show a woman who knows that this is the worst pain she has ever felt, and that such pain must be documented.

A few hours later, Elissa returned from the reading and knocked on my door. I opened it while bracing myself against the frame. "My friend," she said gently, grabbing me in a hug. I felt the delicateness of her shoulder blades, the slight rise of her spine, the flutter of breath under her silk shirt, and I let go. She was bone and flesh, distressingly mortal. We all were, suddenly.

• • •

FOR YEARS, MY MOM struggled with back pain, for which a doctor had recently sent her to physical therapy. After months of
worsening pain, a CT scan had been ordered. As I would find
when my dad passed along a CD-ROM of the images, it showed
a white ghost of a tumor wrapped around her esophagus. A
week after that devastating news, we got an official diagnosis:
stage 4 lung cancer. There is no stage 5. First there would be
radiation, which might shrink the tumor, but, as the doctors
told us, there was no possibility of remission.

What to do with nonnegotiable information like that? I
promptly chopped off my long flowing hair into an angular bob
with blunt-cut bangs. I went from "girl next door" to Aeon
Flux–like superheroine (a wishful act, perhaps). I started talking seriously about getting a tattoo—of the text of my favorite
Wordsworth passage, which shows how laughably pathetic I
was at pretending to be a no-fucks tattoo getter. "A sense sub-
lime of something far more deeply interfused." Once, I felt that
line spoke to the exquisite interconnectedness of the natural
world, but now it signaled the universe's absolute, unerring indifference. The *universe* was a no-fucks tattoo getter, no faking
there. It casually summoned cancer like it was a drunken-bet
tattoo of a dinosaur surfing on bacon.

And then, and then, I brought home a stranger from a bar
and was fucked until six a.m. I hadn't been the type to say that
I was "fucked," but now maybe I was. In any case, it was the
only way to accurately describe such rough, punishing sex. Ian,

a thirty-eight-year-old waiter wearing a wolf-tooth necklace, positioned my twenty-six-year-old body and limbs like I was a sex doll. Spreading, prying, flipping, propping. I greeted his every escalation with an openmouthed, smiling nod and a look that said *More, motherfucker, give it to me.*

He was more than happy to give it to me. "Are you kidding me? You've got to be kidding me," he said breathlessly. "I feel like I'm a teenager discovering *Playboy* for the first time. No, make that *Penthouse*."

What Ian correctly saw in me was a woman who would not only say yes to anything he wanted but "fuck yes." I already felt at the whims of an indifferent universe—why not be at the whims of a desperately horny man? In that moment, my anxious curiosity about what men wanted fused with my grief over my mom's terminal diagnosis. My enduring mission of trying to master "male desire" became determination to validate not only my worst fears about it but also my ability to *withstand* it.

The truth was that I brought Ian home precisely because I suspected he would deliver this kind of sexual punishment. Maybe it was the heavy-handed bad-boy signaling of the wolf tooth, or maybe it was the way his detached smirk at the bar had suggested that he was already flipping my body around in his mind.

As Ian and I lay in bed afterward, he propped himself up on his elbow and told me, "I want to do all kinds of *fucking crazy shit* to you. I wanna stick a candle in your ass, light it, and watch it drip all over your thighs." This sounded as appealing as a dental exam, but I gave him a studied, purring, "Oh yeah?" Later with Elissa, we laughingly christened him Candle Butt Boy, or

CBB for short. Our roommate Jess sketched a crude cartoon of me on all fours, candle aflame, and we snorted until we cried. I didn't register the cruel duplicitousness of this. It just felt like payback, but for what I was not sure.

The following afternoon I pulled down my jeans to show Elissa the palm-size purple bruise left from Ian smacking my ass. "Look at this," I insisted, as breathlessly as Ian had regarded my enthusiasm the night before. "*Look at this.*" I found it beautiful, this abstract watercolor painting just under the surface of my skin. It was proof of life and proof of pain. "Jesus, Tracy," Elissa told me. "It looks like you were beaten."

But these were not just the marks of someone else's aggression. I was angry—at an indifferent universe for giving my mom cancer, and at men for having desires that threatened and compelled me. As women so often do, and are trained to do, I turned that anger inward. There are so many ways to hurt, but I chose sex. I chose men.

MY BRUISES WERE A secret that I carried with me when I went to visit my mom in the hospital a few days later. She had been rushed into emergency surgery to remove a blood clot near her aorta. A drug cocktail seemed to have sunk her into a waking dream state. In a stage whisper, my mom told me that the powers that be had secretly transferred her to a locked psychiatric ward. It was as though in a pharmaceutical fog she was flashing back to the trauma of being committed at the age of eighteen. With pleading eyes, she nodded her head toward the nurse stationed near the door. "Tracy, I'm putting you on notice," she said cautiously. "I have a grave concern about what is happening here."

Same, Mom. *Same.* I wondered whether it was the drugs inducing these delusions or whether the cancer had already ransacked her brain, a terrifying thought. More than anything, my mom *was* her brain. It occurred to me that her body was here but she might already be gone.

Once she was out of the hospital, I came to visit every weekend. Each time, I was greeted by a different stage of the disease. It was like flipping through a childhood photo album, where you miss the intervening growth and see only marked change. These images didn't reflect birthdays, but rather steps closer to death. Some people say, with a cynical, self-amused air, that they are the same thing: another year older, another year closer to death. Those people haven't watched death take over. They haven't seen the way it grows as it negates. One weekend my mom was bright and bubbly, her face flushed, sitting upright. The next, she was disoriented and bedbound, sinking into the sheets. Gray skin, hollowed eyes, plump face gone sharp.

Then I became entangled with Mike, a writer and self-declared "male slut." The smell of whiskey and cigarettes hung not just on his breath, but in the fibers of his plaid button-downs. His forearms were scattered with tattoos, including a small pair of hands in prayer, an ironic plea for mercy from a lapsed Catholic. Mike first kissed me as we sat in my kitchen in the early hours of the morning sipping from a bottle of Bulleit and talking about my mom's death sentence. "You must be having a hard time," he said, gently stroking my thumb, and then he kissed me like the conversation had been foreplay.

During sex, his calloused hands often found my neck and I would lean into his cautious hold, moaning for more. Before long, those hands were covering my mouth, pinching my nose shut, shoving my face into the pillow. His fingers would probe behind my lips, run along my gums, fold over my teeth, press down my tongue. He might tug at my jaw, using it for leverage, or wrap his arms around me from behind, squeezing my torso like a bubble that needed to be popped.

Years earlier, Lady Gaga had crooned about liking it "rough." Now the radio was dominated by Rihanna's "S&M," in which she sang about being excited by "chains and whips." We were a couple of years away from the blockbuster release of *Fifty Shades of Grey*. Fast-forward several more years and Pornhub would report that "rough sex" was one of the tube site's most-searched terms among women.[1] We were on the verge of a massive mainstream cultural shift around BDSM, as well as countless think pieces about a purported, though never reliably documented, "rise in rough sex," but I'd already felt the rumblings of it in my immediate surrounds. Mike had, too, it seemed. "Girls *love* to be roughed up," he declared early on.

Of course, BDSM wasn't anything new in San Francisco, home of the Folsom Street Fair, but I lived within blocks of the historic Armory, a former arsenal for the national guard that now served as the castle-like headquarters of the BDSM porn site Kink.com. You could book a $21.99 tour of the various sets where filming took place: dank dungeons, a padded room complete with a stock straitjacket, and a baroque Edwardian parlor filled with floggers and whips. We lived adjacent to the possibility, the question mark, the "why not" of it all.

I had already ventured into the realm of BDSM porn during my tube site explorations and found that I could mentally edit out the ropes, glossy leather, and cracking whips, leaving just the fundamental act of sexual submission. The aesthetics did not appeal to me, but the subtler power dynamics did. Now, playing out those power dynamics in real life felt like temporary release from my mom's diagnosis.

"Subspace," the altered mental state sometimes euphorically experienced by submissives, is often compared to a runner's high. Researchers have preliminarily proposed that "bottoming" in BDSM is associated with "transient hypofrontality," which is the short-term impairment of the brain's executive function.[2] This state can be associated with "reductions in pain, decision making activity, logic, and difficulty with memory, along with increased feelings of floating, peacefulness, and living in the here and now," as one study put it.[3] In other words, an escape from one's mind. There was nothing I wanted to escape more.

My casual, ill-informed dabbling stood apart from the experiences of seasoned BDSM practitioners, who take skill-building workshops, carefully negotiate boundaries, and often follow a code of ethics known as "safe, sane, and consensual." (It was further still from my fantastical reference point: kink as performed on a controlled film set by skilled actors.) Still, the sense of escape applied.

After sex, Mike and I would lie there talking, his profligate chest hair tickling my nose. He would bruise my ribs with his manhandling and leave me wincing every time I sat down, but then he'd urge me during our postcoital chats to go see a therapist. These conversations often turned to the subject of my mom, as well as my friends' vocal disapproval of our late-night forays, which I recounted to them both with words and with the marks on my body. "I'm going through a hard time and feel pretty fucked up," I told him one night while lying on his chest. "It feels good to spend time with someone who is—"

"A drunken emotional mess?"

"Well." I paused. "You're in the ballpark."

"The *drunken emotional mess ballpark*?"

"Yeah," I laughed.

He began shouting with a smile, "Hey folks, welcome to the drunken emotional mess ballpark! Get your drunken emotional mess popcorn right here!"

Misery loves company as much it loves the release valve of an unexpected laugh. But I also recognized this joke as a light-hearted dig. When the subject of his reputation for sleeping around came up, he often referred to himself as a "dildo with a heartbeat." This quip was justification of his heartbreaking ways, the perfect antidote to accusations of womanizing. Women were using *him*, you see. He wasn't necessarily wrong, but he also seemed to ensure that it was true. Takes one to know one, you might say.

And, actually, he was onto something with the "drunken emotional mess" schtick. During one of our early romps, Mike was rocking against me when he grunted into my ear: "Oh,

Stacey." Then he corrected himself, "Tracy." I let this drunken error pass. I let it pass because I refused to acknowledge out loud that I was having sex with someone so intoxicated that he called me by the wrong name. The next morning, I walked into the kitchen and found him vomiting into a clear glass pitcher. Some months later, I would drunkenly throw up in my own bed and then tell Mike about it. His joking, irreverent reply: "Don't do that again, okay, asshole? Leave something for those of us who have been working hard for a long time at the alcoholic thing."

This was all part of hurting myself. It wasn't just the rough sex, which brought pain with an occasionally redemptive edge. It was also his, and my, drunken recklessness, which had no redemptive appeal at all.

THERE WAS NOW A rented hospital bed in my parents' living room. It was positioned such that my mom became a pillar of light during the afternoon. The heavenly effect of it was unnervingly portentous, even for a nonbeliever like me. When she brought out her wooden pipe, the smoke would slowly cascade up the glowing column, making the act of getting high seem like divine communion. "She's only getting the *primo* dope now," my dad told me.

That she was feeling well enough to smoke weed was an improvement. My mom had rebounded from her initial decline, thanks to radiation easing some of her bone pain. Now she was on to chemo, which had left her with an infant's patchy head of hair until she cut it to a close, fuzzy crop. "It's cute," I told her, earnestly, upon seeing it. Her cheeks were pink and plump again, but when I came to visit every weekend, she only had energy to zone out to low-stakes reality TV shows, like *Cupcake Wars* and *Millionaire Matchmaker*.

Whenever we took a break for a snack, there was the *click-click* of her lighter—the same sound that as a kid I had noted behind her closed bedroom—because weed was the only thing that could stir her appetite. My mom had smoked pot my entire life, but never in front me, not until the cancer. And for this, while lighting up, my mom apologized.

She apologized for everything. *Can you get me a glass of water? Sorry. Can you straighten the pillows on the couch? Sorry. Can you grab me a morphine pill from upstairs? Sorry.* One afternoon, she threw up from the nauseating effects of chemo, heaving into a plastic bag at her bedside. As soon as she caught her breath, she offered up a sincere "Sorry, honey" for my having had to witness it. "I've thrown up *on you*," I said. She smiled. "Yes, honey, but not in *a very long time*."

For her, it was an unacceptable role reversal, but for me it was a relief to experience her as a mere mortal. It would take me many more years to realize that her drive to be a perfect mom— fueled, no doubt, by the need to atone for the adoption of her first child—could be stifling for me. My paternal grandmother, who knew about the adoption, once said of my mom in the beginning of my life, "She cares for her as though she were two children."

Mostly during my visits we napped, falling asleep to the grating lullaby of Patti Stanger shouting at playboy millionaires. My mom would doze noisily in her hospital bed, mumbling vaguely from a morphine dream, as I curled up on the neighboring couch. She wrote me in an email, "When we're both too tired to visit and end up taking naps in the living room I really enjoy that we're doing what we need and being as 'together' as we can be at that point. There is something sweet about taking a nap with one's grown-up child."

This was true—and yet, the guilt. My mom was sick and tired from a terminal illness, while I was sick and tired from boozing and sexing into the wee hours of the morning with Mike or Candle Butt Boy. My mom's death and Candle Butt Boy did not belong in the same chapter, let alone sentence. Both of our bodies were being battered, but only one of us was choosing it. I wondered sometimes whether I was trying to steal the spotlight or make a twisted show of solidarity.

But I also understood the marks on my body to be transmutation. They were a magic trick of pain: a rabbit becomes a dove; all-consuming grief becomes a tiny bruise. Lightly pressing on these marks, I sometimes thought of the girls I'd known as a teenager who took razor blades to their own skin. I, too, was manifesting my emotional hurt by making it physical. In fact, it's suggested that cutting is driven in part by an associated endorphin rush, and something similar is often surmised as the appeal of "bottoming" in BDSM, although there is limited research on the topic. All I know is that I watched with fascination as those self-created marks gradually disappeared—as rug-burned knees scabbed over and healed. It seemed that some day my grief could be transformed, too.

There was something else that kept me seeing Mike, though. Something so much more essential than the pain of the cancer or the anger redirected at myself or the escape of rough sex or the depravity of being called by the wrong name. I try to forget it, I want so much to paper it over, but I see it staring me in the face in my saved Gchat messages from the time.

> **me:** katherine, help. i am going crazy and obsessing
> over why Mike hasn't called me in four days.
> the guy who accidentally called me "stacey"
> during sex
> and who, apparently, was recently hospitalized
> from drunkenly(?) getting severe poison oak
> **Katherine:** so maybe you should just cut it off?
> **me:** i know that I should, but I desperately don't want to
> **Katherine:** well, that's what i figured.
> **me:** i want so much for him to want me. you know?
> **Katherine:** yes. i know the feeling.
> but he is a piece of shit.
> so there are better guys to want/have wanting you.

I didn't think he was a piece of shit, actually. I thought he was a deeply funny, occasionally brilliant, and phenomenally charismatic human being. Lots of women did. His emotional unavailability was a multifaceted gem that glinted with various tantalizing propositions, including the avoidance of my own feelings. Most notably and cliché of all was my aspiration of being wanted in return by such a self-announced ladies' man. But the maintenance of this aspiration depended on the other women remaining abstract and theoretical, which they did not.

One night, I decided to take Elissa to her first strip club. She had been accepted to graduate school in New York, that glittering beacon of possibility where, until my mom got sick, we had planned on moving together. In anticipation of Elissa's departure at the end of the summer, we were checking off a shared bucket list of adventures, and the strip club was my contribution. Here I was, trying to show another woman how men were, letting her in on what I knew, but then we ran smack dab into what I didn't. A dancer stopped at our table and exclaimed, "Elissa?" They were friends from the local writing scene, and they both knew Mike. She crouched at our table and laughed when Elissa mentioned him. "I was just at Mike's house last night," she said with a provocative eyebrow raise. The room tilted and I felt like I might fall right out my chair. I thought: *I was at Mike's the night before last, and the night before that, and two nights before that, and the night before that and . . .*

I pictured them lying in his bed, the sheets unwashed from when I had left them that very morning. I thought of how my sweat, my bodily fluids were on those sheets, how we, she and I, had been closer than she knew—closer, even, than we were now with her exposed flesh. I thought about him grabbing on to me—my ass, my breasts, my face, my hair, how he'd told me, "You have the most amazing tits," as I surveyed hers. I had meticulously cataloged his every expression of longing: "You are gorgeous." "I like you." "I missed you last night." "What is this?" These felt like hints as to how I stacked up against the other women, who I abstractly knew existed. It was quite another thing, though, to run into one in a strip club, a setting that recalled my wishful mastery around men.

The next day, I confronted Mike. Then I went home with him. Mike, ever perceptive, gave me just what I wanted: "Tracy, you're the best. You're the fucking best," he said breathlessly. Afterward, he rolled off me and said, "That might have been the best sex I've ever had." We could both pretend. I had, after all, faked all but one of my many "orgasms" with him. That single one had snuck up on me accidentally when I forgot for a fleeting moment that it wasn't pleasure that I was seeking but a different kind of pain.

AROUND THIS TIME, I was flown to New York for a photo shoot for *More*, a now-shuttered glossy print magazine aimed at women over the age of forty. They were doing a feature on what they dubbed "the new feminists" and, for whatever reason, I had been selected as one of ten for a two-page photo spread. We spent a full day in a Queens warehouse getting blow-dried, painted, and squeezed into Spanx. *Feminism*, you see. They dressed us like first ladies: high necklines, knee-length skirts, Jimmy Choos. I was the only one left in the outfit she had arrived in: a nautical blue-and-white-striped dress. As Elissa had repeatedly observed, "You dress like you're on a yacht." *More* was into that.

Paradoxically, though, after all the prim and proper styling, the magazine would run with the cover line: "Feminists in Fishnets." It seems they couldn't decide whether they wanted to frighten or reassure their older women readers. I was ultimately quoted in the piece saying, "Casual sex isn't either empowering or disempowering. There's tremendous variation, and what works for one person doesn't for another."

Fittingly enough, while waiting for the shoot to begin, I went browsing through the warehouse's aisles of vintage props— gilded birdhouses, fraying armchairs, fractured mirrors—and ran into a young crew member from the photo shoot. He looked like a more handsome, less creepy version of Casey Affleck. We talked inanely about how cool these props would be for various "art projects." Then he, Gabe, asked for my phone number.

The next night, a sticky August evening, we walked the High Line, chatting about Diane Arbus, Joan Didion, and cancer. He showed me his tattoo of the outline of Manhattan, his birthplace. I noted that he, too, had a wolf tooth necklace. *What is it with these men and their wolf teeth?* Then I took him back to my place with a six-pack of beer. "My place" was actually my editor's place in the West Village; she was out of town on vacation, and I was crashing at her studio apartment to take care of her beloved tabby cat.

Gabe and I perched awkwardly on my editor's bed—which had hot-pink sheets and was effectively the living room couch— while surveying the bookshelf over the mantel. "I'm in one of those books," I blurted. Gabe asked which one. I demurred.

Then he pulled *Best Sex Writing 2009* off the shelf with the flick of a finger, holding it up with raised eyebrows. "Yep, that's it," I said, my nerve gone, if it had ever been there. "Just a personal essay . . ." What about, he wanted to know. I fluttered, I reddened. Then he flipped to the table of contents. "In defense of casual sex," he read aloud, smirking. He put the book down and moved toward me.

Then he fucked me, freely and unrelentingly—right off the bed and onto the floor. Did I like it? In theory, sure. Sounds cool. I would return to the memory occasionally: the thrill of New York, of being picked up on a photo shoot, of his beauty, of his fat, fat dick, of his Manhattan tattoo, of wandering through cobble streets mere blocks from the *Sex and the City* house. C'mon. *Come on.* Sometimes over the years I would think: *Man, wish I could do that again.* But, looking back, I'll never shake the feeling that I was barely even there to experience it the first time, like it was a ghost of a girl who did it all for me.

THAT FALL, AFTER ELISSA moved to New York, it was as though the line that had tethered me to this planet was cut and I went spiraling off into the cosmos like a wayward space explorer. She had offered an escape that Mike could not: we'd go dancing in the Castro until two a.m. on a weeknight, take goofy photos in Japantown's green-screen photobooths, and eat Dolores Park weed truffles and then go running through the neighborhood inexplicably equipped with water guns and a board game buzzer.

I had other friends, of course, but Elissa's uniquely depressive sense of humor and taste for absurdist adventure had given me a feeling of partnership in my pain. Now I was desperately grasping for something else to hold on to.

The promise of oblivion through however many consecutive cans of cheap hipster beer was one such graspable thing. Another such thing: a bike messenger with a septum piercing who noisily bragged that he didn't care about making women come. During a party at my house, I latched on to both of these things. I, master faker of orgasms, was *outraged* at a man devaluing women's pleasure just as much as I apparently did. I confronted him in the kitchen, backing him up against the refrigerator. "I think you're scared of women," I shouted, my eyes a pair of binoculars going in and out of focus. "I don't think you can *handle* women. That's why you brag about not giving a shit about making them come."

There was a crowd gathering, tittering with variations on "oh shiiit." He bit his lip. "Well, I don't think you can handle *me*," he said, jutting out his chin, like he was inviting me to deck him, but we all knew what he was really saying. We all knew it's what I'd been saying, too. There followed an escalating exchange about who could handle what from whom and just how much.

Then: kissing and yelling. One of the onlookers swiftly picked me up under the arms and walked me into the other room like a toddler in need of a time-out. "Hey, hey, hey," he said kindly. "Are you okay? Everything's gotten a little out of control." I'd wrapped my arms and legs around him as he lifted me, and now I pulled back to inspect who was carrying me. He had a Yorkshire terrier of a mustache above his lips that narrowed into an ironic curlicue on either end. I smiled at the little lip pet, then collapsed into his neck, drinking down this unexpected tenderness like a quick shot.

He lowered me and as soon as my feet hit the floor, I was hopping over furniture to get back to the bike messenger. To fight him, to fuck him. What was the difference? *Fuck men and their fucking entitlement. Fuck the fucking unfairness. Fuck the fucking fuck. Let's fuck.*

Before long, the bike messenger and I were in my bedroom and he was asking if I had any condoms. I reached into a box on my bedside, filled with a colorful sampler pack purchased at the neighborhood Good Vibrations, *because that's what a sex-positive feminist blogger like me did.* I grabbed a fistful. Then I threw them at him. As they showered down around his feet, I said, "*Fuck yeah*, I have condoms."

I don't remember the feeling but rather the fact of him on top of me. My memory skips and starts. All I know is that at some point, he ripped the condom off and threw it on the floor. Then his hand was gripping my throat and I threw my head back and laughed. I could take it. He pushed harder and my face felt like it might crack right open. The next thing: saltiness flowing over my tongue. No images, just the familiar taste of cum. The next visual: him getting dressed and leaving in a hurry.

In the morning, I woke up to find a few small droplets of blood outside my bedroom door. I followed them down the hall to the bathroom, where I looked up into the vanity and saw reflected back the image of a woman with a fuchsia hand-shaped bruise across the front of her neck. I looked like a victim from my once-beloved *Law & Order: SVU*. Reaching up to lightly place my own palm over the handprint, I noticed a small cut on my finger. I texted with friends and learned that the bike messenger had been seen leaving the party while wiping blood from his lip. The blood, cut, and bruise seemed like clues to a crime, although I had no recollection of anything happening against my will. Then again, there was a lot that I couldn't remember about the night.

That afternoon, I went over to my parents' house with a scarf wrapped tightly around my neck. As we lay there watching TV, I tried to piece together the evidence from the night before: Maybe I had tried to push the bike messenger away as he choked me and there had been a struggle in which I'd injured his lip and cut my hand on his septum piercing. I might have passed out and come to as he finished and rushed off. This narrative seemed plausible enough that within a few days I was on the phone with the frightened and apologetic bike messenger. He told me that during our sloppy make-out, as we ricocheted down my hallway toward the bedroom, his lip had been cut. That I'd told him to choke me. That I'd said "harder." That I'd laughed. That I'd never passed out. That he'd said good-bye but left in a hurry because he felt like he was going to puke, and then promptly did in my toilet.

Suddenly, a memory. After the bike messenger left, I rejoined the party and cracked open yet another PBR. Recognizing that

I'd had too much to drink, a friend tried to playfully grab it from me, but I went to war over that patriotically hued can of beer, crushing it in my grip and diving to the floor to wrestle it back. In the supposedly playful melee, my finger slipped into the sharp open mouth of the can as yellow liquid flooded the floor. *My finger was cut by the beer can, not the septum piercing,* I realized. A sadder sentence had never before materialized in my head.

Of course, I couldn't be certain of all that had happened with the bike messenger that night. All I knew for sure was that I felt queasy any way that I pieced it together.

Many years later, the British media would overflow with stories of the "rough sex defense," in which men claimed to have killed women accidentally, often while experimenting with choking in the bedroom. While the details of these high-profile cases would typically make the likelihood of an accidental death seem highly implausible, I'd interview experts, including medical examiners, who underscored that even light choking, which is accurately called "strangulation," is a dangerous and potentially life-threatening practice. I had no idea.

WHEN THANKSGIVING CAME AROUND, my mom was feeling well enough to host, but not to cook. My dad's two sisters descended upon the kitchen, layering sliced potatoes and grated Gruyère for my mom's signature gratin and basting the turkey with its unctuous juices, as the smell of butter and sage filled the house. We all gathered in the living room to eat in the casual fashion typical of my family: plates propped on knees, stray food dropping to the floor, and my parents' two portly beagles vacuuming up in turn. Only, this time there was that hospital bed, the proverbial elephant in the room, and there was nothing casual about that.

My family had shown up and pitched in. There was every reason to feel full up with love and gratitude, but all I could think as I cut into my second, sickening slice of apple pie was *This is the last Thanksgiving we'll have with her.* An eviscerating thought, one made only more unbearable by its textbook unoriginality. From my brief foray into the internet of grief, I could *just picture* a well-meaning purple-hued hospice website intoning, *Holidays are challenging times for grieving families.*

As soon I got home from my parents' house, I text messaged Mike to let him know that I was coming over. Then I asked: "A request?"

He replied: "Oh, well I could go for a beer, but def not necessary."

"No," I wrote back. "I mean I have a request for you . . ."

"Oh. What's up?"

"Be rough with me?"

"Done," he replied.

Of course, he had already been "rough with me." Now I was vaguely asking Mike to give me more, but without specific directives. I wanted to see what *he* would want to do to me. This was not the careful negotiation of boundaries that accompanies responsible BDSM, but I do recall Mike rapid-fire texting some hypotheticals. That he might do x or y or z thing. And I said yes to all of it.

As I walked into Mike's room, he grabbed me by the hair with a "come here" delivered through clenched teeth. Then he tossed me against the side of the mattress. "Who's in charge here?" he asked. "You think you're in charge?" I could tell from the studied look on his face that I was, that he was acting from anticipation of my wants, not the expression of his own, so I nodded with a smirk. He gave my face the lightest of play slaps and I grinned at the trespass of it. I had never before been smacked in my face. I had never before *wanted* to be smacked in the face. "Harder," I told him, and he complied.

Here I was, a feminist blogger, who had recently written about pop culture sexualizing domestic violence, asking a man to hit me harder. A slap to the face was nothing like a hand wrapped lightly around the neck or some de rigueur slaps on the rear. There was something permanent and symbolic about it. Had I ever been hit by a man? The answer was now, and forevermore, yes. As someone who abhorred the societal ill of men's violence against women, I felt this was thrillingly transgressive. It was, in some ways, a slap in the face of my very sense of self, which was inextricably tied to my mom. Mike was a coach training me for a certain future without her. *Slap, slap, slap.* Toughen up, little girl. Face the darkness. Be brave.

While on top of me, Mike whispered in my ear: "*No, no,* I'm not in control. You have all the power." It was true, I was in charge, and that is the thing about BDSM. It's the bottom who sets the limits. Even in our poorly negotiated power exchange, this vaguely held true. It was clear Mike understood that amid the chaos of my life, asking him to be rough with me was a grab for control. Afterward, with my head resting on his chest, Mike ventured, "So, I'm guessing Thanksgiving was hard." He delicately traced the folds of my ear, waiting for my response.

"It was a reminder of how little time is left," I managed to say before my throat seized up and tears fell. We lay in silence, the same hand that had hit me now gently stroking my shoulder.

The next night, I opened a Word doc and wrote, "It's amazing what you can get men to do to you during sex. Smacking a woman in the face, choking her, tossing her onto the floor? Most decent men would refuse to consider doing such a thing— until a woman is standing in front of them, naked, and saying that she wants it." Those words rang false as soon I wrote them. I wasn't *so amazed* at what you could get men to do to you. I was amazed at my own desires, at what I *wanted* men to do to me. Some of these things I had been curious about before my mom's diagnosis, but most of them, like a slap to the face, only became intriguing in the devastating aftermath. My worst fears about men were, on some level, my worst fears about myself. I had voiced my desire with that vague "be rough" text, and then promptly disowned it. When Mike delivered what I wanted, I smiled smugly at his depravity.

I didn't yet appreciate how I'd been doing a version of this since my AOL chat room days. That game of seeing just what men would *say to me* online had transformed into seeing just what they would *do to me* in real life. "Male desire" was both a moderator of my own wants and, at times, a convenient excuse. I constructed halls of mirrors to feel okay about getting what I wanted from sex. Men were the refractive agents of desires that called insistently from within. What was mine became theirs. This was a socially sanctioned act of sublimation. My mom's death sentence had created an additional alibi: I was just a good girl going through a bad time.

CHAPTER 5

Winning

Live porno wrestling." Those were the words that showed up in my personal inbox just as happy hour kicked off on a Friday at the *Salon* office. Happy hour had once meant that our executive editor would wander cubicle-to-cubicle offering up martinis from a sweating silver shaker. "Anyone want a *martooooni*?" he'd sing, as though offering juice to toddlers. Then we would pile onto the leather couch outside his office or wheel over our desk chairs to shout incredulously about some offensive bullshit that Bill O'Reilly or Tucker Carlson had just said on Fox News. Now, post-layoffs, it meant grabbing a Stella Artois from the fridge and sitting at our desks talking via Gchat until the clock hit six p.m.

It meant a free beer.

This "live porno wrestling" email came from Sam, a well-connected, influential indie author known for his proximity to the BDSM scene. An even better-known local dude writer—*there were just so many of them*—had bailed last-minute on their plans that night, so Sam asked whether I wanted to accompany him as a friend-slash-date to see "live porno wrestling" at the infamous San Francisco Armory. The friend bit I took seriously, and emphatically, because Sam seemed to like the kind of woman who could confidently rock a red latex minidress, and that was not me.

As for the "live porno wrestling," I already knew about Kink.com's site Ultimate Surrender, which was filmed in the building's gymnasium in front of an audience. Women wrestled on padded floors and ultimately had sex with each other, this much I knew from having idly poked around the site. A time stamp on my email shows that I wrote back within a minute of his sending.

I would have said yes to this invite at most any point in my marginally adult life, but I was especially enthusiastic given my recent reincarnation at *Salon*. For the past year I'd been running *Broadsheet*, but my boss had offered to reassign me as a full-time sex writer. This had something to do with my always finding excuses to write about sex. There was also the fact that I had burned out on the grief limbo of my mom's terminal illness, as well as the relentless churn of horrors of that era's online feminism. A headline that I wrote from this period read, "Breast Ironing: Today in Depressing News."

My boss's offer meant I got my dream job. It also meant that I needed to immerse myself in San Francisco's sexual subcultures—*for story ideas, for work.* Another permission slip.

The Armory, a towering brick Moorish building with turrets and a rippling black flag bearing a bold red *K* with a perky devil's tail, spanned nearly half a block of Mission Street. Its imposing figure, dotted with narrow jail-like windows, appeared at the beginning of each of Kink's films along with a foreboding soundtrack of rumbling thunder. That building bore all of the intriguingly sinister symbolism of a cracking leather whip. *Things happened in that building*, we all knew, whether we were watching those videos or just walking by on our way home. Now, walking up the Armory's stark cement steps, I was hit by a bolt of electric excitement.

A beefy security guard opened up the glass-paned front door and ushered us into the lobby with its candelabra-style chandeliers and gray marble baseboards. During subsequent reporting trips I would come to know the entire building well: its creamy terrazzo floors, spiraling staircases, and collection of pornographic oil paintings of gang bangs and rope bondage. For now, though, we were pointed down a stark, militaristic hallway to the gymnasium, where the bleachers overflowed with excess audience members who sat cross-legged on the floor surrounding the large white wrestling mats. I recognized the hip young waitress with platinum hair from my local pizzeria, as well as at least half a dozen other faces that I regularly passed on the streets of the Mission.

At my insistence, Sam and I climbed to the very top of the bleachers, away from the range of the cameras, as he teased that my prudery was giving him a bad view of the action. My reasons for not wanting to be caught on camera were ostensibly professional. At the time, appearing in a porn film, even as a fully dressed audience member, seemed like crossing a line. What was the line, though? What were the journalistic rules for a job that would soon enough involve testing sex toys, watching porn, visiting adult shoots, and writing about the intimate details of my own sex life? A few years later, a woman would ejaculate on my shoe as I studiously took notes for a story on a New Age "sexual healer," and my professional boundaries would start to seem necessarily more porous (or "stickier," I might have said at the time, with an elbow to the ribs).

Still, even then, at this "live porno wrestling" event, I suspected my camera concern had more to do with my own internal identity struggle than with professionalism. In so many ways, from my grief-driven explorations with rough sex and now with my new sex writer title, I was saying: *I'm here but not here. This is me and it's not me.* It was plausible deniability.

I nervously sipped at a tall can in a paper bag. Sam had let me know ahead of time that outside alcohol was allowed in, and I felt I needed it to censor my nerves. There were two referees on the floor below: a man in a traditional ref uniform, and a woman wearing a skintight black-and-white-striped polo paired with booty shorts and knee-high socks. A large digital scoreboard hung on the wall. Four performers in string bikinis marched to the front of the mat and a whistle was blown as the crowd whooped.

Bikinis were pulled off by any means necessary, using fingers, teeth, and bodily friction. I was more than halfway done with my swiftly ingested tall can by the time all the bikinis were gone. Then the competitors, sparring in teams of two, started going for "style" and "sexual humiliation" points—licking, grinding, squeezing, face-sitting. A woman was pinned to the floor and then a hand was slipped between her legs as the referee asked, surreally, "Are you *in*?" There came a nod from the woman digitally penetrating her opponent and then another point popped up on the scoreboard. The referee crouched down for visual confirmation and shouted, "Two fingers in the pussy!"

At this point, I was laughing. Less than shocking or disillusioning, I found it refreshing. Here was an in-your-face representation of how sex, and porn, could be competitive, theatrical, and profoundly ridiculous. This woman thrust her fingers in and out of her opponent while ruthlessly watching as the scoreboard reflected her mounting points in real time. It was like an X-rated episode of *Black Mirror* before there was *Black Mirror*. Meanwhile, her teammate squeezed one of the pinned woman's breasts, each squeeze garnering yet more points on the literal scoreboard.

It was amid this spectacle that I turned and saw—well, let's call him Maxxx. In that moment, the exact explanatory parenthetical that I would use to introduce you to him appeared in my head in screaming all-caps: MY FAVORITE MALE PORN STAR. The experience of seeing him unexpectedly standing a few feet away from me in this crowded auditorium was akin to nonchalantly opening up my laptop in a shoulder-to-shoulder coffee shop only to discover the porn clip I'd been watching the night before playing with full audio. That is how intimately connected he was to my private sexual fantasies. I flushed red. The auditorium wobbled. I pictured myself fainting and tumbling down the bleachers like in a high school assembly horror story.

Maxxx stood off to the side, an oblivious man wearing a plain T-shirt, straight-legged jeans, and Pumas. I knew he had performed for Kink, but the thought of running into him here had not consciously occurred to me. Maxxx wasn't a big name. You wouldn't have any success searching for him on Pornhub, but he was *my favorite*. To me, to my loins, he was a star.

In mainstream straight porn, there were larger-than-life legendary performers like Evan Stone, who had the pecs and golden locks of Fabio. Maxxx worked on the farthest fringes of the industry, doing small fetish-themed shoots. He was pale and scrawny, and looked like he might resentfully make me a cocktail at any number of local dive bars. Discovering Maxxx had felt like the payoff to all my pornographic "research." Even still, I had to mentally edit out the majority of his films. I didn't care much for anything involving ropes or chains or whips, and always watched him on mute, because of the proximity of my three roommates, and because the dialogue about "dirty sluts" ruined it for me.

All I cared for was the maybe five seconds of footage in which all the kinky accoutrements were conveniently cropped out of the frame, with the audio safely muted, leaving just the salient fact of a woman on her knees with his dick in her mouth. It was something about his face, and the familiar everydayness of it, but more so the way that he asserted that dick onto, and into, the woman on-screen. I imagined being able to take his desire as much as being able to express such desire myself—to confidently and literally just shove it down someone else's throat. Never mind that these videos were not a depiction of his desire. Maxxx was performing

that pressing need—the illusion of sexual overwhelm—for viewers
like me.

The women on the wrestling mats were enacting a similar
fantasy. Their flushed-red bodies tangled and twisted in a por-
trayal of sex as battle. There was a winner and loser. Scores were
tallied. Victory meant humiliation of one's opponent. It felt unnervingly relatable. The only way I knew how to "win" at sex
was by negating someone's "sexual humiliation" points with my
enthusiasm. I turned my emphatic enjoyment of their want and
need into its own act of aggression.

AFTER A BRIEF BREAK, the members of the winning wrestling
team emerged wearing strap-ons and the fucking commenced
as audience members laughed and sipped at their drinks. Maxxx
disappeared from sight and that, along with the cumulative effect of the beer, allowed me to refocus on the wrestling match,
clapping and whooping along with everyone else. When one of
the women appeared to have a crowning Hitachi-assisted orgasm, a production assistant yelled, *"Now, now, now,"* and the
sound guy cued trumpeting victory music.

As the audience poured down the Armory's front steps, Sam
told me that he was meeting some friends at Bender's, a nearby
dive known for its grilled mac-'n'-cheese sandwiches. We walked
the few blocks to the bar and soon were surrounded by local
writer people—probably from *Believer* or *McSweeney's* or *The
Rumpus* or *AlterNet* or *Mother Jones* or *SF Weekly*. It was literary
San Francisco circa 2011, back when it felt like the city had

something resembling a writerly scene because we could still afford to live there. I do know that my friend Anna, a fellow sex writer, was there. At some point, even Mike showed up. But everyone else was noise, because I was focused on the distinct possibility that Maxxx would walk through that door—and then he did.

Anna did the honors. "Tracy's favorite porn star is here," she said in a wry deadpan. I had immediately clasped her arm and whispered this fact to her, and she understood it as something that needed to be immediately flung into the sour-smelling dive-bar air. "Who," Sam wanted to know, and I told him. "Oh, Maxxx? He's great. Do you want me to introduce you?" Of course the answer was yes, but I asked for a couple of minutes and pulled Anna to the bar.

Over the course of the next hour, I ordered multiple whiskey shots and cans of PBR, while fretting to Anna about the potential for humiliation of the nonerotic kind. "I'm just some horny girl," I kept telling her. "Just some horny girl" meant "not good enough." Certainly not as good as the women I had watched him have sex with on camera. It didn't help that I had second-day hair pulled up in a messy bun with lazily pinned-back bangs. No makeup. T-shirt, jeans, Converse. This was not how I imagined meeting a man whose image I had masturbated to countless times.

Anna was braver than I, the kind of sex writer who actually did the things that I only privately fantasized about, like going to a sex club and *having sex*, instead of standing on the wall, as I once had. Anna was just the person to give me a pep talk, but really, it was the warm wash of the whiskey that finally made me go up to Sam and say, "Okay, I'm ready."

I stood waiting at the kitchenette where the grilled mac 'n' cheeses were served, nervously sipping my drink. Soon, I felt a tap on my shoulder and turned to see Maxxx standing in front of me, saying, "I hear you're a fan of my work." He gave me a charming, lopsided smile. I had seen that same mouth do many things, but I had never seen it smile. Then our hands met, virtual turned corporeal.

We grabbed neighboring barstools at the kitchenette countertop, watching as tater tots sizzled under a dented silver range hood with big red letters that declared: "HAIL SATAN." Maxxx's voice was higher than I'd expected, more violin than cello, which highlighted how often I'd watched him on mute. I was startled, too, by the beautiful hazy green of his eyes, which I'd never noticed before in his films, because it was never his eyes that were centered in the frame.

More surprising, though, was his eager vulnerability while explaining that he didn't meet many—or any, he corrected himself—fans who were women. There was little evidence of the forbidding dominant that he played on-camera. The one who smacked around women who looked up at him with tremulous smiles. *He's so nice*, I kept thinking.

I talked about being a newly minted sex writer and he talked about the truth of his job. He had a full-time nine-to-five and occasionally performed in porn on the side; I had only made him into a star in my own head. Then he paused, seeming to get into character with a bite of his lip, and asked the dreaded question, "What is it that you like about my work?" I placed my face into my hands and lowered it, making contact with the sticky wetness of the bar.

When I resurfaced, cheeks aflame, I cringed at my own sheepishness. "I like it when a girl . . . goes down on you?" What *about* the blow jobs, he wanted to know. I couldn't look at him. "I like it when you're . . . rough. When you . . . guide them." Then his hand was on my thigh. "That's great, Tracy," he said. He moved his hand up and down my leg, the crooked smile nudging me forward. My favorite porn performer was tenderly coaching me into speaking my fantasy in a crowded dive bar. "I like it . . . when you *fuck their faces*," I blurted, all too loud.

Then his tongue was in my mouth and my tongue was in his, and more than the feeling of it there was the idea of it. The idea being a scenario like one you might read in a tube site video description: "Porn star picks up slutty fan at bar." Then Maxxx leaned back, looked around, and said, "Isn't your boyfriend going to be mad when he sees us together?" I raised my eyebrows. *Boyfriend?* Then I realized: he was improvising dialogue. "Oh, right, yeah, he'll be here *any minute now*," I said in a stage whisper. Maxxx bit his lip again. "We better get out of here, then," he said. I mentioned my roommates were out of town and followed Maxxx out the door.

We walked the few blocks back to my house as he rolled his fixie alongside us, like any other guy I might take home from a bar in the Mission, because he *was* any other guy. Except he seemed to me then like an ultimate arbiter of sexual mastery. "I like it . . . when you *fuck their faces*." He specialized in the very act that had most threatened and compelled me in my early tube site wandering days, that overwhelming representation of women swallowing men's desire. Each step along Eighteenth Street—past one sizzling bacon-wrapped-hot-dog cart and then another—seemed to be taking me closer to a physical confrontation with that symbol. "Take it," I'd heard so many men say in those tube site clips. "*Take it*. Can you take it?"

Well, could I?

As I walked, a faint admonishing voice appeared. *What are you doing? Who are you? What will your mom think?* That voice had always been there in some form, although the mom bit was new. Many women live, and make decisions about their sexual lives, with some version of that voice. As Carole S. Vance wrote in *Pleasure and Danger*, "The tension between sexual danger and sexual pleasure is a powerful one in women's lives."[1] The danger being not just the pervasiveness of sexual assault but also stigma and shame. These threats were key to the traditional patriarchal bargain: be a "good" girl and you'll be protected—by your father, by your husband, by society at large. "Bad" girls, though— bad girls were punished.

Freud famously identified the Madonna-whore complex as a phenomenon among men who saw women as either virtuous wives or licentious sluts. "Where they love they do not desire and where they desire they cannot love," he wrote.[2] Such men could find complete satisfaction only in a "debased sexual object," said Freud, "a woman who is ethically inferior." Of course, the entire culture has the complex: women are often shuttled into one category or the other. Supposedly, I didn't believe in that division, yet it seemed this whole time I had been walking a tightrope between the two. I had plumbed the depths of tube sites to understand men. I'd written about having casual sex, but then validated it with the fact of my committed relationship. I was a sex writer exploring taboo terrain, but it was a job.

There was no hiding in taking home my favorite porn star. There was just me and my desire for this person who, although a man, still represented that forbidden world, that other category of woman, about which I carried such intrigue and admiration. I had yet to connect these feelings to "whore stigma." It's a term, explains journalist Melissa Gira Grant in *Playing the Whore*, describing the societal dishonor placed on sex workers and non–sex workers alike for stepping outside the bounds of what Jill Nagle called "compulsory virtue."[3] As the famed sex worker activist Margo St. James once said in an interview, "The word *whore* is used to stigmatize any woman that doesn't fit the criteria of a good girl. . . . Really, the word *whore* is still used to keep other women in line, all women, but the punishment of the prostitute is the example set by the system."[4] Later, I would find the author Gail Pheterson explaining that whore stigma broadly attaches to "illegitimate or illicit femaleness."[5]

Even if I couldn't name it at the time, I felt the threat of stigma in going home with Maxxx, a kind and degree never experienced with Mike. The only difference being Maxxx was a sex worker whose proximity to "illicit femaleness" seemed to imply my own. As Nagle argued, women are directed to continually prove their "good girl" bona fides. For some girls to be good, though, others must be bad. "If woman is other, whore is the other's other,"[6] wrote Grant. It would be years before I came across the related concept of "whorephobia," which specifically describes fear and hatred of sex workers.

That sense of "illicit" threat, my fear of the admonishing voices, distracted me from the assumptions I was making about Maxxx as a porn performer. I didn't consider the pressure he might feel to live up to my fantasy of him. I thought little of what it was like for Maxxx to be seen by another person in this reductive way. In the bar, he had asked me what I liked about his work, even gently encouraged me to speak it aloud, but I'd failed to ask what he was into. I didn't question whether he personally enjoyed what he performed.

I didn't ask about his fantasies.

USUALLY, MAXXX WAS ON my laptop and but a few inches tall. Now here he was, all six-foot-something of him standing in my living room—and all I was thinking was how I needed to shave my legs.

I excused myself to the bathroom, which sat off the living room with what felt like a paper-thin door. Sitting down on the toilet, I rolled up my jeans and gave a quiet little burst of the faucet to wet my plastic drugstore razor. It was pink and I hated pink, but I also hated shaving my legs and yet here we were. Taking a deep breath, I let the urine flow, thinking, *My favorite porn star is listening to me pee. My favorite porn star is listening to me pee.* A mantra that made the unbearable bearable with the announcement of its unbearableness. Then I dragged the razor across the stubble on my calves, wetting the blade again half-way through so that he couldn't overhear the scrape of it against my skin.

When I resurfaced from the bathroom—the gurgling toilet flush and the all-too-real reality of it making me cringe—he was leaning back with his arms comfortably stretched out across the back of the couch. I was unsure how to proceed, so I sat down next to him and asked, "Can I get you anything?"—meaning "a beer," but also "help me out here." Maxxx laughed, his mouth was on mine, and then he was undoing his jeans. I reflexively kneeled at his feet, just like the women on the laptop screen.

He placed his hand on the side of my face, then he pulled back, pausing long enough that I smiled to show him that I wanted it. Maxxx brought his hand back down on my cheek with a firm smack. It wasn't a warm-up slap; it was the carefully calibrated slap of someone with the rehearsed muscle memory of walking right up to the line without crossing it. It was a smack that said, *I know what I'm doing.* This surety caught me off guard, because it was so contrary to the tentative, sometimes fearful slaps I'd received from Mike. "Harder," I told him. Maxxx's face fell like I'd done something inconceivable. I wasn't supposed to order him around. "What was that?" he asked firmly, as though I'd just insulted his mother. With a smile, I asked, "Harder, *please*?" He ignored me. "Open your mouth," he ordered, and I did.

Before I registered what was happening, he spit in my open mouth. He didn't even have to lean down. Maxxx released this collection of saliva from where he was standing and perfectly hit his target. I'd seen him perform this move on-camera and always fast-forwarded through it. He didn't know that, though. All he knew was that I was a "fan of his work," and he was enacting his oeuvre. I swallowed and opened my mouth again.

There's a one-sided call-and-response that can happen when viewing porn. If an act on-screen rubbed me the wrong way, I would block it out—a version of plugging my ears and going "la-la-la." Or I'd add something in where it was not—a sassy comment, a challenging look. These imaginary edits shaped the content to my own idiosyncratic likes. The action on-screen only had to get close enough. Even with Maxxx's films muted, I could occasionally make out his mouthing that personally cringe-inducing phrase, "Dirty slut." So I pretended it wasn't there.

Maxxx undid his pants and pulled out his dick. Cue angel song. A hard dick can be glorious. Something about the swollen curves and purpling edges. The dual silkiness and rigidity. A hard dick is proof of desire. A hard dick is a man revealing an inner self—sometimes against his better judgment. We worship the *almighty phallus* as a symbol of potency and power, but what a crock, what a compensatory ploy. A hard dick is weakness announced. It is desperate need. It is the soft underbelly gone hard. Often, I'm reminded of watching a slinky, soft caterpillar split open to become a glossy, hardened chrysalis. Contrary to Freud, I don't envy the phallus; I feel sorry for it. And yet I love it all the same.

He stuck his dick in my mouth and clasped my head in an

outstretched hug. I hugged him back—ambitiously, and into the back of my throat. He pulled and thrusted. We were wrestling for power like those performers earlier, only I leaned into his every aggression in a perverted jujitsu, that style of fighting that uses an opponent's force against them. In this instance, it only encouraged him.

He—there's no delicate way to put this—fucked my face so hard that I gagged and liquid, my own liquid, flooded the back of my throat. Was it spit or vomit? I swallowed it back down, all with his dick still in my mouth. *I am a fucking champ* is what I thought. *I've got this* is what came to mind. This was me confronting, conquering, overcoming.

Eventually, Maxxx and I moved to the bedroom. Then commenced the gonzo fucking, the montage of positions, the pornographic checklist. I was *so freaking ready*. I'd prepared for this role for years—for over a decade, in fact—and here was my culminating audition. I met Maxxx's fierce pounding with an equivalently dramatic arch of the back and responded to his forceful grab of my hair with a moan of corresponding strength. These enthusiasms were meant to tell him, and myself, that I could handle it, that I wasn't afraid, as I vibrated with thou-doth-protest-too-much-ness.

I'd been entertained so many times by Maxxx's work, and now it felt I was doing the entertaining. Only there was no audience: it was just us and that imaginary camera that so often found its way into my bedroom and mind. This is what the famed sex researchers William Masters and Virginia Johnson termed "spectatoring," wherein you observe yourself from a third-person perspective during sex, as if outside your own body.[7] Most every prior hookup of mine had followed prevailing heterosexual "scripts," but with Maxxx the script was closer to literal, having been drawn from his on-camera performances. We were enacting what we had previously portrayed or watched. It was a union of audience and performer, screen and flesh.

In terms of actual bodily feeling, there was just the tingling in my fingertips, not from orgasm, but rather the faking of one, and then another. All that desperate air sucking, better known as hyperventilation, will do that. It was obvious during this moment of high-fidelity recital that, for the most part, porn was entertainment, not an instructional manual for pleasurable sex. I already intellectually understood this, but I was coming to actually believe it. There was no denying that in reproducing what I'd seen on-screen, I was finding it less entertaining, less pleasurable, less embodied than with my one-sided viewing. Porn could be an ecstatic form of make-believe, and sometimes better appreciated that way.

Maxxx pulled off the condom and palmed the side of my face, sinking it into the mattress. He thrust into my open mouth, holding himself up by pressing against my cheek, now with both hands. An ache emanated from the joint that connects jaw to skull—I knew it was called the temporomandibular joint because I often ground my teeth at night and sometimes woke up with migraine-like pain radiating from it. That unsexy word—*tem-poro-man-dib-ular*—reverberated in my mind as he fucked my face. Any irritation of that joint could leave me bedbound the next morning, but I said nothing.

There followed the inevitable denouement, our collapsed bodies on the bed, some small talk, and an unexpected second round. Then he stood up, stark naked, and strutted around my room with his hands on his hips. The moon streamed in my windows, giving the lines of his torso the kind of sensual, romantic lighting they never got in his films, what with their targeted audience of straight men. The curtains, I realized, were open wide, revealing us to however many other windows in the tightly packed Victorians across the street.

Maxxx nodded silently as he circled, taking in my belongings. The top of my dresser was occupied by an enormous humming aquarium that I'd purchased secondhand. It was filled with at least a dozen guppies, because the little pervs kept having fish babies, and one day I was going to have to do something about that. In the center of the aquarium, I'd created a lone island and planted it with a bonsai tree. Above my computer desk was a planter mounted on the wall with greenery that reached in all directions. I was a wild mess, and my room screamed it.

The clincher was the black-and-white Diane Arbus print above my bed of two identical twin girls who stared at the camera in a fashion reminiscent of *The Shining*. The poster and its placement said, "I'm weird, I'm dark." I'd rigged my bedroom, and my life, with litmus tests, like I was daring men to run. Maxxx suddenly clapped. "Well, I better be getting home now," he said.

There would be no postcoital snuggling. We exchanged numbers while leaning against the wooden railing at the top of the creaky Victorian stairs. He gave me his legal name and it felt more intimate than the sex. As he was adding me to his phone, he asked, "What did you say you were, that you did?" I offered, "Reporter? Journalist?" Maxxx nodded. "Journalist," he said, typing with his thumbs. "Tracy, the Journalist." And I showed him out.

WHEN I GOT BACK to work on Monday, I was bleakly looking to meet my daily content quota and ended up publishing a brief personal essay about my experience at the event. I was dismissive and distanced in my write-up, which ran with the headline, "The Unsexy World of Porn Wrestling." I wrote of the audience, "Not to sound like a prude but: These are clean, attractive, normal-looking people!" *Oof.* What I meant, or felt, was: Maybe I'm "normal," too.

The piece mentioned going to Bender's afterward and running into some porn performers, but it did not mention that I went home with one of them. (Even still, *Salon* commenters chastised me for venturing into the Armory, while questioning my judgment and psychological well-being.) In response to the essay, Sam wrote me an email suggesting that it would have been stronger if I'd told the full story. To which I responded: "The downside of this daily writing gig . . . is that I rarely have the time to fully process things. And even when I do, it's another thing to work up the courage to tell the full truth, the truer truth, about these taboo topics. It's something I'm working on."

I was still working on my feelings about that night with

Maxxx. After he left, I'd texted my new roommate, Monica, who had taken Elissa's room, that I'd just slept with "my favorite porn star." She was a sex-positive feminist working in public health, and she spoke openly and comfortably about things like STI testing and the G-spot, so she seemed as safe a recipient for this news as I was going to get. I waited, grinning, for her virtual high five. But a bubble of text soon popped up on my phone: "Is this supposed to be a good thing?"

My roommate had passed judgment before hearing any of the details of the encounter; all she needed to hear was "porn star." This was a woman who would later respond to my professional interest in reporting on the adult industry with, "Tracy, they're not curing cancer or anything." (Monica was planning to go to medical school.) I rejected her stigmatizing assessment, but I was beginning to admit that it was not the unambiguously "good thing" I wanted it to be in my mind. Soon after having sex with Maxxx, I Gchatted Katherine, "it was awesome." Then I immediately followed up: "i mean the sex wasn't actually good." And later: "it was just kinda like: weird, cool."

I'd since tried putting my hand between my legs while summoning memories from that night and—nothing. As with many hookups, it had not been pleasurable sex. For a moment, it had been painful. Mostly, it felt like bungee jumping, an adrenalizing physical feat. It was a chemical release, just not the one often associated with sex. I wanted more—say, the engulfing sensations I'd experienced when privately imagining the very same acts with the very same man. It felt like a poor imitation of the real thing.

The "real thing," though, was itself an imitation. Porn often produces an image of "good sex," one that does not always result from "good sex." This recalls the postmodern French philosopher Jean Baudrillard's writing on the "precession of simulacra," in which everything from reality TV to amusement parks generates "models of a real without origin or reality." He calls this a "hyperreal," which is "sheltered . . . from any distinction between the real and the imaginary." Similarly, Butler said that gender is "a kind of imitation for which there is no original," one "that produces the very notion of the original as an *effect* and consequence of the imitation itself."

I find it easy to tumble into nihilism over this realm of thought, which spans from the philosophical to the sociological. If everything is a copy of a copy, if all of social life is a performance, if sexual scripts are adapted from cultural norms, then does authenticity even exist, or matter? But I recognized what felt like clear, unsettling lines drawn between the "real" and "imaginary" in my own physical experience. With Maxxx, just as with most men, I'd repeatedly faked orgasms, moaned through discomfort, and kept buried any hints about what might actually give me physical pleasure. So often, the main gratification sex brought me was that thrilling sensation of *confronting, conquering, overcoming*. That trophy sat on the mantel of my mind, looking increasingly like a dollar-store medal. I had wrestled Maxxx for power, but now I wondered what kind. If this was winning, I wasn't sure I wanted to compete.

CHAPTER 6

Faking

I kept thinking about what this Le Méridien conference room, with its modernist chandeliers and a zigzagging carpet, had previously witnessed. Excel spreadsheets, Power-Point presentations, reams of paper handed out in squeaky binder clips. Those buttoned-up corporate meetings were a far cry from what would soon transpire here: an audience of roughly four dozen watching a woman manually stimulated through fifteen minutes of leg-quaking pleasure.

It was the first day of a weekend-long orgasmic meditation retreat for women hosted by OneTaste, a San Francisco–based center for "mindful sexuality." The center was thrust onto the national stage a couple of years earlier when the *New York Times* wrote about its "shabby-chic loft building" where residents gathered early each morning "in a velvet-curtained room" to practice OMing, as it was known for short. Clothed men stroked half-naked women, explained the *Times* to readers, who no doubt proceeded to choke on their morning coffees.

Since then, OneTaste founder Nicole Daedone, a chic forty-something woman with an enviable blowout, had published a book, *Slow Sex: The Art and Craft of the Female Orgasm*, which earnestly aimed to mainstream the practice of orgasmic meditation. The book and retreat felt timely against the backdrop of the headline-making search for "female Viagra," a pill meant to target the then-estimated $2 billion market of women with low libidos, a "problem" that feminist critics convincingly argued was cultural rather than medical. There was also the unavoidable truth of my personal interest: my only dedicated orgasmic "practice" was faking it, and relentlessly.

The mail that hit my desk at *Salon* was now: vibrators, novelty lube, porn DVDs, and sex advice books. I would be subpoenaed to testify in a federal obscenity trial against a "poo porn" producer and invited to judge air sex competitions, in which contestants performed a naughty version of air guitar. By outward measures, I was a bona fide sex writer who sang the feminist gospel of sexual pleasure—but my personal life made me feel like an impostor. This had surfaced cringingly in a recent phone interview with legendary sex writer Susie Bright when I asked about her youthful explorations with "casual sex." *Casual* sex, she guffawed. Since when was sex casual? "Every time I was with someone it was intimate," she told me. "I just don't find sex to be this jaded, cynical, stoic exercise. How do you manage to do that and have an orgasm? I don't." Neither did I.

Recently, I had started casually sleeping with Tim, a friend of a friend, who told me, smilingly, "You come so easily, babe." The truth: I lie so easily, babe. I didn't know how to stop lying, either. My orgasmic lies spiraled for the same reason that lies generally spiral: the desire to protect the original fabrication. I doubted that orgasmic meditation would provide a solution, but I was intrigued by the promise of Daedone's book: to teach women "to slow down, connect emotionally, and achieve authentic female sexual satisfaction."

The day began with an introduction to the concept of slow sex, which emphasized "sustainability, connection, and nourishment," as Daedone abstractly wrote. OMing, she explained, was the first and most essential step. She detailed the creation of an OMing "nest" (a cozy, blanketed place in which to practice), setting a fifteen-minute timer, and the simple, repetitive flick of the forefinger on the clitoris. The goal wasn't climax, but rather *orgasm*, a word she delivered with such a stony-eyed whisper it sounded like a spiritual state akin to nirvana. She used the term broadly to reflect a heightened, transformative phenomenon of sensation and arousal.

This wasn't the typical "male" model of sexual response: arousal, climax, resolution. Maybe there was a climax, but maybe there wasn't. The aim of OMing was embodied aimlessness, a "goalless" engagement with physical sensation. Borrowing heavily from Eastern philosophies around meditation and mindfulness, Daedone had turned clit rubbing into a spiritual practice. As a result, she had convinced scores of men to seek enlightenment by worshipping at the altar of the vulva. I wavered between seeing her as brilliant eccentric and captivating saleswoman.

After a lengthy primer and a few group exercises, Daedone

stood at the front of the room full of women ranging from their early twenties to sixties. She quietly surveyed the audience, occasionally chuckling softly to herself as though intuiting our deepest secrets. Then she read from a personal manifesto about what she dubbed "the Turned-on Woman," a concept that applied to any woman who was willing to be truthful about her sexual desires. "She does not perform, embellish, or supplement," she read, slowly and emphatically, from the printed-out pages. "Instead she stays present, opens herself to the experience, and *feels her way*."

Daedone frequently looked up from the text and made lingering eye contact with audience members. Each time her blissful gaze hit me, it was as though whatever word she was speaking at that moment *was* me, like my fortune had just been divined and sealed. She continued, "She experiences what is there and asks for what she desires."

We were then instructed to wander the room, whispering previously unspoken desires into each other's ears. "I want to be a sex slave," one woman told me breathily. "I want him to take the object of his choice and stick it in the orifice of his choice," said another as her curls tickled my cheek. There were tamer fantasies about soft kisses and lingering embraces. I can't recall what I whispered, though. It was midafternoon and we'd been there since early morning, listening to lectures and taking coffee breaks. As an introvert, I was peopled out. Now, during this task, I was in something of a social anxiety blackout.

The exercise culminated horrifyingly in all of us speaking our desires at a podium. Then some of us stepped into the "pussy photo booth" set up in the corner of the room. (I did not step within a five-foot radius of the pussy photo booth.) The resulting crotch shots were then strung up along the walls. It was the mirror-between-the-legs consciousness-raising circles of the 1970s, updated for the digital era. A few of us stood there, awkwardly gazing at the labia gallery, muttering things like "neat" and "cool." We were in a communal daze from having norms and boundaries systematically stripped over the course of several hours. There came a disembodied voice from over my shoulder: "I . . . can't . . . tell . . . which one . . . is mine." We were a living Roz Chast cartoon: a bunch of wild-eyed, frizzy-haired women trying, and failing, to pick their own vulvas out of lineup.

As the end of the day approached, after nearly eleven hours of merely talking about orgasmic meditation, a couple of women asked for a live demonstration. Daedone and her close circle of fashionable, cosmopolitan thirty- and fortysomething One-Taste women leaders huddled conspiratorially. Later, in my *Salon* piece, I'd write of them, "Think *Sex and the City*'s Samantha at a Buddhist retreat." The advertisement for the event had specifically said that there would be no "sexual activity," but when the huddle dispersed, a massage table was set up at the head of the room.

Daedone stood in front of us smirking and said, "There's all these questions as OneTaste gets bigger about *fucking appropriateness.*" Everyone laughed. It was in this allegedly off-script moment that she seemed most decidedly on-script. "And there's a *reporter* in the room," Daedone continued, gesturing my way. "But, quite frankly, as a human being I think you're one of us witchy women." Then she winked at me, and it was electric. This capital-T "Turned-on" woman with her shameless clit-stroking agenda recognized me as a kindred spirit, a fellow sex witch. It seemed she was telling me I was part of her tribe.

In that 2009 *Times* piece, former OneTaste members had told the reporter that Daedone had "cultlike powers over her followers." Fast-forward nearly a decade to *Bloomberg* publishing a report alleging that OneTaste was not just cult*like*.[1] In 2018, former members came forward with claims of trauma, sexual exploitation, and massive debt from paying for OneTaste classes. Ex-staffers told reporter Ellen Huet that they used personal information gleaned from "communication games" at OneTaste events—for example, if "a student was recently divorced and lonely"—to sell individual participants on future classes. Senior staff allegedly asked subordinates to focus on "wealthy students who seemed attracted to them or had experiences in common," Huet reported.

Now OneTaste seems to me an example of the dangers of commercializing sexual health. At the time, though, all I felt was the warm wash of having Daedone's favorable attention directed at me. I had no desire to move into the OneTaste loft with its velvet-curtained room. Nor did I even want to sign up to have a "Certified OM Trainer" introduce me to orgasmic meditation. But I did want what Daedone seemed to have: an experience of desire and pleasure that was shameless and authentic. Looking around the ritzy conference room, I knew I was not alone. Every woman in this room—middle-aged divorcées and OkCupid-savvy twentysomethings alike—had paid nearly half a grand to attend this retreat, all for the promise of something more.

Then that something "more," or Daedone's version of it, materialized in the form of a half-naked woman lying on the massage table with her legs splayed open like those of a dissected frog. Daedone pulled her own mermaid locks into a messy bun and gazed between the woman's legs. "Oh my god, it's beautiful," she said breathlessly. "It's an electric rose color. The swelling is already beginning." The women in the audience craned their necks to see the electric rose, the swelling.

Daedone dipped a finger into a container of thick yellow lube and began stroking the "upper left quadrant" of the woman's clitoris. The moans that surfaced from the woman's lips were soft but primal, like in the early stages of labor. Daedone urged her along with things like "good girl" and "reach, reach, *reach*." She was part doula, part porn script.

Someone sniffled and I turned to see a couple of women wistfully dabbing at their eyes like they were watching *The Notebook*. I could have been moved to tears, too, if I'd let myself. Not at the OMing itself, but at this extraordinary symbol of women's collective hunger. This elaborate ritual to achieve orgasm was the ultimate expression of that desperation for something that was ours, that felt right. A dramatic intervention. A validation of pleasure.

"I HAVE AN IDEA," I told Tim sometime after the orgasmic meditation retreat. We were lying in his bed, which sat on the floor of a former walk-in closet of his Tenderloin studio apartment, having just finished watching a movie on his iPhone. The entire time, he had held up the tiny screen, alternating arms as they fell asleep in turn. "I want to try, as an experiment, to delay orgasm," I continued, raising my head from the sweaty nook of his armpit. "I think it'll be even more intense that way."

What I meant was: I've been faking it this whole time and now I want to stop faking it. Instead of saying that, though, I constructed my own version of the orgasmic meditation ritual: a self-imposed restriction on what he believed to be my hair-trigger orgasm. The OMing retreat and *Slow Sex* were a perfect excuse. I was trying to buy myself the time in our sexual encounters to experience an orgasm without having to admit that I had never actually orgasmed with him.

Tim sat up and ran his fingers through his man bangs. "Okay, babe," he said, nodding gamely. "Sounds like some *tantra* shit. I'm down."

Things were not supposed to have gotten serious with Tim, but now Facebook statuses had been changed. He was a thirty-five-year-old artist with an apartment overtaken by canvases stacked in in random, haphazard towers. The art on the canvases was just as erratic: collages of bus transfers, paintings of toasters, a series depicting busty women in space helmets. An easel and paint-flecked drop cloth sat where a couch might be in someone else's apartment. He didn't bother with a couch. There was just his closet bed, across which he'd tossed a thrift store find: a fuzzy blanket featuring an image of a majestic, roaring tiger.

He occasionally worked at a pot farm and sold weed to make ends meet. Tim kept bricks of rubber-banded cash in his freezer. "Yeah, I don't know why I put it in there," he said, shrugging, when I asked about the frozen money. "I should probably hide it somewhere else." Sometimes he would get administrative temp jobs, where he spent his downtime staging photo shoots for Instagram: mostly of him lurking incongruously behind potted plants in fluorescent-lit cubicle mazes. He belonged behind those plants just as much as he belonged in that nine-to-five world.

Eventually, I learned that Tim believed humans were genetically programmed by aliens. He had read some theories about space creatures scientifically engineering and then mating with people. They had built the pyramids, he said. The United States government had undertaken a mass cover-up. There was this amazing documentary series I should see called *Ancient Aliens*. The Illuminati, Sumerian texts, lizard people, the whole shebang. No one could have designed a more perfect deal breaker for me, not even ancient aliens themselves.

But then I found that this man with a tiger blanket, freezer savings, and alien conspiracies was a genuine sweetheart. He would softly pet my shoulder, kiss me on the forehead, and endearingly call me "Miss Tracy." There was little of the games— last-minute flaking, delayed texts—that I'd experienced before. He would plan thoughtfully creative dates, like going to the junkyard to find random objects to plant (one of my frequent refrains at the time being, "You can plant that"). I was still making terrariums like a Mission hipster cliché, and he had learned a thing or two on the pot farm. We would use our bare hands to scoop soil out of a rustling plastic bag and deposit it into various recycled vessels—emptied lightbulbs, antique lamps, and metal colanders. Then we would sit there, picking dirt from our fingernails, as I marveled at the fact of such easy companionship.

That lack of game playing carried over into the bedroom, or closet, in his case. There was lingering eye contact, subtle movement, silent pauses. Tim was *sen-sual*, a word I struggled to say without emphatically corny inflection. I tried to push the ancient aliens out of my mind as best I could. Meanwhile, Elissa claimed godmother of our "alien spawn."

There were moments with him when I could almost take seriously the words that Daedone had read to us at the retreat about "sex that ignites; that lights up the power grid." My orgasmic lie would wait in the wings, though. Impatient, checking its watch, tapping its foot. Then it would burst onstage to perform the operatics.

My inner critic—hands folded, head bowed—slowly raises her gaze with the melodrama of my grade school principal and asks: Why fake it on that first night with Tim? Why fabricate in the first place? What are you, *a liar*? Sure, fine, let me dutifully write out my reasons like a kid in detention detailing sins on a chalkboard:

I was afraid I would take too long.
I didn't want to ruin the moment.
I wanted to be sexy.

My pleasure brought him pleasure.
I cared more about his pleasure than my own.
His pleasure gave me pleasure!!!!!!

That many exclamation points should never be trusted.

It hadn't always been this way. I had never faked it in my first relationship. Sometimes I orgasmed, often I didn't, but pretending never occurred to me amid the dreamy, hormonal haze of first love. It was only as I stepped into the wilds of my twenties that the fakery began. The few times I entered into a committed relationship, there were authentic climaxes, even if they were not nearly as frequent as I would have liked. But of all the casual sex—from college through my late twenties—I remember only one, single genuine orgasm. It was with Mike, who—so cautious about using condoms, categorical about never, *ever* having sex without them—lost himself in the moment, in his desire for me, and slid inside without one.

AT LEAST I WAS not alone in my fakery. I knew the available data. *Half of women report having faked it.*[2] Later research would nudge that figure even higher.[3] Now, I know that the scientific literature provides more than just reassuring percentages. It suggests that straight women often fake orgasms to protect their partners—from insecurity, disappointment, and any other human emotions that might sink a dick. We save men the boner-kill of being with a woman whose flatline vocalizations might seem a commentary on their sexual prowess. (Of course, there lies an ulterior motive: if the dick is sunk, then so might be our ego.) Women fake it for other reasons—to expedite bad, boring, unwanted, or painful sex, for example—but so often the research underscores a sense of necessary self-sacrifice.

It's ironic, then, that orgasms are often talked about in heteronormative discourse as something a man "gives" to a woman, and yet the reverse is rarely true. As Breanne Fahs wrote in her 2011 book *Performing Sex: The Making and Unmaking of Women's Erotic Lives*, straight men are thought to *have* orgasms and *give* orgasms.[4] Women *get* them from other people. If women are faking it as commonly as the research suggests, then—really, truly—it is something that heterosexual women *give to men*.

Heterosexual men seem convinced by these performances: In 2010, the National Survey of Sexual Health and Behavior found that 85 percent of men reported that their partner had orgasmed during their most recent sexual encounter, while 64 percent of women reported having *actually* had an orgasm during their most recent sexual encounter.[5] (The discrepancy was too large to be explained by the small number of men with men for partners.) A more recent study found an actual, rather than perceptual, orgasm gap: 95 percent of straight men reported usually or always having an orgasm when sexually intimate, compared to 65 percent of hetero women.[6]

The stats about orgasms, fake and otherwise, say nothing of the prevalence of subtler forms of sexual dishonesty in hetero sex: the moans throughout, manufactured or magnified. The little sighs, the biting of the lower lip, which in my experience often come not from pleasure, but rather a desire to convey it

and *protect it in him*. Nicole Daedone envisioned and purportedly *was* a woman who did "not perform, embellish, or supplement." This was nearly unfathomable to me.

If everything in social life is a performance, as Erving
Goffman argued, put-on pleasure is just another example of
managing impressions within the constraints of cultural norms.
The norms around women's orgasms are ever in flux, as Fahs
documented. In response to Victorian era repression, Sigmund
Freud famously celebrated vaginal orgasm as "mature," while
deeming clitoral orgasm "infantile." In the 1960s and 1970s,
feminists fought back, hailing clitoral pleasure and "reclaiming
orgasm on women's own terms." This may sound like straightforward political progress, but Fahs argued that the outcome of
this feminist debate was that "women's orgasms came to stand
in for liberation in its entirety—a symbol of women's improved
social and cultural status." Women's orgasms became "a *require-
ment* of sex, rather than a mere pleasure."

On prime-time TV and tube sites alike, there were women
writhing and moaning in ecstasy at a man's slightest touch.
Every single young straight woman I knew dedicatedly enacted
a version of this fantasy of men's supreme sexual competence,
and of our own erotic facility and freedom. Maybe this was why
some of us had to gather in hotel conference rooms and watch a
woman get her clit stroked as an iPhone timer counted down
from fifteen minutes. This points to another climax divide: in a
survey of nearly three thousand single Americans, heterosexual
women reported having an orgasm 62 percent of the time, compared to 75 percent of the time among lesbian women.[7]

Straight men are not the only problem here, but they are a problem. Although penetration is often held as the essential component of cisgender heterosexual sex, it is a poor predictor of women's orgasm. Studies have revealed that women are more likely to climax during sexual encounters that incorporate "deep kissing," cunnilingus, and manual genital stimulation. One team of researchers, having surveyed more than thirteen thousand heterosexual women college students, suggested that satisfaction would rise if only it was possible to increase "men's attentiveness to women's pleasure and women's sense of entitlement to pleasure in hookups."[8]

In my early twenties, I felt it was enough simply to be sexual as a woman, to tumble freely into bed with a relative stranger. However, acting as if traditional gendered expectations have evaporated doesn't make it so. My hookups were thrilling and enjoyable to varying degrees, but my partner's pleasure was typically prioritized—by me, by him, and by the popular directives around hetero sex. I tamped down my own desires for greater pleasure, intimacy, commitment—for anything more than what I got. Faked orgasms were just one manifestation of what increasingly felt like going through the motions of sexual empowerment.

Now, edging into my late twenties, it seemed that I had inherited the right to be sexual, to have sex, but on what terms, and to whose advantage? For years, Laura Sessions Stepp and Ariel Levy had lived in my mind as finger-wagging maternal scolds, but I could no longer deny their shared thread of truth: our culture not only sexually disenfranchises young women, but increasingly does so through the lie of liberation. As sexist and retrograde, caricaturing and polemical as their books may have respectively been, they both made a point plainly underscored by the growing weight of my own experience. The sexual revolution ushered in new freedoms and unprecedented pressures alongside enduring constraints.

Years later, I would discover emerging academic feminist theory attempting to critically map this shifting landscape—with nuance, compassion, and an absence of sexist bromides. This scholarship makes clear that the strictures of the traditional sexual double standard holding men as studs and women as sluts have loosened, leading to a greater range of acceptable, but also mandated, sexual behavior within certain monogamous, heterosexual constraints. At the same time, the virgin-slut dichotomy has morphed from an either-or into an ambiguous continuum with "prude" at its center.[9]

The researcher Laina Bay-Cheng argues that today young women face an additional, intersecting line of sexual judgment: agency. Girls, she writes, "are now also evaluated according to the degree of control they proclaim, or are perceived, to exert over their sexual behavior." [10] She argues that the appearance of autonomy and self-interest—assessments deeply influenced by biases around race and class—can guard against the enduring insult of "slut." In this sense, effortlessly orgasming, or seeming to, is arguably a form of self-protection for some young women (namely white, cis, middle-class, heterosexual ones). So, too, is enthusing to friends about a hookup, despite moments of disappointment or discomfort.

This new standard of "agency" results from individualized and neoliberal notions of empowerment, Bay-Cheng argues. In recent decades, the improvement of women's sexual experiences has been detached from imperatives of social justice and collective struggle. Instead, empowerment is cast as a personal problem, which places pressure on individuals to successfully navigate systemic disadvantages. In other words: If you are not romantically fulfilled, erotically unencumbered, and awash with pleasure, well, hmm. Maybe you should work on that.

And I did. I took it on as a personal project, even though it involved another person, and even though I understood it as a broader cultural problem. That night, lying in Tim's bed, my suggestion of an experiment was taken as foreplay. Here was my opportunity. Here was my moment. Still—I faked it. Of course I faked it. I just waited a little longer before doing so. That became my new norm, which was only a marginal improvement. But happily, my construction of a ritual around delaying orgasm had the unintended effect of making space for more experimentation.

We started trying out the array of promotional vibrators that I was now receiving at the *Salon* office in my name. We did a test run with some egg-shaped masturbatory sleeves, too. Bacon-flavored lube? Sure, what the hell. After I published an article about the growing acceptance of butt play among straight men, we bought a Feeldoe, a strapless strap-on. He gave me some pointers on being the screwer rather than the screwee. "It's all in the hips," Tim told me as he demonstrated his moves on the air.

"All"—thrust—"in"—thrust—"the hips." How sweet, how romantic: my boyfriend was teaching me to fuck him. Soon, I Gchatted with Elissa:

> **me:** last night we smoked pot and then went down on each other
> **me:** he insisted on going down on me
> **me:** and then i sat on his face and moved around so that his tongue touched me in just the right ways
> **Elissa:** You literally disgust me.
> **Elissa:** In terms of how awesome your life is.

I reminded her that I was *not having orgasms*. I wondered about the antidepressant I was on, which was known to carry sexual side effects. Or maybe it was the fact that my mom was dying. She had exceeded her prognosis and now all we knew was that there were *hours or days or weeks or months or years* left. Whenever my parents called and "Fam" flashed on my phone screen, I would sink into the nearest surface, expecting the worst. I kept using the word *purgatory* in therapy to describe this uncertain state of existence.

If I wanted to feel bad about myself, I could find inappropriate parallels between my preoccupation and my mom's predicament, wryly drawing perverse lines of connection and comparison. The little death, the big death. *How dare I even think of pleasure at this time?* said the inner critic. *What a frivolous pursuit, given the circumstances.* Charming French expressions aside, though, my pursuit was more about asserting death's opposite. Sex could be life-affirming—generative not just in the literal, procreative sense.

THIS IS NOT THE part where I magically stop faking orgasms. This is not the part where I ride off into the sunset on a jet stream of "female ejaculate." No. This is the part where I walked down a busy, bright workday afternoon sidewalk in North Beach, past the Transamerica Pyramid, City Lights, and Tosca Cafe. I turned onto a side street, opened a heavy wooden door, and stepped into the disorienting darkness of a bar with its red velvet curtains tightly drawn. There was a naked woman, arms bound behind her back, kneeling on the floor of the bar. Her face and chest glistened with an unknown substance. A dozen people, mostly men, sat on red vinyl barstools, excitedly slurping their foamy beers. I realized that the woman's chest was glistening with saliva and that the saliva belonged to these men.

My longtime friend Jake had been walking through North Beach when he noticed camera and lighting equipment being carried into the bar. As a video editor, he wanted to nerd out about camera gear with some fellow filmmakers. Inside, he found a crew setting up for Kink.com's Public Disgrace. Then he called me at my desk at *Salon* and said a few key words— namely, "filming," "porn," and "They say you can come." I was there within twenty minutes.

As my eyes adjusted in the bar, I saw Princess Donna, the ponytailed dominatrix who ran Public Disgrace, wearing a black

minidress and cowboy boots. Next to her was James Deen, a
porn performer on the verge of mainstream stardom. In a few
years, in 2015, an ex-girlfriend would take to Twitter to accuse
Deen of rape. Still years before mainstream Hollywood's #MeToo
movement, it would unleash a flood of allegations from other
women, ranging from claims of sexual assault to physical abuse,
in some cases on sets like this one. (Deen would deny the allegations.) I'd report on some of these allegations myself, but I didn't
know any of that yet. If I had, I would have turned right around
and left.

Everything in the bar accelerated—not years into the future,
but further into the moment of this dimly lit shoot. I learned
that the bound woman was named Rylie. Her breasts were tied
into bondage such that they seemed to almost levitate off her
chest like two pink hard orbs of flesh. Then she was propped up
on a barstool and a ball gag was placed in her mouth. A red-
faced belligerent man held a beer in one hand and used his other
to prop up her leg as Deen began slamming into her. The red-
faced man unnecessarily yelled, "Fuck her, man!" With a mock-
ing, cartoonish laugh, he shouted right into Rylie's face, "You
fucking love it!"

Meanwhile, two aging frat-boy types in backward trucker
hats stood to one side filming on their iPhones. Red-faced man
was yelling again, nonsensically and in her face: "Are you gonna
buy me a shot? Are you gonna buy me a *fuckin' shot*?" At one
point a guy took a swig of his beer and dramatically burped. I
was sitting there, off-camera, as a point of fact. But many of
these details I only really know because of the video of it that

exists online all these years later. "Hot Blonde Disgraced in Bar" is the title. In truth, I was not very much there, but rather floating somewhere above the scene, distancing myself from the sensation of my stomach scaling my throat.

Rylie had a safe word. She had been warned on-camera by Princess Donna beforehand, "We want you to have a good time. So don't feel like you need to take anything that you don't like, okay?" Rylie *liked* rough sex, she had told the camera in her preinterview. Kink's protocol was for performers to fill out a detailed "dos and don'ts" list detailing their sexual boundaries. This was a staged fantasy of debasement—but for me, these men plucked from the street were too believable in their roles.

Later that night, I sat in one of the Armory's staid conference rooms interviewing Deen. Years down the line, after the abuse allegations, I would have many questions I'd like to ask him. In this moment, though, I relied on what now seem like inexcusably stock inquiries about Viagra and faked orgasms, before turning to perhaps the most predictable of all. "You have so many men, and women, making assumptions based on your movies about what normal or hot sex looks like," I said. "What does it feel like to be influencing the way that people have sex?"

He sniffed in the way people do when reporters ask them the same question that they have already been asked countless times before. "That's way more responsibility than I want," he said. "We do stuff for the camera; we are having sex for the people at home, so not necessarily everything that we do feels good." He said his advice when a journalist had previously asked him how to have sex like a porn star was, simply, "Don't." Deen continued, "I really hope I don't have that responsibility of teaching people how to have sex."

Although it is not the medium's rightful responsibility, porn *is* teaching people—young people, especially—about sex. We can thank the sorry state of comprehensive, science-based sex education for that: research suggests that teenagers look to porn for information about sex that they simply don't get anywhere else. The question of just what porn imparts is up for debate. Adolescent porn watching has been linked to "gender-stereotypical sexual beliefs" and "greater experience with casual sex."[11] That said, a 2019 study found no significant relationship between adolescent porn watching and psychological well-being over time. However, that same study did find a negative link for girls, but not boys, at the start of the study.[12] Many researchers, who could go hoarse trying to remind journalists that correlation does not equal causation, have hesitated to draw definitive conclusions.

It isn't just porn that teaches young people about sex. Portrayals in mainstream Hollywood similarly fill the educational void, if less vividly. Sexual learning has been handed over via neglect to the broad realm of entertainment and commerce, a fact that communicates its own lessons about the meaning and value of the act. Porn, though, is an easier target than mainstream entertainment. It is a convenient scapegoat that takes the blame for societal failures not just around sex education but also around everything from violence against women to gender inequality.

As a teenager, I found porn perplexing and alarming, thrilling and arousing. As an adult, it ultimately facilitated my solitary exploration of desire, pleasure, and sexual possibility. Where things went awry were when my misinterpretations of porn—what it is, what it means, what it reflects—were applied to partnered sex. Now one of the world's most famous porn performers was telling me that what happened on-screen didn't always feel good to him or his costars.

I tried to imagine hearing that fact a decade or so earlier in a high school sex-ed class. My career has often been an exercise in making up for that inadequate education, which is not quite as sad as the fact that many people never get to fill in those gaps.

I walked home zombielike from the Armory, eyes unfocused, feet shuffling. As soon as I hit my bed, the tears came. It was the first private moment I had gotten all day. My feelings at the bar had been stored away in a little velvet pouch, the strings of which I had just loosened, and now everything came tumbling out. I knew about both the pleasure and catharsis of sexual make-believe, that you could symbolically play out hopes and fears, pleasure and trauma, like only the richest of dreams. BDSM in particular allowed practitioners to enter into altered, transcendent, and even therapeutic states via the negotiated enactment of fantasies.

Being spit on and burped at by belligerent frat boys, though, was more of a personal nightmare than a fantasy. I would sooner fantasize about grabbing those men by their throats, dragging them to the floor, and hocking a loogie right in their blazing-red faces. What transpired in that bar might have been Rylie's fantasy—in her euphoric exit interview, she told the camera of the shoot, "It was *awesome*"—but it was not mine. It was like I'd walked into a steak house as a vegetarian, taken a mouthful of bloody filet mignon, and gone with eye-bulging surprise, "*Yuck.*"

No one had told me to attend that porn shoot. No one had suggested that I plumb every popular tube site genre. No one had requested that I relentlessly fake orgasms. I had done these things out of curiosity, fear, and a search for control. That night, I did not feel in control in the least, as I curled up in my bed in the fetal position. One person's sexual spa day is another person's house of horrors.

I texted Tim and asked him to come over, even though it was approaching midnight on a weeknight. I wanted to have sex, immediately. *Mayday mayday may-fucking-day.* This wasn't about arousal but rescue. Not of myself, but of sex. I wanted to have sex not like in the bar, not like on the screen, but like I actually wanted it, whatever that meant. I was learning what it didn't mean, at least. That was something. A starting point.

A FEW MONTHS LATER, I got an email from Dan Savage. "I got an email from Dan Savage" felt remarkable enough, but he was asking me to *field a reader question for him.* For years, I had read his Savage Love advice column, in which he addressed all manner of sex quandary with his signature style of empathy drenched with acerbic wit. Now, having noticed my writing at *Salon*, he was forwarding along a reader letter and asking me to weigh in.

"I am a 23-year-old female, sexually active for seven years, and I can't reach climax," the letter read. "I am extremely frustrated. I have a wonderfully patient and helpful partner. He has tried hard to no avail. I can't even get myself there. I feel like I am broken." Here was Dan Savage asking me to give advice to myself. Worse, here was Dan Savage asking me to give advice to a *better* version of myself. At least this woman, who signed her letter Frustrated Annoyed Person, was not faking her orgasms.

I tried stepping into the role of journalist, detailing a theory about female orgasm that I had recently stumbled across in my research: "Evolutionary selection has *hugely* favored the male orgasm, for obvious reasons. The by-product theory goes that since females share the same embryological origins of pleasure-friendly nerves and tissues as males, they are physically capable of climaxing as well," I wrote. "In this view, the female orgasm is an evolutionary hand-me-down—or, more cynically, mere leftovers." But, I argued, this need not be depressing! Instead, it could be taken as a validation of the full range of women's orgasmic experiences. "This means a multi-orgasmic woman is just as 'normal' as an orgasmless one, a lady who comes from a single flick of the finger is just as 'healthy' as one who requires forty-five minutes with her Hitachi magic wand set on high," I wrote.

My advice now reads to me as defeatist. The factors that interfere with women's pleasure are manifold—from cultural influences, like sexual double standards, to relational issues, like a partner who grunts, rolls over, and falls fast asleep. Just as critics of the "female Viagra" gold rush had argued that it was too simplistic to label women's multifaceted sexual dissatisfaction as a physiological problem in need of a "pink pill," it was too simplistic to label this twenty-three-year-old woman's orgasmless experience as her "normal," a fact in need of casual acceptance.

At the time, though, I was trying to counsel this letter writer in the same way that I counseled myself. "When women have a difficult time getting there, it can be helpful to take the finish line away," I wrote to FAP. "At the risk of sounding woo-woo, I would suggest that she slow down and focus on feeling individual sensations. She'll be most likely to come when she forgets her worries about all that she isn't feeling and simply enjoys what she *does* feel." It was the advice that I was offering myself in those days, but the finish line was never not there; I was just inventing different ways of walking up to it.

Recently, I had experienced a couple of authentic orgasms with Tim, because I'd finally worked up the courage to introduce my plug-in, eggbeater-like Hitachi into the bedroom. Now, Hitachi or not, I was trying to access that woo and *feel whatever I felt*. No pressure to orgasm, no pressure to fake. I had even revived my manufactured "delaying orgasms" experiment. The day that Savage Love column published, I had my first earth-quaking, Hitachi-less orgasm with Tim. As I explained to Elissa via Gchat with a virtual shrug, "I took my own advice."

Then, a couple of months later, I tearfully told Tim that I loved him, and it was as though I'd replaced the batteries on my orgasm. Ah, right, intimacy. That old thing. Within a few months, I was having regular orgasms and no longer faking it. What a turnabout, what a success, what a *disappointing narrative development*. This felt like solving the vexing equation of sex + y = orgasm with the variable of "love." It played right into the same stereotypes—about men's indiscriminate seed-spreading and women's need for commitment—that often fueled criticism around casual sex. *"Admit it,* the bar scene is a guy thing," in Stepp's memorable words. I wanted to be able to drink like a man and watch porn like a man and fuck like a man and get off like a man, not exactly appreciating the distorted stereotype of this guiding inspiration.

No matter, the orgasmic finish line had been crossed. As happens with solved dilemmas, another concern came to fill the void. There was that business about the ancient aliens, after all. I started to worry, again, about those more traditional things—*babies, ovaries, marriage, husband, shit, crap, shit*—as evidenced by a typical Gchat conversation from this period:

> **me:** what am i doing in a relationship with a man with whom i cannot reproduce?
>
> **Elissa:** would you mind rereading that sentence so that you can see how stupid you sound asking such a dumbass question like that?
>
> **me:** but i mean, elissa, c'mon. I'm TWENTY SEVEN.
>
> **me:** THIRTY NEARS
>
> **Elissa:** would you mind rereading that sentence so that you can see how stupid you sound asking such a dumbass question like that?

I reread the question. It sounded like just as I had satisfied one desire, I had gotten back in touch with a deeper one.

CHAPTER 7

Just Friends

I think I'm having lunch with my future husband," I texted Elissa.

This sounds like a binder-paper note scribbled by a schoolgirl, but it's what I typed out as a twenty-eight-year-old woman with an iPhone and a shaky thumb. My "future husband" was in the bathroom of this modern Vietnamese restaurant in San Francisco's Ferry Building, where green waves sloshed against wooden piers. I picked at a neglected plate of crab noodles and sipped at an empty glass of a once-Manhattan. The fashionably oversize ice cube that arrived with the drink was almost melted to normal size. We had been there for nearly two hours.

It was a Wednesday afternoon and I had never spent more than an hour away from my desk. Often, I grabbed a limp compostable box of something to go from the food court in my office building and ate hunched in my cubicle. Even walking the three or so blocks to the Ferry Building felt like a dangerous amount of time away from my computer amid content quotas and the ever-present possibility of breaking news. But two hours passed and I hadn't even noticed, until "my future husband" left for the bathroom and I texted Elissa and *Oh my, look at the time.*

Not that I really cared, given the circumstances. I had been asked out to lunch by a former coworker and casual friend, someone I'd known for several years and never thought of romantically, but with whom I was suddenly envisioning a lifetime. Only in the abstract, of course. On the level of a single phrase that I had never before written or uttered or even thought. I realized how it sounded—airheaded, foolhardy, traditionalist, anti-feminist—but I had to write it for the record. I called it via text message: future husband.

WHEN CHRISTOPHER'S NAME HAD shown up in my inbox the week before with an invite to lunch, I thought what I usually thought about him: *That freaking guy. I love that guy. What a great guy.* He wrote, "It's been forever, which is mostly my doing. I have recently emerged from relationshibernation and I'm sheepishly asking myself . . . where did I put everybody?" He was working as a programmer in the beckoning sparkle of start-up land and his new office was a couple of blocks from mine, the one we had once shared.

Christopher used to work in *Salon*'s art department, designing the site and doing illustrations for feature stories. We first met when I was a twenty-three-year-old feminist blogger and he was a twenty-six-year-old new hire. He was a skinny, sensitive indie rocker type with long, mussed hair and a pair of sailor-esque swallows tattooed above either clavicle. He wore T-shirts featuring bands I didn't know. I immediately wrote him off as not my type but soon found that I adored him as a friend. *A buddy. A pal.* I wanted to be closer friends, in fact, but he seemed busy with his serial, cohabitational monogamy. Plus, he lived in the East Bay, a whole twenty minutes across the bridge. Another universe, practically.

Christopher lasted a couple of years at *Salon* before leaving to tour with his band. At the time, a higher-up at the company joked at an all-hands meeting that Christopher was leaving us so that he could go "choke to death on his own vomit" like a true rock star. But then there he was playing at South by Southwest, doing glamorous photo shoots, and very much not choking to death on his own vomit. In fact, he looked a lot happier than any of us who had stayed in our ghostly post-layoffs cubicle farm.

Over the years, we had stayed in sporadic touch. When I competed in Literary Death Match, the site of my love match with Elissa, Christopher showed up. Afterward, he came along with me and my friends to grab a bite at Taqueria el Buen Sabor, where he accidentally dropped his burrito in his lap, leaving a greasy crotch stain on his chinos. Bars were hopped, drinks were had, and then we all walked past a freshly fallen scoop of ice cream on the sidewalk outside an organic ice cream parlor. "You should lick it," I said impishly. Christopher nonchalantly got down on his hands and knees and took a lick, and then another, and then a bite. Someone whipped out a phone and snapped pictures.

Later, one of my friends asked me to set her up with him.

Christopher made lap burritos and sidewalk ice cream oddly charming.

Whenever his band played locally, I would show up and watch him hop around with his electric guitar on stage at Cafe du Nord or El Rio. I might shout-talk over the music with his live-in girlfriend of the moment, and then chat with him afterward about the guy who currently wasn't texting me back. Indie rock was not my thing, just like Christopher was not my type. I had at one time blamed this musical aversion on the "neener-neener" of guitar, the very instrument he played. After one of his shows at Rickshaw Stop, though, I wrote to John about having watched Christopher "rock out." He was "really good," the "band was great," I was "super impressed," it was "very good, inventive, interesting and unique stuff."

Occasionally, I emailed Christopher to get quotes for articles— say, a piece about the difficulties of talking about porn in relationships—and he thoughtfully obliged. One of these conversations led him to write about how his bumbling interpretation of feminism had paved the way for some very bad sex in college. Christopher had read *The Whole Lesbian Sex Book* in what he described as a "misguided attempt to learn how to be a non-heteronormative lover." He avoided anything that might make him appear "sexually aggressive or dominating in any way." This led one partner to ask whether he was gay and another to exclaim, mid-coitus, "Come on. I want *you* to fuck *me*." His email continued, "I was just trying to avoid being the stereotypical tin-eared, jack-hammering brute that I was fairly certain women didn't respond to. Clearly, I was overcompensating, but I had no idea."

At the time of this email, I failed to see our similarities, that we were trains on parallel tracks: him trying to be what women wanted, me trying to be what men wanted. Instead, I read that email—from a feminist guy comfortable talking about sex and using terms like *heteronormative*—and I thought, as usual, *That freaking guy. I love that guy. What a great guy.* It didn't occur to me that maybe I should date that freaking guy. I wrote back to say that his email made "me feel better about The State of Dudes Today—even though you're not an average dude." Why, one might ask, had I spent so much time optimizing for average?

So, when I got Christopher's lunch invite, I thought nothing of accepting, despite having a boyfriend. Tim and I were still going, if not strong. Christopher and I were friends. *Just friends.*

THE CHRISTOPHER WHO WALKED into the restaurant was not the Christopher I expected. He still had his neck tattoos, but the messy rocker hair had been handsomely cropped and he was leaning more J.Crew than thrift shop. He strode in, smiling when he saw me seated at the bar, and I thought, *Oh, hello.*

What followed is one of the more important conversations of my life, but I remember only disjointed frames. His eyes pooling with tears as I told him about my mom's illness, and my parents' nearly thirty-five years of a happy marriage. The visible thump of a pulse under the soft of his stubbled neck as he shared plans to soon quit the band for good. The way his lip slightly caught on a charmingly askew upper tooth as he smiled at my dilemma of having a sweet boyfriend who believed in ancient alien conspiracies.

We covered all the best topics: relationships, therapy, religion, marriage, books, nature, death, food, money, politics, writing. All of them except for sex, but I already knew plenty from my emails with him over the years, including how often he watched porn and his feelings on butt stuff.

The conversation wasn't flirtatious or romantic, except that we were two people talking about wanting the same things. The obviousness of this filled the air between us like an overpowering scent that we refused to name aloud, even as our nostrils visibly flared. Then there was this: "I just want to be a rad mom," I told him, the words escaping before I had time to censor. These were not words that you said aloud as a hetero woman to a man of interest, lest you scare him off. I can't recall what he did in response—a tilt of the head, a lean forward. I knew he wasn't afraid. This time, my eyes teared up—not at his lack of fear, but at the shock of recognition in my word spillage. I meant what I said, and I felt comfortable saying it to him. When he left for the bathroom, I texted Elissa.

I had a model for this kind of love story. My parents had been "just friends" as roommates in Berkeley in the seventies. They were emphatically not each other's types. My dad was too much of a thrill-seeking, skateboarding wild child, and she was too retiring and modest for him, with her dog-eared copy of *Lyrical Ballads* and buttoned-up peasant blouses. When they started sleeping together, they were still "just friends." At the time, my mom wrote him a letter reading in part, "From the beginning, we both knew that ours would not be a love relationship. Clearly we are not the fulfillment of each other's needs and desires in that way." They got married six months later. My mom would tell me of her earlier certainty about being just friends, "I was such dummy."

Despite the audacity of my "future husband" text, it took a little over a month, and one more platonic lunch with Christopher, before I broke up with Tim. I didn't know whether Christopher felt the same way about me, and I had little faith in the possibility of finding someone else like him. I was terrified of being alone—in the world, and in my mom's illness. I recognized the selfishness of this calculation, the greedy exploitation, even, of another person's heart and body. I've seen all but the bravest among us do this to a degree. We hook ourselves up to another person like a form of life support and live in fear of pulling the plug, of finding out whether we can breathe on our own.

I CASUALLY ALERTED CHRISTOPHER to the breakup in an email PS. The tone was, essentially: Thanks, bud, for helping me come to my senses. I didn't want him to think that I'd broken up with Tim for him. *Hahahahaha, of course not.* Christopher went on a final two-month-long summer tour with the band, a last hurrah, and we emailed each other nearly every day. He wrote of dry desert thunderstorms, lush green rivers, bending reeds, and melting heat. In New Mexico, he offered to bring me back some alien tchotchkes. In the Midwest, he told me about the platinum records sitting next to the hand soap in a famous musician's bathroom. I tried to make my life—writing an article about STI testing, making an appearance on the *Savage Lovecast*—sound equally exciting.

Things stayed platonic, save for the constancy of our emails, but I spent those months longing for Christopher, living in my head about the idea of him. At a friend's cabin in Tahoe, I cut up apples and oranges for a picturesque sangria, while imagining the resulting Instagram photo and how Christopher might comment or "like" it. Back in San Francisco, while running through Glen Canyon Park, jumping over tree roots and stopping to admire sun-bleached succulents on craggy cliffs, I wrote a witty email to him in my head.

It was all reminiscent of a single memory from the summer after sixth grade. One afternoon, as I rode along in a van filled with other camp kids slathered in sunscreen, I looked out at the passing eucalyptus trees haloed by sun and noted my own twelve-year-old reflection in the window. For the rest of the drive, I imagined I could see the face of Adam, my school crush, in place of my own. His porcelain skin and nineties mushroom cut were superimposed on my olive complexion and tangle of long hair.

This memory sticks because of what it now seems to represent: Life passing by while living through some boy. Subsuming my identity to some boy. I had spent most of my life doing this. I was never alone. There was always a fantasy of *some boy* watching and wanting me, making me better. Making me whole.

• • •

THE FIRST WEEKEND AFTER Christopher got back into town, he emailed to say that he was going shopping at a vintage furniture store near my house and then to my favorite plant shop. "Maybe the lovely Tracy would like to look at furni and plants too," he wrote. I stared for a few beats at the word *lovely*, noting the tonal shift, before writing back. A couple of hours later, he was picking me up in his zippy two-door VW hatchback, which still had new car smell. It felt adult—suburban, even. A confession: I liked it.

We spent several hours hopping in and out of shops, before grabbing takeout containers and cans of Tecate from Bi-Rite and sitting in the park: a cliché surrounded by clichés. By the time we returned to my house, night had fallen, and goose pimples rose on my arms as we walked up the endless steps to my front door, and then up again to my shared flat. We had spent two months emailing constantly. He thought I was "lovely." My roommates were gone. Something was going to happen.

We sat facing each other on the couch in my living room and looked at each other silently. *Do it now, do it, do it now, you obviously must do it now.* Christopher laughed unevenly, mumbled some false starts, and glanced at the door. Then he said, "I should go home." He touched my hand and said with equal parts irony and earnestness, "I intend to *court* you." I might have been less shocked if he'd suggested double anal.

Christopher stood up to leave, told me he was going to plan us a date, and said, "I'm going to kiss you on the cheek now."

Then I felt his lips, the sandpaper of stubble, press into my face, and he was gone.

This was endearing, but more so annoying. I didn't require delicate courting. Not that indelicate courting had worked so well for me in the past, judging by many measures (orgasms, tears, text message exegeses). I wanted to have sex with this man. Why couldn't I *just have sex with this man*? Courtship seemed rigid, proscriptive, inhibited. I wanted to throw my wanting into the wind and see what happened. Hadn't all that chaste emailing counted for anything? What about those lingering lunches? It didn't occur to me that he was the one who needed to be courted.

On our first date, Christopher showed up at my door with a bouquet of miniature calla lilies in his hand. *Nature's dick pic*, I privately mused, seeing a penis where others would have seen a vulva, and avoiding the unnerving thoughtfulness of his gesture. (Those flowers were enough of a shock, and my content quota was such that I wrote an entire personal essay for *Salon* framed around them.) Then he took me to the Independent, where a friend of a friend of a friend was playing a show. We went out afterward with the band, and then wandered off on our own, drinking Fernet and talking at great length about the pigeon sex I had recently witnessed on the ledge of my bay window. I am quite the lady and conversationalist.

Eventually, we spilled out of a bar and he pulled me into a set-back storefront with a "c'mere." He kissed me, and it was not a chaste kiss or a courting kiss. It was jumping into a hot tub after a pool, my skin freezing and aflame. But back at my house, while we made out on my living room couch, he pulled back and said, "I should go home. I think this is a good note to end on."

The skyscraper fall of rejection. He had been able to withstand my charms. He had been able to pull away and summon an Uber. The cultural narrative around men's desire was that it didn't, it couldn't stop once activated (see: blue balls). This was the same narrative so often used to justify violence against women—the one exemplified by "He couldn't help himself" and "She asked for it." It also turned a man's ability to stop into a personal insult. If a man could walk away from you, well, what did that say about you?

Christopher had seen the flip of this with that former partner asking if he was gay. I knew something of what she might have felt: the frustration, insecurity, and confusion of the disrupted narrative. Either he was gay, or she was undesirable. I realized how little room there was for heterosexual men's sensitivity and feeling in sex when these are the stakes, when anything short of ravishment was both an insult to a partner and an indictment of one's sexuality. I wondered how much I had demanded of my past partners without knowing it. *Take me. Want me. Do unto me.*

If your desirability was proven by a man's intensity and unflappability, his brutality and selfishness, there was no room left for your petty pleasures, let alone nuanced feelings and expansive longings. Hadn't faking it been on some level about not disrupting men's wanting? About not reminding them of their soft, tender selves, lest their dicks follow suit? As far back as high school, I had tuned in to the atomic subtleties of my boyfriend's hard-on, calibrating accordingly, prioritizing his erection over my own pleasure. I had been protecting men's boners—and consequently, all egos involved—the whole of my sexual life.

Protecting men's boners was about more than just sex. It was a perspective, an outlook—a beneficial political stance, even. In my early twenties, at a woodsy *Salon* staff retreat, I'd gotten into a discussion beside the campfire with a decades-older man high up at the publication. I was an intern at the time, and I wanted desperately to belong even in the approximate vicinity of these writers, some of whom I'd been reading since college. Everyone else had gone to sleep in their tents, but there I was, accepting proffered swigs of eye-watering grappa and trying to get cerebral about *what else but porn* while quoting some Camille Paglia, who was then a frequent *Salon* contributor.

Then this man—a liberal intellectual, a literary bon vivant—patted me on the thigh and said, "I'm glad you're not one of those feminists who think that erections are evil."

ON MY SECOND DATE with Christopher, we went to Zuni Café, a bistro with floor-to-ceiling windows looking out on the restored vintage streetcars that hummed along Market Street. I wore a tight black dress and heels, feeling like I was cosplaying as a San Francisco socialite. During a brief weekend-long foray into online dating via OkCupid, I had gone on first dates to a dive bar in the Haight and a taqueria in the Mission, but never to a restaurant that accepted reservations. I knew the gist of what misogynistic trolls, who continued to haunt the comments sections of my articles, might say about this: Why buy the cow, et cetera. Intellectually and politically, I did not believe this nonsense. Yet I was pleasantly surprised that Christopher was so insistent on taking this free cow out on a date.

It's not like I hadn't *been out*. For most of my twenties, I had slept with men and platonically dated women. We ladies—*hey lady, love you, lady, you're my lady*—provided each other with emotional support. We shared our hard truths. We went on vacations together. We celebrated Galentine's Day. We went out to dinner, taking turns grabbing the bill, and joked about cohabitating and raising kids together if things didn't work out with these men.

I was familiar with the spate of trend pieces and blog posts lamenting the decline of courtship. "The Demise of Dating," warned a 2008 *New York Times* Op-Ed headline. "Romance Is Dead: Reflections on Today's Dating Scene," read the headline of a 2010 *Psychology Today* blog post. Soon, a *New York Times* headline would ask, "The End of Courtship?" (Skip ahead several more years and *Vanity Fair* would declare: "Tinder and the Dawn of the Dating Apocalypse.") As Moira Weigel explains in *Labor of Love: The Invention of Dating*, "experts" have announced the end of courtship for well over a century. When the concept of dating arose around the 1900s, it wasn't thought of as the wholesome affair romanticized today. In fact, women were *arrested* for going on dates. "In the eyes of the authorities, women who let men buy them food and drinks or gifts and entrance tickets looked like whores, and making a date seemed the same as turning a trick," writes Weigel.

In the decades that followed, dating kept reinventing itself, from the "petting parties" of the 1920s to going steady in the '50s to free love in the '60s. Each permutation brought with it handwringing about the decline of dating. That said, from the 1920s to the 1960s, there was consistently "an assumption that a series of dates would lead to sexual intimacy and emotional commitment." Of course, that dating script has since been reversed on college campuses, where instead of formal dates, students "hang out" in mixed groups and sometimes pair off to hook up. That thing we now think of as "traditional dating"—sitting across from each other at a candlelit table—might come after, or not at all. That dynamic had defined not just my college years but also most of my twenties.

Perched on a barstool at Zuni, having arrived early, I nervously fumbled in my purse every couple of minutes to check the time on my phone. Many time checks later, Christopher sent a text. He was late, but on his way—a meeting had run long at the office. I can still feel the outsize smart of that text. *I allowed myself to believe in this man, in the romance, the safety of it all. How dare he be late. How dare he make me hope.* This slight "misstep" felt like a brutal rejoinder, a taunting "I told you so." But then there he was, twenty minutes late, wearing a dress shirt and thin black tie, looking sharp as heck, and apologizing profusely for running behind.

For a long while, I had protected myself from letdown with the low expectations of late-night texts and no-strings sex. I pretended—to men, to myself—that it was *all good*. "No worries," I'd text, with a calculated delay, when some dude or another took a while to text back. This wasn't all that different from faking orgasms to protect boners. Maybe it was *all* about protecting boners.

We slid into a corner booth overlooking an alley strung with white lights and talked openly about what we each wanted in life, the subtextual hope being that we would find it together: a dog, a garden, a kid. "I just want a cozy life," I said, feeling self-consciously conventional. After draining a bottle of wine, we went back to my house and got into bed, rolling around in our underwear for hours. Then, at his suggestion, we went to sleep.

Each date that followed was like this. There was the hike in Point Reyes followed by a make-out on a lichen-covered rock in the woods. The home-cooked dinner at his tiny shingled rental cottage in a wooded creek-side oasis near downtown Oakland, to which I brought a bouquet of flowers as a gesture of equality. ("Men deserve flowers, too," I told him.) The movie in the park, where we made out under a blanket until someone screamed, "I'm so honored to watch you conceive your first child!" Another piece of clothing removed, the advance of a hand or mouth, but no *sex*-sex. "I don't want to rush," he said.

Weeks passed. I Gchatted with friends about this remarkable, UFO-level occurrence. "Have you had sex with Christopher yet?" they wanted to know. I had not. "Still, no." "Nope."

"Nada." Looking back, I know that we were already having sex. There had been mutual orgasms, just no PIV, as the sex researchers that I routinely interviewed called it. Somehow this didn't count, even though it had brought me more pleasure than all the "real" sex I'd had before. Sexual scripts don't just shape the experience of sex, but the very definition of it. *Dick in the pus', dick in the pus'*, sang the puerile mantra in my head. My validation and power, a fantasy of order and control. Getting to know him before *getting to know* him? Developing intimacy before being "intimate"? I was walking around without skin, all nerve endings and exposed tissue.

And he noticed. On one of those early dates, Christopher looked at me and said with the shock of recognition, "You're just a *sweet sweetie.*" He had thought of me as a daring, irreverent sex writer who had not too long ago written an essay titled "In Defense of Casual Sex." The one who visited porn sets, judged air sex competitions, and got subpoenaed for a federal obscenity trial. My friends had tried to tell me: *He is terrified. Who wants to sleep with a sex writer? You're mailed dildos at the office.* His hesitation hadn't stemmed from retro romanticism, paternalistic caretaking, or a lack of attraction. He wasn't cozy yet.

Then he got cozy. A month in, lying on the brown leather couch in his woodsy cabin one Saturday afternoon, we did it. PIV. Except it was more like: Sweat dripping. Tears, too. The well of skin between his shoulder blades, my fingers sinking into it like warm, still water. Stubble sloughing off my surface, exposing the underneath. My hair in his mouth, my mouth, and neither of us removing it. Bodies slipping against each other like they were trying to find balance. Sunlight and leaves. Flying and crashing. I hadn't slept with a new person without the assistance of alcohol in over a decade.

MY UNSPOKEN RULE WAS there would be no more faked orgasms, ever. I resisted the temptation to fill ear-thrumming silence with false moans. The quiet felt like failure. I was used to feigning pleasure for men's benefit, but Christopher was turned on by something I couldn't fake: connection and closeness. *Damn it.* Occasionally, I felt my consciousness rising out of my body during sex like sweat evaporating from skin. Then I'd be over there, standing in the corner of the room like a voyeur, watching us having sex. Christopher would sometimes pull back, like he had noticed this leering third person in the room and wanted to show them the door. "Hey." Kiss. "Just . . . want to reconnect for a second."

It's not that I suddenly eschewed sexual make-believe. Now, though, I was feeling less like an actor handed a script and more like the ink-stained playwright. We turned his bedroom into a test kitchen in the interest of frothy two-dollar-a-word freelance pieces for magazines like *Cosmopolitan*. For one such article, we experimented with role play, acting out my enduring fantasy of a masseur with wandering hands. Of course, that fantasy, with its eroticization of abusive trespass, was formed by an alchemy of mainstream pop culture, hard-core porn, and the societal water in which I swam; none of us are authors un-touched by outside influence. There is no pre-cultural self to which we can return.

I carried a casual mistrust of my desires and their origins at the same time that I enacted them. Occasionally, I mentally scrambled for more philosophically palatable turn-ons, but as Sallie Tisdale wrote, "Parts of my consciousness refused to rise, staying far below the sanitized plain of social politics."[1] Authenticity is hard to define and can become its own pressure, a directive to portray just another sexual ideal. The researcher and psychologist Sharon Lamb, writing of adolescent sexuality, warns against romanticizing notions of a "'natural girl' whose own authentic desires will come free once she recognizes commercial and ideological forces."[2] Sometimes, a girl might look inside only to find "another packaged version of teen sexuality"—say, the "slut" reformed by love.

Of course, that is just the conformist reversal threatened by my own developing narrative. After dating for several months, our abstract discussions about wanting a "cozy life" transformed into specific ones about a cozy life together. There was a ring at a local jewelry shop: a tiny triangle-shaped diamond on a rose-gold band that I saw on my way home from work. I had never been a fan of diamonds, for reasons aesthetic and ethical. I had never been a fan of engagement rings, either, because I detested the lopsided, patriarchal tradition of men proposing to women. But I started dropping in on my walks home to visit the ring, try it on, and talk to the shopkeeper about the feel-good origins of *this* diamond.

Scholars have suggested that diamond engagement rings arose in the 1930s as collateral against a woman's virginity. It was common at the time for women to have sex with their fiancés, but then engagements could fall apart. When they did, a woman's "value" as a future bride would be diminished if she'd had sex, but at least she would still have that valuable hunk of rock. A writer for *The Atlantic* dubbed the engagement rings of that time "virginity insurance." Well, I wanted death insurance. My mom was now occasionally using an oxygen machine and frequently wheelchair-bound. She had exceeded her prognosis by nearly three years. She was among the statistical few whose time with stage 4 lung cancer could be measured in more than months. I understood this luck—more so than diamonds—as a dwindling resource. My mom would soon be gone, and then I'd be left bobbing in the middle of the ocean.

Christopher was land and lifeboat. I wanted a life with him because of love, and I wanted to get engaged *as soon as humanly possible* because of need. I Gchatted Elissa about the ring: "i want it to symbolize something that it can't possibly symbolize . . . which is that everything will be okay always from here on . . . that i've figured everything out . . . mission accomplished." After years of eye rolling at De Beers commercials and *Bachelor* finales, my inner capitalist had in my weakest moment emerged from underground holding a tiny, glinting three-sided diamond to the sky. As though its shape and size separated it from the traditional romantic fairy tale. As though that wasn't exactly what I sought, especially in this moment of mortal terror.

Some six months after we'd started dating, I was ordering a custom engagement band for Christopher, he was buying me that irregular diamond, and then we were standing on a cliff in Point Reyes, proposing to each other. I decided to move into his creek-side cottage, leaving most of my years-old Ikea furniture on the curb on Eighteenth Street. While sweeping the bare wood floors of my old room, which was about to be put back on the market with a four-hundred-a-month price hike, I watched through the bay window as passersby picked over the remnants of my single life. A man pulled up in a pickup and loaded up my couch, the same one I'd posed on in those labia-spreading pics coolly received by John. My rug—the one I'd collapsed onto after my mom's news, and upon which Candle Butt Boy had flipped and propped and ground my grieving body—was rolled up and tossed in next.

The man saved the mattress for last. I loved that mattress and everything that had happened on it, even though I'd lied through so much of it. I adored many of those men. Their heft, body hair, and gravel throats. Their freedom and entitlement, too. Shimmering shards of otherness, as alluring as they were alarming. I'd met that otherness with my naked body, attracting, absorbing, and surviving it; and then feeling victorious. Naked, but never fully. Always with my armor.

Along the way, that old mantra of "Yes, girl, you are a goddess" had started to feel more like an affirmation whispered on the way up a mountain: "You can do it." I had done it. *I had done it.* Now for a different climb. The scariest one of all: intimacy. I had started to write about all this for *Salon* and women's magazines like *Elle*—the years of faking, the pleasant surprise of going on real dates, the insecurity of waiting to have sex, the reappraisal of just what casual sex had and had not given me. The trolls and conservative culture warriors took notice, and some seemed to be genuinely worried about my future romantic prospects.

Just as I started dating Christopher, the website Hooking Up Smart set its sights on me. It was run by Susan Walsh, a blogger who routinely targeted feminist writers with conservative anti-sex rhetoric and attracted an enthusiastic readership of MRAs and PUAs. She published a two-thousand-word blog post titled "The Abject Failure of Sex-Positive Feminism: A Case Study." I was the case study. "As a sex blogger, Clark Flory doesn't have the luxury of hiding her past—any guy who chooses to date her is clearly cool with her Google search results," she wrote, dropping the hyphen from my last name, as sexist trolls often did. Walsh continued, "If she's lucky, she can step off the carousel"—the "cock carousel" being a term frequently used by PUAs to describe women who slept around—"and give monogamous commitment a whirl." *If she's lucky.*

After I wrote about my engagement, the "manosphere" blog Free Northerner declared me "The Archetypal Modern Woman." The post detailed at length my "descent into absolute sluttery," only to emerge with a fiancé in my late twenties. This was, the post argued, so often how it went these days. Women slept around with "alphas" only to eventually marry poor "betas," who acted as the burdened financial providers for their "ex-slut" wives, as one commenter put it. "Alpha fux, beta bux," they called it. Never mind that few of the men I'd either slept or relationshipped with fell into stark survival-of-the-fittest categories.

Then the author of the blog posted an addendum: "To the guy marrying Tracy: RUN AWAY. Run as hard and as fast as you can before you are legally bound to her." In the thread below, a commenter wrote of my engagement, "It is stories like this that make me want to doubt the existence of GOD." He was convinced that given my past "sluttery," I would soon divorce Christopher, leaving him "on the hook for child support, alimony, and lawyer fees and he'll never be free of any of it."

At the time, I laughed. It seemed outrageously funny, but only because this was the year before twenty-two-year-old Elliot Rodger went on a shooting spree in Santa Barbara, killing six people. He was driven in part by rage over being an "involuntary celibate" (or "incel" for short). These incel communities had begun to emerge within the larger anti-feminist manosphere. Women were free to make their own sexual and romantic choices. The outrage. *The injustice.* Many incels, quivering with white entitlement, saw this as disenfranchisement, rather than a righting of the scales toward equality.

The year after Rodger's massacre, eighteen-year-old Ben Moynihan would stab three women after explaining in a prerecorded video: "I think every girl is a type of slut, they are fussy with men nowadays, they do not give boys like us a chance. . . . I am still a virgin, everyone is losing it before me, that's why you are my chosen target." He waved a knife at the camera and asked, "Shall I stab you in the neck or in the heart, shall I slash your throat or should I just cigarette lighter you or just fire you? I do not know where I could get petrol from but how hard can it be to come by?"

Years later, when those and far too many other similar stories would unfold, I'd inevitably think of the men in that comment thread, raging over my "sluttery," sending digital smoke signals to my fiancé, and doubting the existence of a god. All because I had some sex, wrote about it unabashedly, and then decided to get married. (And to think that a man would even have me.) In their eyes, I'd gotten away with something. I had escaped the usual punishment. "Here's to you Tracy Clark-Flory," the blog post concluded. "You won the mating game."

Still, these men tried to have the last laugh. In the comments, a contentious debate was sparked about my relative attractiveness. The original poster suggested that I was "fairly good-looking, a solid 7," but commenters took offense. "That girl is a 5. Maybe a 6 on her best day," sneered one fellow. Said another gentleman: "More like 4.0-4.5." And another: "I not only don't find her attractive, I find her repulsive." The discovery of my dad's Perfect10.com subscription, and indelible memories of watching strippers rated numerically on *Real Sex*, had helped set me off on this journey across the sexual landscape to confront my fears—and now here were faceless men on the internet evaluating me on a 1-to-10 scale. How exquisitely, excruciatingly, poetically perfect.

It was men like these—with their resentment, anger, and entitlement—who made my mom worry for me. "You're so much braver than I was," she had said. My mom had been more severely and irreparably punished for her sexuality—having been sent away to protect the family from shame and stamped with a scarlet letter. In one generation, the personal and societal circumstances had improved immeasurably, but plenty remained the same.

"I DON'T KNOW IF it makes sense to plan around me, honey," my mom told me as we discussed nearby wheelchair-friendly venues for a wedding date the following summer. "I'm not sure that I'll make it, sweetheart."

The cancer had taken a turn, she felt. It was the thickening in her lungs, a whistling in her breath, and the sleep that fell over her like a blanket of intergalactic dark. We decided to fast-track the wedding, wanting her presence more than a Pinterest-perfect day, which had never been Christopher's aim, anyway. "We could get married on a pile of dirt for all I care," he had told me early on in a fit of hyperbole as I, previously more of a city hall type, fretted over venues. All that fell away when she told me she might only have a few months left. We chose a date three months out, printing out invites on our LaserJet and stuffing them into envelopes with hastily scribbled addresses.

Weeks before the wedding, my dad called unexpectedly. It was that same solemn tone again, the one that had delivered the first bad news, and I collapsed onto the couch like I'd collapsed onto my floor years earlier. For three years, I had prepared for this moment, and it didn't matter.

"Mom's gone," he said. "I'm so sorry, honey, but she's gone."

I whimpered in words: *what, how, what, how.* "I'm sorry, honey, I just tried to wake her—" His throat seized. "She's gone," he choked. "She's not breathing. There's no heartbeat." I put palm to chest to check that mine was still there. My dad continued in my silence, "She was taking a nap and slipped away. She's not here anymore." There were so many ways to say that someone was dead, and you had to say them all before it began to make any sense.

Christopher turned from the sink, holding a sponge and cereal bowl covered in suds. The infuriating absurdity of the everyday next to my mom's forever end. I wanted to throw that bowl, shatter it on the parquet floors, create chaos to match my insides, just like I had right after her diagnosis. Instead, I filled my palms—and then the crook of Christopher's neck—with breath, tears, and snot. Then we got in the car to go see what was left of my mom.

I STEPPED ONTO THE sunlit porch of my childhood home and paused before the threshold of the living room, where I knew that her body lay. Sitting down in the doorway, I stared at the tear-blurred image of wisteria arcing over the front gate.

That wooden fence, standing five feet tall with a section of flower-dotted trellis running along the top, had been there most of my life. My mom told me early on that she had it built after my birth because she wanted to keep me safe from passing cars and strangers. This was as comforting as it was distressing for what it suggested of the outside world. In a recurring childhood nightmare, the Big Bad Wolf would pace outside that gate, huffing and puffing as his shiny, predatory eyes and bulbous cartoon nose peeked over the top. He was trying to get in.

Sitting in the doorway, I was a dreamer at the transitional moment when you can decide to rouse and save yourself the terrors, or else move deeper into a waking nightmare. Meet the wolf or go running to your mom—except now those were the same option. I stood up, clutching the doorframe, and stepped inside.

CHAPTER 8

Heartbeats

There was no mom there. Just an empty shell, a human suit. I don't know what I expected: a muted, inanimate version? A lingering, tangible essence to which I might be able to say good-bye? Instead, "she" lay on the hospital bed in the middle of my parents' living room, head tilted to the sky, mouth agape like it had provided her exit, like she'd left the door open on her way out. Christopher placed a cupped hand on either of my shoulders. My dad, head tilted, said, "She looks peaceful, really." Face frozen to stone, chiseled as though mid-snore. How could this hollow artistic rendering be said to be a "she," let alone to look peaceful?

It was as if my mom had tucked a crude dummy of herself into bed and vanished, like those prisoners I'd learned about on countless field trips who attempted escape from Alcatraz. Where had she fled? A globe spun in my head as a toy plane hovered, like an interlude in a vintage TV mystery. Then I flashed, absurdly, to my earliest childhood memory: My mom leaving me on the first day of preschool. She disappeared behind a looming wooden gate and didn't come back, not even when I wailed. She was gone and I was left behind. A teacher had promised, "Your mom will be back."

No, she would not.

The Berkeley "family" descended upon the house with food, tears, and lingering hugs. Did I eat? Who knows. Did I pee? Can't recall. It's certain that I breathed, but hard to believe. At one point, someone tenderly asked if I wanted to hold my mom's hand. I said, "No thanks," and thought bitterly, *That is not my mom.*

I took the rest of the week off work, but I spent my days researching mortality like it was my job. I read about the cultural history of witnessing death, from the Victorian practice of postmortem photography to the modern decline of open-casket funerals. Then I came across an *Esquire* article about a controversial photograph from the 9/11 terrorist attacks of a man jumping from the North Tower, which read, "He appears relaxed, hurtling through the air. . . . He does not appear intimidated by gravity's divine suction or by what awaits him."[1] A photographer had captured a dozen images of his ten-second fall. I navigated back and forth between each frame, seconds farther from or nearer to death. As I clicked and scrolled, he plummeted and rose, hovering in the before.

I searched for photographs of the other "jumpers," who had been forced by fire and smoke from the upper floors of the building. Then I typed in these terrible words: "9/11 bodies on sidewalk." Maybe I was trying to replace one horrific image with another—trade my mom's gaping mouth for the bloody body of a stranger—or maybe I wanted to understand the how of death so that I could negotiate with it.

I kept rewinding the imaginary mental tape of my mom's death: At what precise point had she been irretrievably gone? Or was it not a definitive black-and-white moment but a gradual negation? Had she become less alive and less alive until she was dead? What if my dad had woken her up a moment earlier?

Other Google searches: "atoms and death," "definition of death," "moment of death," "stages of death," "revived after death," "near death experiences."

In between these searches, I would sometimes navigate over to a tube site and click through gang bang videos filled with women splayed, gasping, crying, heaving. Ejaculate gargled in the throat and webbed across bloodshot eyes. Orifices pried open, the camera seemingly intent on burrowing inside. I wanted all the horrors, the body in its extreme forms. Then I'd have a tiny orgasm, the petitest of petite morts, followed by more actual death.

"Sex seems like the worst thing in the world," I told Elissa in those first weeks. Now whenever Christopher touched me, it burned like betrayal. *How dare I feel pleasure? My mom is dead.* I turned to him and confessed, "I don't think I'm ever going to have sex again."

I started to think in ghoulish specifics about my mom's body. Had they cremated it yet? Maybe I could place an urgent phone call and ask them to wait, to save me a whole piece of her. A thigh bone, perhaps. A lock of hair. I pictured her heart floating in a jar of formaldehyde. Her brain encased in resin. I imagined visually tracing the cauliflower contours of that brain, over and over again until I memorized them. As though learning the topography of her mind was a form of resurrection. I sent Elissa Gchat fragments:

> when people are brought back to life
> after drowning
> it's just. where is the person? the brain?
> i want to freeze her brain

Elissa wrote back with a quote from *Buffy the Vampire Slayer*. It was a line said by an ancient demon turned human grappling with mortality after Buffy's mom dies: "I knew her and then she's—there's just a body. And I don't understand why she just can't get back in it and not be dead anymore."

Despite the thigh-bone thoughts, I was too afraid to look when my mom's ashes arrived. All that remained of her body sat unopened in a heavy black box on my parents'—*my dad's*—mantel. Meanwhile, a part of me felt that my mom was impishly hiding under the bed or in a closet somewhere. Then I reasoned with myself: She was never one for pranks.

In the evenings, Christopher would come home to an unspooling of morbid facts. "I read today about a mortician who saw her first dead body when she was five," I told him flatly one night. "A child fell over the railing at a mall." Another night, said with zero affect: "Did you know that people can intentionally move their eyeballs after having their head chopped off?" This continued even in the weeks and months after I got back to work, as I was required to write about death's near opposite. Soon I would be filing mindless, disengaged listicles with headlines like "The 10 Strangest Facts About Penises." My grief turned out to be great for *Salon*'s traffic. Then I would write a post titled "10 More Strange Facts About Penises."

Eventually, my gruesome obsession turned to my own body. Over dinner, without segue or explanation, I asked Christopher, "What if my face burned off in a fire?" Later, while I changed for bed, he told me, "I love your boobs so much." Without missing a beat, I replied, "What if I lost them? What if I had to chop them off?" One day, he asked rhetorically, "Baby, when did you become Wednesday Addams?"

In those first weeks after my mom's death, I lay on our couch, thinking, *When will this death fever go away? Maybe if I lie here for a few more days I'll get better.* As though I could sleep off grief like the flu. Of course, I wanted to: there was our wedding, which we had fast-tracked just so that my mom could make it, in less than two months. Now our marriage was about to be forged in the fire of her death.

MY DAD STARTED HAVING an affair with an unhappily married woman who lived down the street. At the same time, he was getting back in touch with a former girlfriend from his twenties and talking about feeling alive again. He would come over to our little shingled cottage and it felt like our lusty teenage son—driven not by hormones but by a desperate flight from death—was home visiting from college.

During one of those visits, my dad casually revealed that he'd had an "infidelity" at the beginning of his marriage to my mom. "You cheated on Mom?" I screeched. He leaned back like I'd thrown a punch: "I wouldn't say it was cheating. We hadn't talked about monogamy. Your mom didn't *like* it, but she allowed it. Things changed, though, once we had you." I was crying, then hyperventilating, as Christopher rubbed my back and seemed to hold his own breath. Earlier in my career, I had written extensively about polyamorous, open, and monogamish relationships, and even talked at length with my parents about these pieces. At the time, I had wondered: Can I be monogamous long-term? Do I want to be? They didn't bother to mention that their monogamy had ever come with an asterisk.

Just as we were about to walk down the aisle, my one-dimensional vision of my parents' relationship went 3D. My dad had held the marriage up to the light at a slant, and I suddenly saw its subtle, unpolished textures. Still beautiful, but multifaceted. And then there was this confronting fact: even after decades of a happy marriage, one of us could end up alone and in need of desperate reinvention. Marriage, I'd previously thought, would mean security and companionship. It would be like finally arriving home.

I knew the divorce rate, but hey, it had worked out for my parents. I also understood that marriage was, for good reason, what happened off-screen after the fairy tale ended and the credits rolled. In the late 2000s, the artist Dina Goldstein took a series of photographs depicting Disney princesses after the wedding. In one image, which I'd used as my desktop wallpaper, Snow White props a baby on either hip as a toddler tugs at her gown and the Prince drinks a beer, feet up, while zoning out to TV. Marriage, domesticity, and motherhood especially could trap women, shrink their ambitions, limit their options. I had vaguely tried to guard against that threat with my choice of fiancé: the kind of man who had elected to take a women's studies course in college.

Of course, I understood myself to be embarking on a ritual entrenched in sexist convention, one specifically used historically to control women's sexuality. But: lalalalala. Somehow, I'd even picked out a virginal white dress. Compromises and concessions, all to be a human participant, a member of the tribe. It wasn't so different from my experience of our sexual culture. Nothing belonged to women; everything was laced with poison. I had clung, however, to some feminist convictions in an attempt to fend off patriarchal trespass: I was keeping my hippie, hyphenated last name, and my dad wasn't going to walk me down the aisle to "give me away."

You couldn't mitigate marriage's existential threats, though. Your face might burn off in a fire, as I had morbidly pointed out to Christopher before asking, "Would you still love me?" Your boobs might be cut off. ("Would you still love me?") You might spend three years devotedly taking care of your spouse as cancer advances, retreats, and then overcomes. Yes, everyone dies alone, and sometimes, you're left alone (and that might feel like its own kind of death). You could make each other promises, but there were no guarantees. There was no way to guard against that fact, not with a diamond ring or an overpriced ritual.

There was just wanting to do it anyway.

A FEW WEEKS AFTER my mom's death, Christopher and I were circling each other in the kitchen, making coffee and pouring cereal, when our bodies brushed together. We stopped to kiss. He pulled back, scanned my face, and pushed me up against the refrigerator. The soft impact of my shoulder blades against the textured black plastic knocked down all the walls I'd built around my body. He was late to work, but it didn't matter. Lucky us just to not be dead. Clothes were torn off, innovative surfaces employed—it was like a scene from the tawdry D.C.-based political soap opera we were bingeing at the time.

I straddled him on the kitchen floor and orgasm vaguely approached, like an oncoming sneeze. Then my mom's dead face popped into my head. Her mouth hanging open, body tense like stone. I pushed the image away. *The Falling Man.* Pushed it away. *The bodies on the sidewalk.* Pushed it. *Rotting fruit.* Pushed. I clung to Christopher's elbows like he was pulling me over the side of a cliff and fell onto his chest, frenzied. Then: the Tilt-A-Whirl. It has the makings of a *Cosmo* cover line, but there is no other way to put it: best orgasm of my life. I was flooded with tears and laughter. "What are the feelings? Tell me the feelings," he said gently. What I thought but didn't say was: *I'm alive.* "It's life flipping death the bird," a Lorrie Moore character said of dance in *Birds of America*.

The next time we had sex: multiple orgasms. These weren't the orgasms of the before. Those had been waves of pleasure washing over me, and this was more like getting swept out to sea. It was what I always knew sex could be but had never experienced. All the horrors—illness, death, decay—had brought me into my body better than any sex tip ever had. It gave me something to fight against, too. Sex was the perfect antidote to mortal dread: the pursuit of pleasure for pleasure's sake; the potential, even, to generate life. Hence the cliché of the funeral hookup. It seems so ghastly, so inappropriate, which doesn't exactly dampen its appeal.

No mainstream women's magazine editor wanted these hot sex tips: terminal illness, death, grief, existential terror. That was not a traffic bonanza of a listicle. But it was the truth: good sex often had less to do with aesthetics or special moves than it did with feeling. Those things that were harder to summon or sell.

WHEN WE WALKED DOWN the aisle in our slapped-together ceremony at a local restaurant, it was to the *Mission Impossible* theme song. Nothing to set the mood for a wedding quite like reminding your guests of the *impossibility* of marriage and discouraging divorce statistics. But they dabbed at their eyes all the same when we swapped vows, what with me choking up while mentioning my mom's conspicuous absence and Christopher committing to a shared vision of a "cozy life."

After we exchanged our "I dos," Meredith, my best friend

from middle school and our officiant, read the script we'd prepared. Instead of introducing us as Mr. and Mrs., she declared,
"Now I'd like to introduce to you: Tracy and Christopher . . .
the same people they were at the beginning of this ceremony."

It wasn't long before I was back to using our sex life as fodder
for my writing. I requested a "review copy" of an Autoblow 2, a
so-called blow job robot, and had Christopher give it a try.
The device was a rubbery tube with a pair of fake lips on one
end. It plugged into the wall and moved a sequence of beaded
rings up and down the shaft for a pleasurable hands-free experience. "Sounds brilliant, sounds awesome, sounds like THE
FUTURE—until the future is on your genitals, sounding like
it might spontaneously combust," I wrote, before describing the
horrifying vacuum-like noises it made once placed upon his
most delicate body part. I watched, taking literal notes, and told
him, "It looks like you cut off part of a dead chick's face and are
boning it." At this, he lost his erection. All of which I detailed
unflinchingly in my piece.

In response, a writer at the feminist site Jezebel wrote a blog
jokingly declaring Christopher a "BRAVE HERO MAN" for
his adventurism. A brave hero man is how many people seriously seemed to regard him for having married me. It was one
of the most common sentiments expressed in reader emails and
Salon comments whenever I wrote about him. A family member
had even offered up a version of this during a toast at our wedding. The meaning was often clear: not only was I a feminist
who wrote about sex on the internet, but I had developed a supposed expertise around men's fantasy worlds. As one reader

wrote me at the time, "Your poor husband must consider himself enormously lucky and hugely intimidated at the same time."

Except that my prior wisdom vis-à-vis men was seeming increasingly questionable the more I actually talked to them.

I started emailing with "Dave," a man with a micropenis, who reached out in response to one of my articles. "Think the size and shape of a sewing thimble soft, wine cork erect," he said in his first message, adding that his scrotum was "sized to match." With my permission, Dave sent along a photo of himself naked, save for an unbuttoned baseball jersey and an anxious expression, which documented the truth of the sewing thimble comparison. He agreed to an email interview and told me about high school locker room ribbing, a humiliating "first time," and the ex-wife who divorced him after declaring his penis too small to satisfy her.

Now, though, he was happily remarried with kids and talked about sex with no-nonsense wisdom. "I'll never give a woman toe-curling screaming orgasms through penetrative intercourse alone," he said. "No tragedy there." He continued, "I view vaginal penetrative intercourse as an appetizer or a dessert and never as a main course. I have ten fingers and a tongue, a fit body and a creative mind, and I use them all." Dave added with a virtual shrug, "I experiment, respond to her pleasure signals." I had spent years interviewing sex experts with all manner of tips and tricks, but Dave had cut to the heart of the thing: creativity, adaptability, experimentation, consideration. More simply: a departure from the penis-pounds-vagina mandate of cisgender, heteronormative sex.

Before Dave, I'd interviewed Jonah Falcon, the man purported to have the world's largest penis at 13.5 inches long. Contrary to the rock-star lifestyle such a man occupies in the public imagination, he detailed to me a "depressing" existence working a grinding nine-to-five data entry job, playing video games in his spare time, and having little to no interest in romance. "Sex just isn't a priority anymore," he said. It was only when I asked him questions about his taste in music and movies—subjects that had nothing to do with his headline-making penis—that his disengaged monotone suddenly brightened. At that point, Falcon had been ensnared for nearly fifteen years by international media attention. The enduring frenzy had everything to do with us and our collective obsession with dick size, and little to do with Falcon and the reality of his experience with a large penis.

Biggest penis, tiny penis. At one point, I'd even written about a man who lost his penis in a childhood accident. I was like the Goldilocks of phallocentric sex writing. My survey of the penile landscape wasn't intentional, but it seems in retrospect like a ham-fisted climb toward a more nuanced understanding of dick-havers. You might notice: I wasn't interested in vulvas.

Years earlier, I had started a sex advice column at *Salon* that attempted to use legitimate experts and scientific research, rather than any purported personal wisdom, to answer people's sex questions. Tongue firmly in cheek, I titled the column "Am I Normal?" because it was the sentiment at the heart of most every reader question that I received. Everyone worried that they were abnormal, so here I was to tell them that sexual variety and diversity were what was *actually* "normal."

I was also telling it to myself, over and over again. Guys wrote in about fantasies involving everything from wearing women's lingerie to happy ending massages. There was a sixty-something man worried over his diminished orgasm, and a young guy anxious that there was something wrong with him because he didn't want to ejaculate on his partner's face like he'd seen in porn. No singular narrative arose from the scores of letters, except for one of tantalizing, sparkling individuality, like pebbles in a riverbed. What a corny, inexcusably romantic thing to say, but it's how I felt. My wishful mastery and distant gawking were giving way to sexual empathy—for men, of course.

Back when I was starting as a full-time sex writer at *Salon*, I had reported on a "kinky foxhunt" at a nudist retreat in the mountains of Santa Cruz. I'd tagged along as a dozen or so people dressed like hunters, horses, and hounds pursued a latex-clad "fox" deep into the woods. It was Old English countryside with a twist of BDSM. The hunt would culminate in a play party back at the retreat. As I scaled a hillside, one of the horses—clad in black spandex and a full horse mask, with "hooves" tied behind his back—neighed realistically behind me. It was, I realized in that moment, an adult version of hide-and-seek.

The day after the foxhunt, I went out to a dim sum brunch with Susie Bright—*the legendary Susie Bright*—who happened to be in town. We'd first met when I interviewed her for *Salon*, and then we'd kept in touch. She picked me up in her car, which

I falsely remember as a convertible because she had the windows down, and because that was just her embodied, carefree vibe. She whisked me away to a restaurant in Daly City as short wisps of hair blew across her face and she shouted comfortably into the wind. At the restaurant, a series of sizzling dishes were placed upon the white tablecloth while I regaled her, wide-eyed, with the story of the kinky foxhunt. *Neighing men in spandex! A dude in a latex fox costume! Could she believe it? How cray-zee.*

She smiled, utterly unscandalized, and said with such tenderness that it sent me flying back in my seat, "I'm so glad those sweethearts have each other to play with."

"JUST IMAGINE YOU'RE A giantess stomping on the buildings and cars below." That's what the photographer told me as I stepped in front of a green screen with a self-conscious grimace. I placed my hands on my hips, raised one foot a few inches off the ground, and attempted a scowl while resisting a smile. In a few days, he would send over the resulting image of me edited onto a New York City skyline. There I'd be, taking down a skyscraper with one of my peep-toe Hasbeens clogs while gazing warmly at the tiny imperiled humans below.

This green screen presented the opportunity to have oneself rendered in the proportion of King Kong or Thumbelina, and it was one of the chief draws of SizeCon, a gathering for well over a hundred people with kinks involving shrinking, growth, and disparities in scale. *Macrophilia* is the catchall term. There were sexual fantasies about skyscraper-size women who might crush you with their well-manicured feet, as well as teeny-tiny model-train humans who could be inserted into orifices. Some liked the idea of being shrunk to the size of a crumb, while others dreamt about specific body parts (breasts, butts, penises) grotesquely and uncontrollably inflating under the influence of a magic spell.

I had left *Salon* many months earlier for a gig at Vocativ, a well-funded media start-up equipped with the resources to send me on reporting trips. This meant I was able to finally get out from behind my desk and into the real world—of fantasy. Which is how I found myself in a sprawling Manhattan event space decorated with imagery iterating on the iconic poster for the 1958 sci-fi film *Attack of the 50 Foot Woman*.

An oversize crayon leaned against one wall. The event's bartender handed out miniature drink menus that had to be flipped through with delicately pinched fingertips. VR headsets allowed attendees the firsthand visual experience of being tossed like an insignificant piece of popcorn into a woman's wet mouth, or slipped into her sweaty, heaving, lingerie-clad bosom. Vendors had set up booths to display their artistic renderings of breasts inflated like beach balls or half-dressed giantesses daintily picking up men who windmilled their arms in terror.

I chatted with a thirty-two-year-old man wearing a bright pink headband, flowing sundress, and high heels, who went by Miss Kaneda online. In the real world, he wore a suit every day to sell furniture in Massachusetts, where he lived in a home with his wife, two young sons, and a few immediate family members. He hid his collection of women's clothes and the hours spent on giantess message boards from all but his wife, who knew about his fantasies but didn't share in them.

SizeCon was the first time Miss Kaneda had gone out in public in a dress. It was also the first time he had spoken freely in person about his fantasy of being a giantess who stomped on people running around at her feet like pathetic little bugs. Talking about the euphoric relief of the experience brought tears to his eyes.

Then I met Jim, a stocky twenty-seven-year-old of average height with fantasies about being shrunken to four inches tall. Did his family know? "I plan to take it to the grave," he quickly answered, before mentioning the recurrent nightmares in which his dad found out. Shifting from foot to foot, Jim traced the origins of his kink back to a memory of himself at five years old seeing a group of girls gathered around a ladybug on a playground. "I walked up to look at it and they were like, 'No, you're gonna hurt it, you're gonna kill it!'" he said. "They made me feel like a monster, and I hated that." Jim wiped his forehead with a shaky hand. "I remember feeling, like, I wish *I* was the ladybug," he said.

Later, in a series of email back-and-forths, he would open up about a particular fantasy of living under a couple's floorboards and coming up once in a while, like a mouse, to "collect useful objects, crumbs of food." Eventually, the couple would discover and catch him, storing him away in a shoe box or in a hamster cage, after which they would neglect him. "It's that lack of concern for me as a human being, and more as something like a pet that is a turn on," he told me. "I like the idea of being forced to watch them make love, maybe at the side of their bed in a jar."

He described the possibility of being spanked with "the tip of a finger" or a nail file.

So many of the people I spoke with at SizeCon described similar scenarios infused with shades of BDSM. Themes of power differentials and loss of control were standard. So were early childhood memories like Jim's about the ladybug. One man recalled being aroused as a kid during an episode of *Tom and Jerry* where a mouse desperately dodges a troupe of high heels; another guy remembered the slack-jawed effect of seeing Ursula sinisterly swell in size in *The Little Mermaid*.

Jim's words, "I wish *I* was the ladybug," stuck with me. They sent ripples across the surface of my heart every time they came to mind. His vulnerability and tenderness were the opposite of what I had originally set out to find in probing the world of straight men's fantasies. That had been my first mistake: assuming the existence of a uniform, homogenous straight "male desire." Already, I'd subjected Christopher to cross-examination about his porn-watching habits, and his desires didn't fit any of what I "knew" about men. While I had been trolling tube sites filled with face fucking and gang bangs, he had been looking at solo nudie pics, *still photographs*. Often, they were photos women had posted of themselves to the internet, more nude selfie than *Playboy* centerfold.

Men like Falcon, with his record-breaking penis and nonexistent sex life, and Dave, with his micropenis and well-adjusted approach to pleasure, complicated my deeply baked assumptions. So much of the cultural wisdom around love and sex failed to pan out.

• • •

I INHERITED SOME MONEY after my mom's death, exactly enough
for a down payment on a house. Magic money. Tragic money.
How else, even with the luck of a decent paying job, could people afford to buy houses in the Bay Area? There aren't many
other ways; soon, friend after friend would start moving away,
back to more affordable hometowns, and the market would sky-
rocket such that we wouldn't have been able to buy even with
the magic-tragic money. After a year of searching, we found a
house that we could, disbelievingly, call our own. We hadn't
even offered the highest bid; the eighty-year-old widowed seller
had simply liked our offer letter, which described it as "a perfect
place for us to start our family," just like she had done half a
century before.

As soon as we closed on the house, there was a collective
throat clearing in our creek-side cottage, which was filled with
reclaimed wood that perpetrated gnarly splinters and had a perilous staircase leading to a single loft bedroom without a door.
This apartment was a dream, but no place for a baby. ("Maybe a
baby could go in the closet where you store your music gear," I
had feebly ventured at one point. "How about the kitchen pan-
try?") We knew we wanted to have a kid at some point, and now
the house had given us enough nerve to leap off the cliff into
potential parenthood.

Our first weekend in the new house, boxes still sealed tight
with packing tape, I realized that my period was late. Then I
watched as two pink lines materialized on a pregnancy test. I

stared at those two lines until they blurred from tears of joy, then I sentimentally placed the test in one of the drawers of our new bathroom.

Several weeks later, at our first prenatal doctor's visit, I lay on an exam table with a vaginal ultrasound probe between my legs as Christopher softly petted my hair. The nurse holding the probe was quiet, then spoke. "I'm not finding a heartbeat," she said. I gazed at the unmoving uterine ghost on the ultrasound screen. This was what they call a "missed miscarriage." The fetus had stalled in development, failed to thrive. It was supposed to be the size of a kumquat but was more like a shriveled pea. It had been a something, and now it was a nothing.

Life isn't experienced in symbols, except when it is: I was lying on my back, legs spread, with a person between my legs. Inside me: a phallic probe—and it was covered by a condom, no less. I'd often used sex to feel in control and powerful, which required a denial of the fullness of my own desires. Now here I was, vulnerable and exposed in the unfulfilled wanting I had directed at that ultrasound screen. It was irrational, possibly a result of the hormones roiling in my questionably pregnant body, but it felt like getting screwed by my own desire. I had wanted too much: not just a marriage, a house, a baby, but also the freedom and exploration of my twenties. There rose up the voices that had haunted my earlier years, the admonishments and warnings from all corners, the refrains of feminist backlash insisting that trying to "have it all" would make a fool of me. I was Icarus flying too close to the sun.

Just as quickly as the punishing thoughts came, they left.

The doctor started explaining that I could wait for the "products of conception" to pass naturally, but that I might risk an infection. It was time to be a mother to myself, the kind my mother had been to me. I scheduled a dilation and curettage procedure, or D&C. "There is a dead fetus in my uterus," I told Christopher. "I want it out, now."

In the meantime, I had all of the dreaded first-trimester symptoms: My breasts ached like someone had poured concrete into them. I woke in the morning, and unless I was a quick-enough draw with the Saltines on my nightstand, I would dry heave over the side of the bed. It was the work of pregnancy with none of the promised reward.

Afterward, when well-meaning friends would tell me, "I'm so sorry for your loss," it felt like they were suggesting I should feel other than I did. At least, that is what I told Christopher at the time. The brief stirring of potential life inside hadn't felt like a baby to me, I explained. This was true and yet maybe those messages of "loss" felt like an affront precisely because they spoke to a truth. I had lost my mom and then, in short order, lost her again. Although I hadn't told anyone, it had felt like the pregnancy, through the voodoo of DNA, was summoning her back from the dead.

Instead of trying again, I went back on birth control, and we decided to take an ambitious international trip. In Vietnam and Cambodia, we ate ecstatically while hunched over plastic side-walk tables, stood silently with the remnants of war atrocities, rode motorbikes through lush green countryside, explored ancient temples overtaken by jungle, and rode tuk-tuks down long dusty roads with potholes that launched our luggage into the air. Once home, we revisited the baby talk and decided instead on a dog: a wiry, floppy-eared little ten-week-old rescue pup we named Hank. We were the portrait of over-involved dog parents: reading all the popular "how to raise a puppy" books, keeping potty-training logs, and standing side by side at his obedience classes.

After more months passed, there was baby talk once again, but instead we went to couples' therapy to iron out some wrinkles in the relationship. I got my own individual therapist who thought that, oh, maybe I hadn't fully dealt with my mom's death. We grew up a little more, together.

Then came the caterpillars. I brought two in from our yard, placed a bouquet of dill on my computer desk, and watched these plump green bugs with yellow-dotted black stripes scrunch their way along bending branches. They chomped at starbursts of yellow flowers and dropped poop the size of poppy seeds onto my workspace. I watched as the caterpillars attached themselves to the plant, shrugged off their exteriors like chain mail, and exposed the squishy insides, which swelled and hardened into opaque chrysalides resembling dried leaves. Inside the chrysalis, they would go through a process of self-digestion resulting in what one blog bracingly called "caterpillar soup." From this soup, butterflies would emerge.

As I waited, I stumbled on a quote by the writer Richard Bach: "What the caterpillar calls the end of the world, the master calls a butterfly." After several days, though, I found myself worrying that they might not hatch, that it *was* the end of the world. I cried at the thought. Who could say how things would turn out? Then I laughed through my tears and ventured out loud what I already knew: "This isn't about the caterpillars."

A few days later, I woke to find the chrysalides cracking open. Out crawled a pair of butterflies with wet, folded wings— snowflakes cut from tissue paper. They had an iridescent coloring of yellow, blue, and orange, so finely rendered it seemed painted on with pollen. I gently guided the butterflies to an open window, where they sat on an exterior ledge, drying their wings in the morning sun, before flying away.

Butterflies. *God.* I wouldn't ever intentionally choose such a cliché representation of metamorphosis, but there it was. I needed to believe again in the miracle of nature and biology, to come to terms with my lack of control, to surrender to vulnerability, before I could try again for a baby. I had already recognized the tenderness of my interview subjects—"those sweethearts," as Susie put it—and was starting to get in touch with my own. "You're just a *sweet sweetie,*" Christopher had said early in our dating. Despite my best efforts, he had glimpsed the squishy insides.

A year and a half after the miscarriage, we decided to try again. The two pink lines appeared. Once again, I lay on the exam table and spread my legs. There was a heartbeat.

CHAPTER 9

Porn Valley

The San Fernando Valley is a dry stretch of land bisected by highways and surrounded by mountains. These are not the stretches of pristine beaches and rolling aquamarine waves that tourists imagine when visiting Los Angeles. But leaving the Burbank airport in my white four-door Kia rental car, I happily rocketed away from that iconic coastline, windows down for the still-warm late-December air. The valley, perhaps best known as the birthplace of vocal fry and upspeak, is also home to a great number of porn sets, hence its other nickname: Porn Valley.

Despite reporting on sex for a decade, I had never before gotten the chance to fly the couple hundred miles south for a real live, in-person story on the mainstream adult industry. This was the source of the box-cover features that were among my early introductions to porn as a sexually intrepid teenager. Now I was a thirty-two-year-old woman in her first trimester of pregnancy, with the under-eye circles and queasy pallor to show for it. In my purse was a ziplock baggie full of dusty snacks: trail mix, wheat thins, dried apricots. If I went too long without nibbling, I would without warning start retching into the air. At six weeks pregnant, "morning sickness" seemed a misnomer for all-the-time sickness.

This was unexpected context for my first visit to Porn Valley, but it was a period defined by surprise. Months earlier, Donald Trump had been heard on tape bragging about nonconsensually grabbing women "by the pussy." Now he was about to be sworn into office. We had nearly elected our first woman president. Instead, an admitted sexual predator was set to become the commander in chief.

Exiting the highway in Chatsworth, I turned down a bleak thoroughfare where one large cement rectangle bled into the next. Then it was on to side streets filled with nondescript business parks with building numbers that featured more prominently than business names, a colorless landscape dotted by for-lease signs and metal roll-down doors. The few visible windows were darkened like an old man's transition lenses, and the streets and parking lots were filled with cars, but there wasn't a soul in sight.

I imagined faceless employees contained within cubicle farms. This was watercooler talk and wilted desk salads, not splayed pussy lips and fountains of ejaculate. It was all so contrary to the vivid, fluid-filled world of porn that I felt like I couldn't be at my destination yet. This was corporate, not corporeal. My phone kept telling me to turn on such-and-such street that I had just blown straight past. *Really, here?* Here. What had I expected, an

X-rated amusement park filled with glory holes, Sybian rides, and vendors selling cream pies?

I knew better, having visited porn shoots in San Francisco. There had been the time I saw a naked woman get chained to a sparse metal bed in a faux dungeon and then brought to ecstatic screams by a motorized contraption featuring a series of hot-pink tongues on a conveyor belt—a cunnilingus chainsaw, a tool for temporarily splitting open the body and mind. Everything on-camera in that dungeon shoot seemed designed to evoke the horror of being imprisoned by a psychopath: metal chains dripped from patinaed brick walls, and the black bed frame was extensively chipped at either end, as though worn through struggle.

Off-camera, though, outside the frame of fantasy, there was the solicitous assistant equipped with gloved hands and a squirt bottle of lube. There was a table laid out with wet wipes, hand sanitizer, moisturizer, hair ties, and an assortment of trail mix and granola bars. There was another table that practically glittered with no fewer than three dozen jewel-toned sex toys; an assortment from which the performer could pick, so as to maximize her comfort and pleasure. There were the sober contracts detailing the parameters of her consent. I had seen that porn was watercooler talk and wilted desk salads, but there lingered a teenage fantasy. It was as though I expected the landscape itself to manifest the glossy glamour of those early box covers.

Porn Valley was the adult industry's mainstream hub, or so it had been said for decades. More recently, the internet had unlocked countless forms of virtual, independent sex work: webcams, Skype sessions, for-pay Snapchat access, custom fetish clips, financial domination via payment apps. People could create their own adult content and profit from it without ever setting foot onto a mainstream porn set, without ever setting foot in Los Angeles. Porn was so often talked about as a monolith, as though all X-rated content was produced by the same sweaty, gold-chain-wearing stereotypical producer of yore. Now many performers were their own producers. Still, this little stretch of desert was the closest thing that this increasingly fractured and decentralized industry had to a home base.

I walked into one of those cement blocks and found a fluorescent-lit office with a collection of props scattered around the room: vintage desk, hospital gurney, textbooks, plastic houseplant. Beyond another door, the low-ceilinged room suddenly opened up into an airy warehouse with today's set at its center: a black platform placed in a dark body of water. A fog machine sent drifts of smoke across the surface of this shadowy pool, creating the illusion of an eerie abyss. Back in the prop-filled office—which was probably more of a set of an office, I realized—I sat on a couch chatting with Kayden Kross, the film's director and a mostly former performer who had started her own independent porn studio.

Things had changed for women in the adult industry, Kross told me. Back when she entered the industry in the mid-2000s as a twenty-one-year-old, women performers could land a lucrative contract with a studio like Vivid, which is exactly what she did. "You used to have these huge superstars, and now superstars don't exist," she said. This was part of the wreckage left by tube sites: people stopped paying for porn, which meant the pool of financial opportunity for adult performers dried up. Women, especially, had to start doing more for less.

"It used to be that anal was very few and far between with the girls who did it," Kross explained. "Then it became this thing where everyone has to do it."

Things had changed for men in the industry, too, Kross explained. In the nineties, studios would hold casting calls with hundreds of guys from all over the world. "It was almost barbaric the way they did it," she said. This mass of men would be ordered to drop their pants and get a hard-on. Maybe ten would make it to the next round of elimination, whereupon they would be challenged to stay hard while receiving a high-pressure blow job in front of their potential employers. Kross once dated a man who got into the industry from a cattle-call in which "three people got hard out of three hundred," she said.

That's a 1 percent success rate. Eventually, though, "directors started handing pills to guys who couldn't really do the job," said Kross, referring to Viagra. Although she didn't mention it, I'd also written before about industry use of Caverject, a drug injected into the base of the penis to stimulate a powerful, long-lasting boner. I'd learned about the drug after it landed a performer in the hospital with a painful, persistent erection (or priapism, in technical terms, which an expert likened to "a heart attack of the penis").

Whether it's getting hard amid a cattle call, popping Viagra, or shooting up a dick to get the job done, it seemed to me that the implications were profound for performers and viewers alike. Many viewers see this kind of 1 percenter, medically assisted sex and believe it to be the correct, aspirational way—as opposed to exceptional and impressively unobtainable. Similarly, the ubiquity in porn of certain sex acts may seem a straightforward reflection of viewer desire, as opposed to the result of unseen economic pressures on performers and a ravaged industry desperate for eyeballs. A frequent refrain I'd heard from performers: You shouldn't take notes from porn any more than from Hollywood blockbusters.

And yet many people do. I did.

MANY TIMES BEFORE, I'VE tried to describe to friends what happened next on this porn set, but their responses always miss the intended mark. "Then *Tommy Gunn* walked into the room," I'll say. And they go: "Huh?" or "Who?" or "Are we talking about a weapon?" I'll explain, "No, no, Tommy Gunn, the porn star. Tommy Gunn! Tommy. Gunn." These friends, even the casual tube-site wandering ones who have no doubt seen him perform, don't recognize his name, because they have not thought quite so much about porn.

I had already met the star of today's shoot: Katrina Jade, a performer with jet-black hair and a spiderweb inked on her temple. But I hadn't been told the names of the two men she would be performing with—then, in the middle of our conversation, Kross warmly exclaimed, "Tommy!" In he walked and I felt the electric neural zap of any mainstream celebrity sighting.

The first time I saw him perform must have been well over a decade ago. He was an inescapable figure in those days of big studio productions and contract stars. Now approaching fifty, having been inducted into an industry Hall of Fame, Tommy Gunn was a legend. A legend wearing a nondescript T-shirt, jeans, and practical black sneakers. A legend who was soon showing me cell phone pics of his beloved truck, a military vehicle meticulously renovated by hand and lovingly named Big Momma. He spoke with a playful, folksy lilt. Like so many actors, he was eager to please, to yuk it up.

Charles Dera, a late-thirties, square-jawed performer, showed up next wearing a muscle tee and gym shorts. Soon I would discover that one of his pecs bore a tattoo of the word *marines* in all-caps, a remnant of a former life. He had also been a Chippendales dancer and *Playgirl* centerfold, having come from the realm of straight women-centric sexual entertainment. He was all macho swagger: gravel voice, well-groomed beard, frequent mentions of jujitsu. I doodled in my notebook as Dera launched into a conversation about protein supplements.

The defining image of a porn shoot isn't sex. It's a handful or two of friendly people lounging on couches, waiting for something to happen. Hair and makeup are done. Wardrobe decisions are made. Snacks are consumed. Cute dog pics are swapped. Lightbulbs blow. Cords are tripped over. *Who unplugged this light?* Coffee runs are made. The camera guy is MIA. Lipstick touch-ups are needed. *Ah, look at the time, let's order dinner.* Call time is eleven a.m., but the shoot doesn't begin until dark. So much of what happens on porn sets happens while hanging out on couches waiting for the sex to start.

I was hanging out on a couch waiting for the sex to start when I heard those words: "Girls these days." We've already been here; you know what happened next: Talk of girls growing up watching porn and "thinking that's what sex is." Gunn comedically humping the air and Dera asking, "Where the *ladies* at anymore?" Girls sending naked selfies. Jokes about anal as "the new first date," "the new handshake." Then an on-set visitor, a man in his late thirties who was friends with Kross, jumped in to ask sympathetically whether sending a pussy pic was equivalent to a smiley emoji for this generation. This cracked up Dera. "That's the 2016 greeting," he joked. Then Gunn exclaimed while grabbing his stomach, as though hit with the full force of *Girls these days*: "Oh gawd!"

I felt the impact, too, but for a different reason. These guys were telling me that porn is make-believe, that it isn't a guide for good sex, that it isn't necessarily the truth about what men want, even when the men in question are the ones performing on-screen. I knew this, *of course I knew this*—and I didn't. I'd heard these messages delivered countless times before, but I still found it hard to believe, impossible to fully incorporate, like the time as a four-year-old during a Disneyland trip when I witnessed a Minnie Mouse costume malfunction right in front of me and went on believing in the magic, regardless.

In the coming years, these messages would gradually start to set in with yet more illuminating on-set moments. I've watched as someone hollered, "Where's the Cetaphil?" and an assistant ran off and came shuffling back with a blue and white bottle with a pump top. *Squirt, squirt, squirt.* The milky, gelatinous face wash was dispensed in oozing blobs on four women's chins and chests, and voilà: a facsimile of a facial. The photographer resumed snapping photos of the performers posed with mouths open as if mid-moan, portraying satisfied astonishment at this impressive load of fake jizz.

There was the time I sat on a prop couch in front of a false-front building as a legendary performer told me that he doesn't watch mainstream adult content, because he likes the authentic feel of amateur porn. Once, I chatted with a longtime performer known for playing the creepy stepdad, who told me, "I just like to cuddle," of his off-screen sex life. The most thrilling on-set moments would continue to be revelations of the details omitted from the idealized, fantastical frame: when costars negotiated boundaries off-camera, a performer paused to ask for lube, the photographer politely asked for a body part to be moved for a better composition, or laughter exploded at the inevitable awkwardness of improvising positions in a gang bang.

All that was still to come. So were my future listens to the recorded audio, when I would begin to understand that Gunn and Dera were not just engaging in familiar forms of "Girls these days" critique. They were also expressing frustration with the ways that as porn performers they are equated with their work. They talked about girls sending pussy pics in general, but also girls sending unsolicited pussy pics *to them*, perhaps assuming these men to be sexually available because of their jobs. I would type out Dera's words, "Then *pay me*, because this is work now," and think of taking home my "favorite porn star," indirectly asking him with my blushing face and blurted fantasies to perform his job, and for free. They were talking about the ways they were personally impacted by the misapprehension of pornographic fantasy as reality and the denial of their work as *a job*.

All I heard in the moment was that there was no winning. Young women could opt in to popular visions of sexiness and find themselves critiqued by sexist traditionalists, men's rights activists, feminist commentators—and one of your unwitting teachers, no less. If you attempt to opt out, well, you might be deemed a prude, a killjoy, a stick in the mud. You're the lone kid standing on the wall at the school dance after everyone else has been pulled out to the floor. There is only impossibly shifting terrain: game but not too game, sexy but not too sexy, desiring but not too desiring.

That is part of what I was afraid of all along: being not just undesirable, but too desiring. Pursuing straight men's fantasies as a subject to master allowed me to acceptably reroute my own yearnings through men. This was exactly what girls and women were supposed to do, right? Make themselves desirable, reduce their wanting to being wanted. Maybe more traditionally through diets and makeup and depilating all but the tops of our heads instead of porn and strip clubs and faked orgasms, but close enough.

Of course, in the process of investigating "male desire," I'd started exploring my own. *Whoopsies. Accident. Not my fault. Hands up.* I have always been skilled at indirectly feeding my own hunger, constructing safehouses for the exploration of my own need. This was a doubly useful form of erotic subterfuge: while being overpowered by men's need—whether through a bracing scroll of top-viewed tube site videos or with a hand gripping my throat—it's impossible for my own wanting to be too much. I have the deeply baked belief that my sexual drive is excessive—which, because I am a straight woman, is to say that it exists at all.

I could have just said all that aloud. I might have told Gunn, "Actually, I came of age watching you perform." Instead, I laughed along, trying once again to be one of the guys.

The talk continued onto a reminiscence of the porn of yore: dirty mags, VHS tapes, the slow-loading nudie pics of the early internet. I mentioned the scrambled channel and there was a collective enthusiastic shouting of, "Yeah!" Meanwhile, the question swirling in my belly wasn't just whether I had been the dupe, but whether my theoretical daughter might become one, too. What would it mean for her to walk that impossibly shifting terrain, that perilous tightrope? I had inherited the caveated freedom of my mother's generation. Now what might I pass along to a baby girl, or boy?

AT THE HARD ROCK HOTEL in Las Vegas, a line of men snaked clear across the smoke-filled casino floor and continued through the building's front doors, then curved down the sidewalk out front. Button-down shirts, gelled hair, hard-soled shoes. These men looked like they were going on a date or trying to get one. Walking by, I caught a whiff of cologne: cedar and vanilla. All these men, young and old, collegiate and graying, were here for the AVN Adult Entertainment Expo (AEE), a yearly event that gathered porn performers into a harshly lit conference hall for autographs and photo ops with hundreds of fans. The longtime event was an opportunity for adult production companies to advertise themselves in booths with screen-printed backdrops featuring blown-up logos and URLs, but its true raison d'être was simple and clear: fandom.

It drew journalists like me from all over the world, many of whom were hungrily searching for a sexy story angle. Less sexily, I was planning to write about the porn industry bracing for the inauguration of Donald Trump, who had signed an anti-porn pledge circulated by Republicans. Despite, or maybe because of, his own links to the industry—performer Jessica Drake had recently accused Trump of sexual misconduct—there loomed the threat that his presidency could mean the revival of obscenity prosecution. Of course, I was also drawn to the event by my personal fascinations, which included these waiting men.

Not even a line surpassing that of the DMV would turn them away, not when there was the prospect of a signature scrawled on the back of their T-shirt, taking a selfie with an arm draped tantalizingly around a shoulder, a friendly hug that brushed a perfumed strand of hair against a cheek. The guys shifted foot to foot, not speaking with each other, while waiting to obtain their individual plastic entry badges strung on lanyards branded with an adult company's logo. Watching porn was so often solitary and yet public: clicking through tube-site videos, there was always the unavoidable presence of ratings, viewership numbers, and user comments. Alone together, same as with here.

Some of the men had put in less visible effort: clunky sneakers, baggy T-shirts, and multi-zippered backpacks carrying memorabilia that they wanted autographed. But what stood out were all the freshly shaved faces and crisp collars. What I saw, stepping into the casino, were men hoping to impress women.

I had to laugh, not at them but at myself. Earlier, my stomach had tumbled—not, for a change, from morning sickness—as I clomped in my Vegas-inappropriate clogs down the sidewalk from my neighboring hotel. I'd anxiously anticipated masses of men drunk on sexual power, something akin to the *Girls Gone Wild* commercials forever imprinted on my brain. A frat party in which all women were potential property to be aggressively claimed or dismissed. *What if they grope me? What if they ignore me?* (A study of AEE attendees would find these "porn superfans" are no more sexist or misogynistic than the general population, and on some measures hold more progressive beliefs around gender.[1]) Now here they stood so fully on display—vulnerable, even—in their wanting.

Still, I envied their playground, this monument to their desire. *Where was my conference? Where was my expo filled with scantily clad men catering to straight women's sexual wants?* I could sketch the whole thing out, however improbably, in my head. Booths featuring famous men doing physical labor—say, Cole

Sprouse digging a ditch. The main attraction: Lining up to pose for a biceps-squeezing pic with Dwayne "the Rock" Johnson or reenact lines from *The Notebook* with Ryan Gosling ("It *still* isn't over," he would repeat, again and again, until he lost his voice and it was truly over). But this daydream ignored the teenager who worshipped Jenna Jameson's blow job skills, the twenty-something who had bookmarked dozens of YouJizz clips. This was, imperfectly and troublingly, my expo, too.

Soon, I was browsing aisles of newfangled penis pumps and stacks of "male enhancement" pills whose packaging screamed things like "ROCK HARD" and "NO HEADACHE." I considered the full range of products telling guys that their penises weren't big or hard or long-lasting enough. This was hardly a Shangri-La of progressive, affirming sexual messaging. Men might be recognized as sexual subjects, but they are also commodified as such.

On the main expo floor, guys lined up once again to get autographs from their favorite mainstream performers. I tried to hide my spectatorship, digging in my bag for a ginger chew, then taking on the furrowed, lip-biting look of someone searching for a friend lost in the crowd. At the front of the line, when pictures were taken, these men might smile shyly or give the camera an enthusiastic thumbs-up, but the photo often seemed less the aim than a point of fleeting connection: a one-armed side hug or whispered exchange.

Not all of these men wanted to just chat or laugh, of course. A VR booth allowed a man to strap on a clunky black headset, tilt his head crotch-ward, and behold the virtual mirage of a naked woman kneeling right before him and taking his (suddenly longer, fatter, harder) dick in her mouth. There were displays of Fleshlights, flashlight-like tubes with silicone labia molded directly from popular performers' vulvas. There was all manner of limbless sex doll torsos slapped upon tabletops for curious passerby to poke and prod, evaluate for verisimilitude. These products promised the illusion of partnered sex, or the masturbatory approximation of it.

What a thing, being pregnant and walking by a truncated torso, a woman blatantly reduced to her essential parts: breasts, vagina, anus. I felt similarly reduced—only to a reproductive rather than sexual aim. This already beloved parasite had taken over, my every waking moment filled with fatigue, nausea, and brain fog. For two months now, every little thing that I ate or drank had been filtered through considerations of the fetus's needs, its safety. Fearing listeriosis, the bacterial infection dreaded by all pregnant people, I spurned blue-veined cheeses, aioli, salad bars, precut fruit, sushi, and deli meats. Alcohol was avoided, coffee minimized. "Biology is fundamentally sexist," I had told Christopher bitterly at the end of a workday, splayed on our couch, my suddenly too-tight jeans unbuttoned and unzipped. At the conference, I held my breath desperately and anxiously while walking through the casino's incessant clouds of cigarette smoke. Then, crouching in a bathroom stall in between interviews or lying in my hotel bed at night, I'd google "cigarette smoke pregnancy," "secondhand smoke fetus," "how much secondhand smoke harmful to fetus."

Days later, after returning home from Vegas, I received the

results of an early blood test screening for fetal chromosomal abnormalities. A single piece of information jumped out, even before the text notifying me that mine was a "low risk" pregnancy. It was the heavily bolded Mars symbol at the center of the physical page of test results, which had been scanned and uploaded to an online patient portal. In my home office, my mouth dropped while I stared at the computer screen: A circle connected to an arrow that pointed up and to the right, like a map to uncharted terrain off the edge of the page. "Fetal Sex," it read. "Male."

Christopher and I hugged and high-fived when he got home. But what did "Fetal Sex: Male" mean, anyway? We weren't going to respond by painting the nursery blue or buying a bunch of stuffed power tools. Soon I would buy a "gender is a construct" onesie. I understood that a baby's sex didn't tell you much about the person it would become, just the cultural expectations and political realities it would encounter in the world. This fetus was a future person, details TBD.

It was International Women's Day 2017, the first after Trump took office. I stood in a basement warehouse where dozens of headless naked bodies dangled from the ceiling, strung through a bolt in the back of their neck onto a metal chain, which attached to a laundry conveyor. It lined them up front to back like so many pieces of dry-cleaning, as breasts bumped into shoulder blades and limbs stood rigidly in something like rigor mortis. This was the factory of RealDoll, the famed manufacturer of six-thousand-dollar sex dolls.

All around the world, women were striking from work and taking to the streets to protest gender inequality with signs bearing slogans like IT'S WOMEN'S TURN and KEEP YOUR ROSARIES OFF MY OVARIES. I might have been doing the same, except that I was busy hanging out with a bunch of silicone dolls (well, they were doing the hanging). The symbolism was grimly perfect: a visit to a factory dedicated to the literal objectification of the "female" form, and on this day of all days.

The timing had been accidental, the result of an assignment to write a story on RealDoll's new sex robot. On some level, I'd wanted to come here for just under two decades, having watched founder Matt McMullen and his creations on an episode of *Real Sex* in the late nineties. The dolls, as with so many things, had made me wonder, made me worry, about men and their wants. But soon after greeting RealDoll's office manager, a middle-aged woman with dark curly hair and kind eyes, she illuminated the reality of the customer base.

Yes, she told me, there were men simply looking for a sexual outlet, an enhancement to their masturbatory routine, but many were seeking a fantasy of companionship. This was shades of that Ryan Gosling movie, *Lars and the Real Girl*, in which a socially awkward man falls in love with a sex doll. Some of these customers had lost lifelong partners to terminal illness and in their grief sought out a silicone replacement, she explained. Later, McMullen himself would tell me that many customers lacked the social skills to find a human partner in the first place; that's part of why RealDoll was creating an interactive robot. Now more than ever, my expanding body defied the idealized proportions of the supersize Barbies displayed at the front of the office, but instead of feeling threatened, I was kind of touched.

The RealDoll office manager walked me through the warehouse with such composure, we might have been surveying Xerox machines instead of sex doll body parts. In the workshop above the basement, rows of bald silicone heads sat on sticks. The skin was flat and chalky, but soon to be dotted with freckles. Hyperrealistic eyes would be popped into vacant eye sockets. Tidy, arched eyebrows would be meticulously pulled through foreheads with needle and thread: human face as embroidery piece.

At the back of an industrial work desk: pallets of shimmering, powdered makeup—from dusty purple to electric fuchsia—just like you would find in any drugstore. It was dabbed onto brushes and painted on the dolls before being sealed with silicone, creating permanently glossy lips, smoky eyes, and rouged cheeks. Two identical face molds sat on sticks next to each other: one fully adorned and the other just bare, molded flesh. Here was the evolution of doll to woman, a workshop of femininity. Pinned on the wall was a black-and-white calendar featuring a close-up of Marilyn Monroe giving an open-mouthed smile, America's iconic sex symbol now watching over the creation of countless sex dolls.

Beyond industrial racks filled with fully made-up heads, and tags bearing customer names, the human body was fragmented into its component parts. A young woman—an artist in her off hours, she told me—sat painting irises onto white globes of plastic. For the "hi-realism" eyes, which cost fifty dollars extra, she even placed red string on the corneas to subtly render blood vessels. Glass jars filled with multicolored eyeballs sat on the shelf above her desk.

Pinned to a bulletin board were various styles of pubic hair: light to dark brown, compact rectangle to full beard. Forty-two different nipples hung on the wall alongside labels reading things like "standard," "perky 3," "XL puffy," "mini 2," and "half dome." They went from light to dark, smooth to bumpy, flat to puffy, the size of a penny to beyond currency. One of the nipples was roughly three inches in diameter with a scattering of large bumps on the areola, looking like a beige chocolate chip cookie.

There were so many choices for customers to make: eleven different kinds of vulvae, for example, which were pictured in close-up on the website looking like various types of flayed squid. Hooded with a surgical slit. Parted with a slight ruffle. Peek-a-boo clit. There were sixteen different types of stock body: boobs came small to big, but all leaned skinny; none weighed more than 105 pounds. You could pay close to a grand just to increase the breasts by a cup. It was ninety-nine dollars for custom nipples, and twenty-five for a custom nipple color. That's to say nothing of skin color, hair type, nail polish, freckles, piercings.

It wasn't so different from how I'd regarded myself, shopped my own body at times in my life. As a teenager, I'd wished my breasts bigger and bought padded bras. Shaved my pubes into a triangle, then a landing strip, then off entirely. Depilated my body, took ruler to labia. For a brief phase, I baked my skin in tanning beds. I bought hair products promising an unobtainable frizz-free facade, slathered my pimpled face with this brand then that brand of benzoyl peroxide, and when they didn't work (they never worked), I'd start in on my skin, picking, popping, prodding, making myself bleed, relieved to surface the inner gunk, that sickening, purulent imperfection.

I'd wondered things like: Are my nipples too big, too small, perky enough? When I felt such questions couldn't be answered objectively, I'd pose in the mirror—lips suddenly slackening to a pout, one shoulder twisting back, ass arched up—just like I'd seen in magazines, TV, mainstream movies, and porn. *Passable, good enough, not horrific*, I told myself. Still, I wrote in my middle school diary, "I feel like a monster." On the cover of said diary I made a collage of images cut from magazines: I pasted a toad next to a butterfly with a little "vs." written in between. It was hope for the future, for evolution. I know women who went through much worse, who taped images of Kate Moss next to their bedroom mirrors and drew copious black lines on their bodies like pint-size plastic surgeons.

All of us, though, had done the work of comparing and contrasting, reducing ourselves to a collection of body parts, some better than others. We lusted after perfection, as defined by a capitalistic caricature of what straight men wanted. Here, in this sex doll factory, there were the usual clichés to be found about that wanting, as well as plenty of pleasant surprises. Bumpy dinner-plate nipples! Beard-like pubic hair! Men's desires were different and varied and *how wonderful for them*. I'd spent the majority of my life comparing myself against and modulating my own desires through the ever-shifting figment of "what men want." Now I stood in a warehouse that took a receptive, accommodating feminine ideal and turned it into a literal physical object. This was a factory of the fantasy I'd enacted for so long.

I stared with such intensity at the glass jar of eyeballs, each looking unnervingly in a different direction, that it seemed my own eyes might go askew.

CHAPTER 10

"Moms"

I was four months pregnant with a swollen belly and a desire to get off: Hitachi in hand, deranged gang bang in mind, and a comforter tented over my knees. Then came a voice: *You can't think about this, you're pregnant.* I lifted the vibrator from between my legs, causing it to buzz emptily like an idling car. I flipped through the slides of my recurrent fantasies, the ones that reliably sent me hurtling—breathless, face flushed—into another dimension. Glory hole, casting couch, creepy masseur, dick-sucking frat boys. I kept flipping, finding each scenario untenable in my expectant state.

Then it was back to the original image: five middle-aged white men with tiny dicks, beer bellies, and a sheen of sweat on their brow. They groped and prodded: hungrily, desperately, disbelievingly. They wanted—oh, right—*my body*. The me on the screen of my mind wasn't occupied by a rapidly growing fetus, but here, I remembered once again, *I'm pregnant*. It felt indecent to be gestating a life while picturing such things. This was a run-of-the-mill orgiastic turn-on, the most basic of "naughty" fantasies, but I turned off the vibrator. I put away the Hitachi.

Pregnancy came down on my body like the thought police. *You can't think about that, you're pregnant.* All that sense of permission I'd accumulated while poking around men's fantasy worlds evaporated. Mothers are supposed to be selfless, controlled, and risk-averse. The training in this regard begins even before conception, with the Centers for Disease Control and Prevention infamously decreeing in 2016 that if a woman has the potential to become pregnant—regardless of whether she's trying—she shan't consume a single drop of alcohol. As a baby incubator, the training continues—with cautions to avoid not just foods and drinks that might harm the fetus but also hypothetically risky behaviors, like riding a roller coaster, lounging in a hot tub, or, I suppose, having real fun of any kind.

Christopher and I had been having sex, but it was fairly vanilla, married-person sex. Some missionary, some cowgirl. Nothing too wild, nothing that challenged this emerging identity of Mom. Meanwhile, though, my belly grew and grew—and the prohibition on my fantasies expanded, proportionally, into reality. Eventually, my stomach started making a *smack-smack-smack* sound during sex. This wasn't the matter of some extra weight; it was the matter of a baby. We had just recently seen it—*him*—in great detail at the twenty-week ultrasound: bright white spine, rapidly pulsing heart, and ski-slope nose. Now, approaching the third trimester, he was announcing himself, basketball-like, in between our naked bodies. I was no longer just a woman with an idea of herself as a soon-to-be mom, but its physical embodiment.

Of course, there is the concept of the "mother I'd like to fuck" (MILF), but the very phrasing betrays an underlying belief that most mothers are not fuckable. A more accurate phrase might be: This Mom Is Notable Because She Is Actually Fuckable Unlike Those Other Moms (TMINBSIAF). But here's the thing: Whose boner was I concerned about deflating? An honest answer: mine. To whom did I want to be fuckable? Me. Christopher didn't care. He *really didn't care*. "Your sexuality is so . . . pure," I told him. "So wholesome." The guy had started running his hands over my belly just as he would my hips or breasts, not because he'd developed a pregnancy fetish, but because it was part of my body. The problem was I couldn't get hot for myself, not when I thought about that imaginary camera, which still sometimes found its way into my bedroom.

Instead of banishing the camera, I looked for new reference footage, poking around in the niche of pregnancy porn. On one clip site, where performers sold short fetish-themed videos, "pregnant" was the second most searched term. I pitched a story on said genre and interviewed a pregnant dominatrix who wielded her belly like a whip, a cam performer who threatened to blackmail viewers for child support, and a woman who had once filmed a custom video for a loyal fan while timing aloud her wincing contractions. Then there was Madison Young, a feminist porn director, who performed in several queer films during her pregnancy and explained that she wanted to "honor the natural presence of sexual desire and sexual identity in all stages of our life."

"What does it *mean* to be a sexy pregnant woman?" I asked several of these performers, perhaps a little too pleadingly. One time, the silence that followed was so complete I had to check that the line was still connected. It was like my interviewees didn't understand the question or suspected they had misheard it, because from their perspective what *wasn't* sexy about a pregnant woman? Glowing vitality, amplified curves, proof of fecundity. On the kinkier end, all of the deep anxieties that straight men felt about pregnant women—from uncertainty about paternity to women's power to generate life—could be eroticized. I watched as these ladies stroked their round bellies, stared into the camera, and purred things like, "You didn't get me pregnant; a *real* man did."

It would be nice to say that this instantly made me see myself as a fertility goddess deserving of erotic worship. Instead, biology intervened. The hormones flooding my pregnant body silenced insecurities, introducing a louder and more insistent voice. People like to joke about pregnant women's hunger—the demand of a late-night grocery store trip for ice cream and pickles—but they don't tell you about the other kind of desire: brain-melting horniness. Multiple times a day, I padded barefoot into our bedroom to pull out the Hitachi from its bedside drawer. Increased blood flow meant amped-up sensation; orgasms were instant and epic. I stopped even putting the Hitachi away. It just lay plugged in next to our bed, perpetually at the ready.

"I'm kind of obsessed with my body," I told Christopher one night, early in the third trimester, my stomach bulging with a cabbage-size fetus, my breasts folding over the cups of my elastic XXL maternity bra. "Join the club," he said, but I hadn't been waiting for the validation. I was in my beige, stretched-out underwear in front of the mirror, twisting this way and that, rubbing my curves, marveling at the bodily transformation. I could reproduce that signature magazine cover pose, the one pregnant celebrities from Demi Moore to Jessica Simpson have struck: hand across the breasts, thigh or arm acting as fig leaf. And I did, I would, whenever getting out of the shower. Inevitably, though, my arms would fall out of the pose, and I'd just stare. The successful fulfillment of the pose was nothing next to the feeling of those biological gears turning inside me. The more this reproductive script took over, the farther away that camera seemed. The more my body—swollen, spilling, blazing with hormones—asserted itself, the deeper my consciousness sank down into it.

IN PREPARATION FOR LABOR, I made a playlist of flute-filled music and contemplated buying a Tibetan singing bowl. We met several times with our doula, a woman with a flat, earthy affect, and practiced various positions: bouncing on a yoga ball, crouching on all fours, slow dancing with arms slung around Christopher's shoulders. I decided on a relaxing visual for when things got tough: one of my dad's dogs, a beagle with velvety brown ears and Precious Moments eyes. The doula had me fill out a "birth plan," which indicated that I didn't want any pain relievers and wished to avoid a C-section, before I picked out the essential oil that I wanted diffused in the labor room. It was a bit "woo," but how else did you prepare for "natural" birth?

All of a sudden, I had plenty of time to prepare: a month and a half before my due date, the well-funded media start-up I worked for decided to "pivot to video." All the writers and editors were laid off. I received the news with a hand on my belly. Then, throat choked with terror, I managed to negotiate severance to cover my "maternity leave." Now, though, it would be leave from nothing.

On the final meeting with the doula before my fast-approaching due date, she asked about my fears—aside, obviously, from the pain. I didn't tell her running out of money, never getting another job, losing myself to motherhood. Instead, I said something equally true: "I'm afraid I won't be able to let go and moan freely." She had spoken several times about the power of releasing sound during labor, of moaning through the waves of painful contractions. The doula smiled politely and told me that this was unlikely to be a problem. "The other thing," I continued, "is I don't know if I will be comfortable being naked? I am not a naked person." I was a prude when it came to nonsexualized nudity, the lone weirdo wearing her bathing suit to the all-women's sauna. We'd talked about the possibility of using a warm shower at the hospital for pain relief, and here I was, a few weeks from my due date, wondering if I could get away with wearing a bikini during labor. I was a sex writer, and once master faker of orgasms, afraid of moaning and being naked while giving birth to her child. The irony, or tragedy, wasn't lost on me.

A couple of days later, I was wailing on a hospital bed, buck naked and on all fours. The sound coming out of my mouth was a mixture of the throaty vibration of a moan and an all-out horror movie scream. It was a noise of attempted personal escape— a vehicle speeding out of the echoing caverns of pain and into the sterile hospital air, where other non-hurting humans shuffled around the room, checked charts, and futilely massaged my back. When I'd pushed mom friends for analogies for the pain of labor, most demurred, describing it only as "unimaginable" or "unparalleled." One offered with a shrug, "It's like being run over by a garbage truck." I could understand the lack of appropriate words now: It wasn't a localized pain like a broken leg or a stubbed toe, but a mortal fever pervading all body parts and thoughts. Food poisoning to the nth degree.

I time traveled in my pain, flashing to historical labor images of questionable legitimacy: mostly women who looked like *Game of Thrones* extras, crouched and sweaty, a stick between their teeth. Previously, I had thought there would be something transcendent about accessing the unadulterated physical experience of labor, tapping into a timeless, essential phenomenon. Now, though, I'd pulled open a mental door on roughly rendered women lacking access to the wonders of modern medicine, and all I wanted was to slam it closed. *This isn't the Dark Ages*, was a thought that kept ringing in my head. For the past hour, I hadn't spoken to or made eye contact with Christopher, the doula, or the nurses bustling in and out of the room. But now, fourteen hours after I'd gone into labor, I stopped wailing, looked at Christopher, and said with total clarity: "This is *absurd*."

I had set my sights on "natural" childbirth with a feminist understanding of how labor is often defined by the interests of doctors and hospitals (for whom C-sections can be seen as both more efficient and remunerative). Certain medical interventions, like getting an epidural, could raise your likelihood of having a surgical birth, and the C-section rate in this country was, and is, inexcusably high. Those cold, hard facts were motivating, but so was the rhetoric around "natural" birth. Amid this medieval torture, though, "natural" felt like its own form of tyrannical control. I was being drawn and quartered in the town square while my doula whispered into my ear, "You can open, Tracy. You . . . can . . . *opennnnn*."

I emphatically declared it epidural time, and these *idiots*—my loving husband and empathetic doula—resisted me on it, just as we'd planned, but I held strong. As soon as it took hold, I announced of the anesthesiologist, "I love that man, I *love* him. Can he come back so that I can thank him? Can I write him a card?" I'd been crawling across the fiery depths of hell, only to stumble into the express elevator going up. Now the contractions happened on a bedside monitor, where a bright green digitized line showed their climb and fall, and I felt nothing. I clicked on the TV, crossed my ankles, and snuggled into the pillows like I'd arrived at a swanky hotel with crisp Egyptian-cotton bedsheets.

Then began the pushing—three hours of it, multiple life-times of it. At one point, the baby's heart rate plummeted and they declared the need for an emergency C-section—then, just as swiftly, it was determined a false alarm. "You're amazing," the nurse said. "*Push, push, push.*" And then: "I can see the baby's head. I can see it." And even: "He's coming soon. He's coming!" But when the lead doctor came in to check the baby's position, she said plainly, "It's *never* gonna happen." The baby's head was tilted to the side, efforts to reposition him were unsuccessful, and I'd already been in labor with my water broken for twenty hours, and that got doctors worried about infection. Soon I was being wheeled into an operating room with Christopher appearing bedside in scrubs.

On the operating table, my limbs jerked uncontrollably, like shivers on steroids or that phrase "crawling out of your skin." The anesthesiologist told me it was the drugs and draped a weighted blanket on my chest, but it felt like a physical manifestation of my terror: they were about to cut me open, rearrange my insides. I looked at the operating light above me and then, once I saw my own reflection in it, up and beyond until I could see the blurry undersides of my eyebrows. Even a fleeting glimpse seemed like it might cause me to disintegrate into a collection of body parts and viscera, no longer a unified whole. I imagined pooling red, a dark chasm, guts. I thought, *I will never be the same after this.* This was true, but it had little to do with the C-section.

They prepped the incision site and I felt a light weight

pressing on my stomach. I anticipated the feeling of the blade, and then, and then—this freaking duck started quacking. "Quack-quack, quaaack-quaaaaaaack." The cutting had already begun. In fact, it was over. The duck was not a duck. "He's out, and he's perfect," a voice said. The doctor held a pink, squalling human child above the blue paper tented above my stomach and my mouth fell open. "It's a baby!" I exclaimed, in earnest. "It's a baby. It's a *bay-bee*."

He was wrapped in a pink-and-blue blanket dotted with cartoon animals. A nurse held him so that his face, red and sticky, touched mine. "Here's Mommy," she told this baby, *my* baby, his face contorted in a quack-cry. "Hi, honey," I told him—already feeling him my honey at this first meeting—and he stopped crying. The figures standing around the operating table were already sewing me up and obediently *aww*-ed from behind their papery blue face masks. The baby's eyes—dark, dilated, alien—seemed to find mine. Weeks earlier, I'd downloaded an app that purported to simulate what a baby could see at various ages of development. It told me that, at minutes old, he saw me as just blurred grayscale.

Here was this new body, from my body. A separate person with different contours and boundaries. Someone so deserving of his own story, I can't bring myself to even write his name in these pages.

WHEN WE RETURNED HOME from the hospital, already delirious from sleep deprivation, it was to the curtain-less bedroom of the now so obviously childless couple of before. The baby fed around the clock, sometimes as often as every thirty minutes, which meant that day and night were spent sleeping, trying to sleep, or thinking that we should be sleeping. All forms of light were experienced as an assault on the baby's rest, which was in turn an assault on *our* rest. We'd bought blackout curtains and planned to get around to putting them up before the baby arrived, but then he came two weeks early, before the hospital bag had even been packed. Now, in the middle of the night, I'd shoot daggers at the unobstructed white glow, thinking, *What the fuck, moon.* In a near-sleepwalking fury, we taped up thick black garbage bags with duct tape, leaving the brand-new curtains piled in their boxes.

For those endless night feeds, we rush-ordered a special lightbulb that supposedly wouldn't suppress melatonin or interfere with sleep cycles or something—who really cared about the science or lack thereof because it was hope. Then came the rush-ordered magical swaddles promising sleep with their Velcro and hidden zippers and complicated arm flaps. (Around this time, I wrote a mom friend a middle-of-the-night four-hundred-word email all about swaddles, while propped up in bed, baby on my boob, thumbs flying on my iPhone.) Then came the rush-ordered sleep books from experts who contradicted themselves on nearly every vital point. This is what those early days were like, desperate and deranged.

Christopher returned to work and I started going to a weekly bougie mom's group at a birthing center in Berkeley stocked with yoga balls, plaster pregnant-belly molds, and a bulletin board advertising mind-bogglingly expensive lactation services. Just under a dozen of us sat in a large circle of gliders as our babies kicked on blankets, snoozed in strollers, or rooted around in our shirts.

During that first mom group meeting there were some new-parent platitudes: "I'm living on coffee," "Who needs sleep anyway?" Mostly, though, there was talk of the prior miscarriages and IVF attempts that had led us here. We shared our labor stories, most of which went counter to plans of vaginal birth without painkillers, and which included a C-section experienced with an ineffective epidural and, yes, the dreaded episiotomy, in which an incision is made between the vagina and rectum. The tales ranged from amusingly tumultuous to legitimately traumatic. There were stories of cracked nipples, sleepless nights, unsuccessful breastfeeding, and mastitis, a painful infection of the breast tissue.

Meanwhile, tits out. No nursing covers for this group, no way. The first of us to breastfeed set a standard, casually whipping out her bare boob. We all followed suit, fully flipping down nursing tanks and deeply unbuttoning blouses. I had not one, but two different kinds of nursing cover in my bag: a light swaddle blanket covered in baby giraffes and an apron-like doohickey that promised a no-hands nursing experience. I might have been more comfortable sitting feet away from bouncing breasts on a porn set, but I left the nursing covers buried in my bag. Better to expose my areola than reveal myself as uptight, as adolescent, as the creep in the corner sexualizing everyone else's boo—*breasts*. Outside that room and my own home, though, a nursing cover always came out.

Later, I told Christopher about the class discussion—the cracked nipples, episiotomies, and ineffective epidurals.

"Wow," he said. "Sounds depressing."

"It was amazing," I corrected. "It was energizing and real."

I went in an overachiever, devoting myself not just to the one mom group, but two. This was partly due to my fears about the postpartum period and the specter of becoming the weepy, depressed mom from countless articles I'd read. It was also the reality of being a motherless new mom: Maybe I was hoping to find a mom for myself—and in a way, I did. The bougie group had a paid leader, a woman in her forties with long brown finger-combed hair who worked part-time as a nanny and was always ornamented with objects that conveyed a certain rooted spirituality: flowing fabrics, mixed-metal baubles, and clinking bangles you might purchase at a New Age gift shop. But then she also wore leather boots that belonged on a motorcycle—a modern earth goddess interpretation. She talked in a way that one might learn from years of talk therapy in the Bay Area, pointedly using the word *grief* when one woman spoke about having to give up on breastfeeding. Most important, she had a child and had been through all of this before.

Both groups gave sanity-saving structure to those otherwise shapeless days and weeks. But they also gave me, god, here come the words, just like the tears did in those days: *a community of women*. This was different from having women friends;

this was a group of women united around an experience that was at turns alienating, traumatic, hidden, and joyous. Late in my pregnancy, a mom friend who was offering advice told me, "You're joining the biggest, best club ever." At the time, I'd wondered if there was a way to be a mom without joining. Maybe I could leave my application blank. Who wanted to be a part of that club, really? Now, though, I found myself using the word *sisterhood*. Then I'd laugh, but still mean it.

WITH BOTH MOM GROUPS, we would park our strollers en masse at a popular family-friendly biergarten where other peoples' kids scarfed down chicken nuggets before wreaking greasy-fingered havoc on the resident sandbox. These visits felt like ironic performance art—because strollers, lol. *Look at me being such a mom*, I thought ("mom" said with a drawn-out vowel, as in, "Mahhhm, stop embarrassing me"). It wasn't just me: One afternoon at the biergarten, a handful of us sat in a circle of Adirondack chairs while delicately sipping low-alcohol beers in between breastfeeding sessions and joked about how every public mom action seemed to come with exaggerated air quotes. "I'm gonna go grab my 'diaper bag' from my 'stroller,'" one of us said. "Yeah, I'm gonna 'nurse' my 'baby,'" said another. I laughed so hard tears seeped from the outer corners of my eyes.

We had lived the entirety of our adult lives with the awareness of being seen as women and watching ourselves as such, mostly through men's eyes. As John Berger famously wrote in *Ways of Seeing*, "Men look at women. Women watch themselves being looked at." The same phenomenon applied, but now we belonged to a different category of woman: mom. We had inherited the mantle of every cultural judgment, dismissal, and mockery of motherhood—from endless reporting on trumped-up "mommy wars" to viral SNL skits about frumpy "Mom jeans" (which, despite their newfound hipness, had not made actual motherhood any more attractive). We contended with it every time we went out in public and experienced ourselves as being seen by others. On another biergarten meetup, Stacy, a therapist with an enviable Topanga Canyon aesthetic, rolled up to the group and laughed surreally: "I just had that realization again: I'm *that mom* walking down the street with her stroller."

Implicit in our air-quoted sense of motherhood was the truth of how many people saw moms, but also our own prior assessment of those stroller-pushing women. It was a means of detachment and self-protection. As Susan Sontag once scribbled to herself in a journal, "Camp: irony, distance; ambivalence (?)."[1] I was not conflicted about parenthood, but capital-M Motherhood felt inherently satirical. We had to keep telling each other versions of: I am a "mom." You are a "mom." We are "moms." My childhood friend Meredith had given birth within days of me, and in those first postpartum weeks she used the phrase "technically moms" in a voice-mail message. As in, technically we are moms, but our own sense of identity was still catching up with that factual reality.

A couple of months postpartum, I met up with some mom group friends for a "mommy and baby" yoga class where you pay an extra five bucks for "baby holders." We placed our infants on pastel blankets in front of our pastel yoga mats, and the fussy ones were swept up by these assistants so as not to interrupt class. One baby holder was a college-age man wearing a "Nevertheless, She Persisted" T-shirt. Another, a woman in her third trimester of pregnancy, held the squirming creatures precariously over her globelike belly. When the fussing babies outnumbered holders, an assortment of bouncers and Rock 'n Plays were deployed. Mid-class, a woman wearing a tank top reading "Mama Bear" in glittery gold script huffily leapt from her mat to retrieve her baby. "He's spending too much time in *devices*," she said, the final word spit like an obscenity.

There was plenty to be made fun of here, plenty from which to protectively distance myself, but then it was the first time I'd worked out since giving birth. There was nothing ironic, nothing satirical about the tender muscles newly flexing around that pink three-inch C-section scar. For weeks, I had avoided the fact of even having a stomach, or a body separate from my baby. I did downward dog, plank, child's pose, all while staring down at my years-old yoga mat, which was disintegrating in spots shaped like fingers and toes. At the end of the class, I lay down, limbs splayed, eyes closed. A buzzing resonated at the center of my forehead and I felt myself rising up and up through an endless black.

This happened to me in yoga, the buzzing and rising. This time, though, it was different: *My mom is here.* A silly, mystical thought, but I allowed it. *I miss you, I miss you, I miss you*, I told her. *Isn't my baby just so beautiful, so perfect, so wonderful?* I was floating in a dark, warm bath of primal soup. *I wish you could hold him, feel his warm squish.* Like a camera lens folding in on itself, I sensed the closing of a portal to—not to an afterlife, which I didn't believe in, but to the mom embedded in me. *Thank you, miss you, love you*, I said, rushing out the words.

The teacher was playing a loudening sound track of chanting monks, and the babies decided to join in with a crescendo of cries as we all lay determinedly on our mats, savoring these lasts moments of calm, such as they were. My belly trembled with laughter, and tears slipped down the sides of my face. We were a roomful of women nevertheless persisting.

Afterward, I went walking the several blocks back to my car. My little bundle, strapped onto my chest, facing inward, started wailing. He rubbed his face aggressively against me, trying to push beyond the slick cold of workout tee to warm, bare skin. Filled with ferocious hunger, he rubbed himself red. His intent singular: nipple, mouth, nipple, mouth. The street was busy with slow-going cars. Across the way stood a group of teen boys, kicking aimlessly at the sidewalk. Ahead of me, a construction crew in reflective vests building scaffolding on the face of a building.

My nursing cover was stuffed in the bottom of my bag. The baby carrier only disguised so much. "Screw it," I said aloud to myself. *"Screw it."* I hiked up my shirt, unclipped my beige nursing bra, and fully popped out a sweaty boob. It was weighted and tingling with milk, singularly focused just like the baby. I shoveled it into his waiting mouth and the wailing stopped, flailing limbs went soft, eyelids fluttered closed. Nothing else— not the cars, the teens, the construction crew, not my exposed boob and soft belly—could possibly matter more. It was just a breast, just food, just my body, just love.

MY DAD STARTED COMING over twice a week to watch the baby for four-hour stretches so that I could rush, hair in a precarious bun, to my local coffee shop to hammer out a few hundred words. On my first outing, I cranked the radio on the drive over and here, as always, came "the dancing woman" sashaying across my mind. The hair-flipping, hip-rolling sprite of my imagination had been with me for almost two decades now. She had even followed me into *this* life phase, I marveled, while avoiding rearview mirror glimpses of the empty car seat behind me. Inside the coffee shop, I watched the young barista wearing high-waisted jeans, serviceable clogs, and a cropped T-shirt and thought: *Me, before.* Then there I was, after: stretchy maternity jeans, saggy wire-free nursing bra.

I cracked open my laptop, then scraped at a spray of dried, flaky breast milk on the mouse pad. Back home, the stuff stiffened our bedsheets, flecked our bathroom mirror, and dotted my bedside table, leaving behind whiffs of sour milk. It leaked, dripped, and when I gave a squeeze to relieve the pressure, arced across the room. Years earlier, a friend had irreverently joked about the realities of a teenage boy's bedroom: "Cumcovered everything." My reality: breast-milk-covered everything.

Stepping out into the world without my baby, I felt not unlike that stereotype of a teenage boy. My breasts were engorged, of course, but so was my vagina. (I say "vagina" instead of "pussy," you might notice—not dirty talk, just basic biological fact.) Blood pulsed and flowed. Everything enflamed, electric. Was this hormones, the physical experience of a body healing after labor? I had no clue, nor did I really care. Here's what I knew: I felt like hot shit. This sense of hotness was outsize, having nothing to do with any purportedly objective outside measures of it. Maybe that just means that for the first time in my life, it was correctly placed.

Crappy pop music blared in my ears as I clacked away on the laptop and started to subtly rock back and forth in a state of flow. I was writing about being on a porn set with two men riffing on "girls these days." I rearranged a couple of sentences, made an exciting connection between ideas, and suddenly my breasts felt like water balloons swelling at the tap. I glanced down, half expecting to see milk leaking through my shirt. Not that it, or anything, could make me leave this coffee shop before my four hours were up.

I was no longer "girls these days," that was clear. I'd exited to the other side, to lesser cultural relevance. I was no more the young, single, middle-class, white, cis-het woman upon whom the mainstream critiques and warnings and trend pieces— whether around "female chauvinism" or un-marriageability or depleting oxytocin stores or egg freezing or rough sex—would be directed. Now I had stepped into the realm of maternal import. There were a million different "shoulds" around breastfeeding and sleep training. I had read all the major baby books, dog-earing pages and making notes in the margins, and routinely called the advice nurse with questions such as: "I accidentally

splashed some water in my baby's mouth during bath time and
he coughed. Do you think he's okay?" (Translation: Will he die?)

Of course, there was also the breathless cataloging of celebrities' post-baby weight loss and the existence of "mommy
makeovers" that lifted breasts, tucked tummies, and "rejuve-
nated" vaginas. In this moment, at least, I was impervious to
those superficial forces. I thought of the porn performers who
had been rendered speechless by my question about how to
make pregnancy sexy. *I gestated a human. A baby was cut out of
me. I survived. Now I'm sustaining that baby with my body.* I'd
always associated sexiness with feeling powerful. That hadn't
changed, but now my sense of power came from a different
place.

At the coffee shop, as always, I had an awareness of the men
all around me. They comprised a morphing blur in the corner of
my eye: flirting with the baristas, stirring in sugar, looking for
electrical outlets, spreading out belongings alongside women
who in turn shrank to make space for them. In a reflexive return
to habit, I imagined how this new body of mine might be judged
by these unseen men: stretch-marked breasts, darkened nipples,
jiggle of tummy, and that pink, puckered C-section scar at the
start of unshaven pubes.

The make-believe judgment—a row of twos and ones held
overhead—made little sense next to the tens indicated by this
newly raging, roiling self-regard. *You motherfuckers have no clue*,
I thought, smiling at the choice of the curse word, these imagined "motherfuckers" specifically not being fuckers of mothers
but rather the kind to joke about "saggy mom vaginas." I wasn't

cursing the real men in the room so much as the simplistic caricature of sexiness and straight "male desire" that had haunted
me for the entirety of my postpubescent life. *It* had no clue.

I GOT BACK HOME from one of those early coffee shop visits to
an eerily silent house. My dad sat on our couch with a folded
newspaper and pencil in hand. Picking up the baby monitor
from the coffee table, I saw the rise and fall of chest, and let out
the breath I'd been holding without knowing. We talked mea-
surements: ounces of milk, degree of nap-time fussing, minutes
spent sleeping. Then my dad, glasses sinking on his nose, set
aside his crossword with a smirk. "I guess I didn't do a good
enough job hiding my porn," he said, seemingly apropos of
nothing. I laughed unsteadily: Hah-hah-hah. Then, serious:
"What do you mean?"

Here was a sixty-eight-year-old man with an ungroomed
fluff of a beard gone white, but then he broke into a grin and the
small gap between his front teeth, the rising apples of his cheeks
made him seem boyish. He was the same little imp who in oft-
repeated family lore had discovered some matches as a five-
year-old and, whoops, set the sandbox aflame. "I found some
pages laying around. I thought maybe you'd left them out for
me to read," he said unconvincingly. There was that laugh of
mine again—hah-hah-hah—as I tried to remember what, exactly, I'd written. Something about finding his porn as a teenager. Had that draft included the bit about masturbating to his
Perfect 10 membership? I sat myself down.

"Your mom wasn't so clueless, you know," he said, eyes glimmering. They had watched porn together, sometimes, at her suggestion, he told me. Stuff for couples, some of it by that feminist pornographer I'd interviewed for the college newspaper—what was her name? Oh yes, Candida Royalle. Words kept coming out of his mouth—and my brain, usually ace at recording dialogue, went off-line. It was just: unexpected verbal diarrhea about my mom and sex. How much she loved it. How back in the day she read the dirty stories in *Penthouse*. How she stumbled on this one article about spanking that gave her an idea. Did I remember that reading I did at Good Vibrations? She noticed a riding crop that night and, well—

What I have retained from this much-too-much conversation is just enough. Here is what matters: When I found my dad's porn all those years back, I told myself a story about my poor, pathetic mom, his poor, pathetic wife. *She must not know, he keeps his secrets, how embarrassing for her, I don't want to become that*. I didn't stop to think about her secrets, or that she might have any. Soon enough, I'd learned about the teenage sexual rebellion, unintended pregnancy, and pressured adoption. The camp for unwed mothers, the mental institution. Of course, my mom proved to have more sexual secrets than my dad.

She hadn't been a poor, pathetic mom or wife. This isn't to suggest that her early *Penthouse* meanderings and Good Vibrations explorations in middle age were equivalent to my dad's access to sexual entertainment and validation as a straight man. This isn't to suggest that I'd been wrong in identifying a gendered power imbalance that would soon be mine. But it is to suggest that I had unthinkingly desexualized her as a woman, and as a mom. Therapist Esther Perel writes in *Mating in Captivity* of the "sexual invisibility of the American mother, which is so deeply rooted in our psyche that men and women alike conspire to deny maternal sexuality."[2] Daughters conspire, too.

I'd never even thought to go looking for my mom's porn.

CHAPTER 11

I Want

I was led down a moodily lit hallway that descended steeply into darkness. It had the mystery and intrigue of walking into a Prohibition-era speakeasy, save for the thrumming Katy Perry song surfacing from below. The stairs opened up to a lounge area outfitted with pink Art Deco couches: an Instagram trap. A framed black-and-white photo of a man's washboard abs hung on the wall and I stopped to take a picture on my iPhone as a pair of women flung themselves onto a nearby lounger. When I looked up, a smiling, attractive young man with puppy dog eyes greeted me with a "miss" and asked for my ticket.

The feminist website Jezebel had hired me as a staff writer just as my "maternity leave" ended and flew me to Las Vegas to cover the 2019 Adult Entertainment Expo. I'd spent all day reporting at the convention, petting limbless sex dolls and watching VR shot from a man's perspective. Now, in my off hours, I was going to see *Magic Mike Live*, which promised to be a modern reimagining of the stereotypically cheesy and crass "male revue." The show is the brainchild of the actor Channing Tatum, who starred in its Hollywood precursors: *Magic Mike* and *Magic Mike XXL*. The stated purpose of the stage adaptation was to take heterosexual women's desire seriously. Well, here I was trying to take my *own* desire seriously after spending over two decades primarily experiencing my sexuality through straight men—their desire, their pleasure, their sexual playgrounds.

The young man with puppy dog eyes ushered me down a set of stairs to another young man with puppy dog eyes. It was at this point, before any men had even taken off their clothes, that I decided I loved *Magic Mike Live*. It took so little: intentional scene setting, an artsy nude, catered attention, and some crappy dance music. This wasn't a facsimile of my interior erotic life—my Pinterest board for the space would have been much less pink—but it acknowledged that my interior erotic life might exist.

The stage sat in the center of the windowless room, surrounded by bistro tables. If it weren't for the blaring pop music, it would have seemed a high-scale jazz club instead of a woke Chippendales. On two sides, the dark platform was flanked by long pink couches with backs that rose and fell in a Cupid's bow, as though the stage was placed ever so unsubtly between a woman's lips, a pill perched on a waiting tongue. The imagery suggested that the audience would collectively swallow these men whole, but as I sat in the second row, waiting along with four-hundred-plus other women for the show to begin, my mood was more anxious anticipation than ravenous hunger. I was filled with *Don't let me down*.

A stubbled waiter wearing a crisp white button-down and old-timey suspenders chivalrously kneeled down next to my table to take my drink order. I heard a woman across the aisle wearing a "21st Birthday" sash whisper to her table of women, including her mother, "Even *the waiters* are hot." The hot waiter's reverential body language recalled Prince Charming preparing to slide the glass slipper onto Cinderella's foot. In truth, I realized, he was trying to upsell me on my drink order.

He pointed to a line on the menu reading, "Triple the size" and "XXL." "You get three drinks for the price of two," he said, delivering the sales pitch in the singsong style of a flirtatious compliment. In a too-chipper tone, I replied, "No thanks! I promised myself I'd only have *two* drinks tonight." I held up a pair of fingers like a peace offering. He quickly countered with a wink, "You can always throw out the third drink if you don't want it." I was but a few minutes into my empowering, feminist, sex-positive *Magic Mike Live* experience and a man was already trying to talk me into drinking more, and with the assistance of unsubtle phallic references. How quickly this sexual utopia had transformed into a canny money grab.

Soon, the lights dimmed and a man with crunchy hair, an oversize diamond-encrusted necklace, and the voice of a shock jock appeared in the audience, mic in hand. I shifted uneasily. Rock music began to blare and a group of dancers looking like a discount version of the Village People descended upon the room. This MC launched into rapid-fire raunch, shouting things like "Oooh that made my nipples hard" and "It's getting moist in here so take off all your clothes." A woman was pulled onstage and a man dressed as a firefighter pulled out a can of silly string, which he held at crotch level. Then he sprayed her in the face, mimicking a cum shot.

It was at this point, as I imagined reaching for my purse to leave, that she screamed, "*Unicorn, unicorn, unicorn,*" and everything suddenly came to a halt. The whole thing had been a setup. The audience member was not an audience member; she was part of the show. In the universe of *Magic Mike Live*, we learned, *unicorn* was a safe word with the power to summon the voice of Channing Tatum in the rafters. As if speaking from the heavens, Channing's prerecorded audio breathily told her, "You can have *anything* that you want. You just have to ask." The show was transformed into a fantasy of her own making.

Tears pooled in my eyes as I fought my crumpling chin. I took a deep, wavering breath. I was crying in *Magic Mike Live*, a statement of fact nearly as horrifying as the prank that had just transpired. A grown, adult woman brought to tears by a male revue. They were tears of relief—at being rescued from cum-shot imagery, and at the nod to the steaming platter of crap that is so often served up as "female desire." The faux audience member transformed into the night's real MC, replete with her own rhinestone-encrusted mic, which she proceeded to thump desirously against her crotch. She was the comedic embodiment of tongue-wagging wanting. Now I was grinning, watching these men follow her every request through the luster of my own tears.

The guys, now clad in T-shirts and denim, swarmed the stage, awash in smoky purple light. They danced in unison and then broke out into individual routines with one of them springing into a backflip. Shirts came off, revealing Ken-doll pecs and climbing walls of abs. They artfully humped the stage all at once and then jumped up to scan the audience with come hither looks as all of us screamed and clapped wildly. This might have been a cheap, superficial acknowledgment of "female desire," but I drank it up like a bottle of water discovered in the middle of the desert.

It's tricky, though, holding on to sexual subjectivity in a one-size-fits-all enterprise. Toward the end of the show, a shirtless gentleman with heavy-lidded eyes hopped off the stage as the spotlight followed him over to me. He raised his eyebrows and held out his meaty hand, and after a pause, I stood up and gave him mine. Then he wrapped my arms across his broad, bare shoulders, picked me up by the thighs, and laid me on the edge of the stage.

What happened next blurs; there's just the visual of this man looking at me fiercely from between my legs, me closing my eyes in cringing anticipation, and then the *bam-bam-bam* of his slamming into me. I was surprise-fake-fucked in front of a room full of cheering women. There was no whispered, "Would you like me to hump you?" Just wham, bam, back to your seat, ma'am.

How quickly this tightrope walk had teetered from the revolutionary embrace of the "female gaze" to being an object upon which things are done. We could look, we could squeal, we could sip our XXL cocktails, but *Magic Mike Live* seemed to assume that the height of women's sexual desire was to be taken, to be aggressively wanted by a man.

Once delivered back to my seat, I wanted to feel empowered about it, to rejoin the room's chorus of woos. Just a little light-hearted humping, right? Not enough to derail an otherwise enjoyable evening. If anyone could merrily shrug this off, you'd think it would be me: I'd once casually conducted an interview with an erect penis at eye level and mere inches from my face. But the ice knocking around in my stomach suggested otherwise. Then came the self-recrimination: *Well, you did give him your hand. What did you expect?*

I sucked uneasily at my empty drink. I wasn't traumatized, but I wasn't happy, either. The show had been inspiring and moving, and then it wasn't. Even writing this now, I think about the well-meaning folks behind *Magic Mike Live*—including sweet, dimpled Channing—and not wanting to hurt *their* feelings. There's the weight of their imagined expectations. There's the familiar pull to pretend, to be the cool girl once again, but women's desire often gets distorted because of the drive to meet expectation and protect men's egos. The point of this *Magic Mike* excursion wasn't just getting in touch with my own wants but also getting in touch with what I didn't want. The point was to be able to say: I didn't like that.

I didn't like that.

ON MY FINAL NIGHT in Las Vegas, I found out I wouldn't be able to finagle a ticket to the AVN Awards. Cardi B was to perform and organizers were not going to waste those tickets on reporters. Back at the hotel, I brushed my teeth and changed into my pajama top: an oversize promotional T-shirt for a strap-on company that read, "sticking it to the man." I pulled the blinds against the neon aura of lights from the Strip and crawled into bed. On the nightstand was a fake dollar bill with a half-naked man on it: a memento from *Magic Mike Live*. I flipped through Twitter looking for updates on the awards show, then I tapped my way over to my digital photo album.

Nestling into the over-bleached hotel sheets, I flipped through videos of my baby giggling hysterically at Dada blowing raspberries on his belly, riding Mama like a horse, and doing his signature foot-thumping dance. It's not supposed to be so easy to incorporate motherhood into all this: "sticking it to the man," Vegas lights, porn Oscars, *Magic Mike*. I was a woman who had eagerly left her baby and husband back at home in order to go to a porn convention and attend a male revue, and I also was a woman who eagerly wanted to return to her baby and husband back at home. That was the simple reality of having multiple desires that you not only acknowledged but also acted upon.

After glancing at the glowing bedside clock, I forced myself out of bed and pulled out my pastel pink breast pump. I was still breastfeeding twice a day and didn't want my supply to dry up, which meant pump and dump. Fifteen minutes later, I poured two bottles of milk into the sink, watching the ivory liquid splash against the bleached white porcelain and feeling keenly aware of myself as a biological being, as standing outside the mainstream fantasy realm of pigtailed babysitter or busty MILF that I'd steered earlier that day while reporting on the expo.

This was just me, my body, and the simple fact of milk pragmatically emptied down the drain in the same way I might remove and flush a tampon. It was the private, prosaic experience of encountering my body and any number of its various functions that are supposedly disgusting, abject, verboten—lest some man somewhere find it sexy. Of course, the behind-the-scenes reality of the convention itself wasn't as simple as the illusion it portrayed. Earlier in the day, I had grabbed lunch with a woman porn director who also was a mom. We had shifted easily between talk of parenthood and squirting, kid birthday parties and double anal without missing a beat.

The answer to the question of what I desired didn't live in the vacuum of sex and sexuality. It was a borderless hunger that touched every area of my life. It didn't distinguish between "mother" and "sex reporter," "wife" and "that weirdo crying during *Magic Mike Live*." My mom had often referenced the classic F. Scott Fitzgerald quote, "The test of a first-rate intelligence is the ability to hold two opposed ideas in mind at the same time and still retain the ability to function."

The ability to hold two opposing ideas in mind is also essential to surviving as a complex, fully realized woman. The world shuttles us into categories, often asking us to make a fractured or dichotomous choice. The flip side of pleasure is danger: physical and reputational. If you can't hold these contradictions, you are a woman reduced.

THE NEXT MORNING I found myself at the Las Vegas airport walking the jetway to my Oakland-bound plane as slot machines dinged in the background while thinking, *I don't know if I'll come back*. To the expo, I meant. Not *I won't come back*, but a lightly held *I don't know if I will*. This was a different feeling from my last expo visit, after which I knew that I would return, because I felt a thrumming need.

Porn had provided me with personas to try on, awakened my own fantasies, and sparked an appreciation for the glittering range of human sexuality. It taught me about the cathartic eroticization of real-world inequities, not just by men but also by women like me. Less optimistically, it reflected sex through the distorting lens of capitalism, and within an industry increasingly anxious for viewers. It mired me in men's perspectives and pleasures, just as with most mainstream entertainment, until I found the pockets of the industry that spoke more comprehensively to me.

My most significant education, though, came from peeking behind the curtain as a reporter to witness the business, choreography, and movie magic. I opened the seams on sexual performance, expectation, and fantasy, and as a result, I was able to fashion for myself a more spacious sex life and sense of self. My career allowed me to learn the things I could have been taught a long time ago.

On this trip, I sat down for lunch with porn director Holly Randall, the daughter of Suze Randall, who ran one of the first porn sites I'd ever visited as a teenager back in the nineties. The same one that had advertised things like "Stacked blonde pornstar gets poked poolside" and "Jaded jizz junky begs for the big fix." What happens if you come full circle and keep going?

Then again, that's what life often is: traversing the same

hillside, passing familiar signposts, noticing earlier footsteps, cutting new paths. What I realized, walking down the jetway, was that if I did return to the expo, it wouldn't be because I needed something personally from porn, but because it is an industry and entertainment medium worth writing about. If I needed something from porn, it would be direct and unfiltered: to watch and enjoy.

It was all too easy to view sex workers as symbolic stand-ins for sexual fearlessness and inexpressible desires. I saw this tendency in myself as much as in the men standing in windingly long lines waiting for autographs. We all wanted something from these performers, some of whom sat on literal pedestals at the expo. We could get our interviews or autographs without suffering any of the precipitous social, political, and potentially criminal consequences that come along with being a sex worker. That is true just as the aesthetics of sex work are co-opted by mainstream culture as a titillating but not too threatening form of rebellion.

Sex workers are often wedged between two extreme and competing narratives: a "radical" one of all-pervasive exploitation and a "liberal" one of empowerment, as Lorelei Lee would soon write in an *n+1* essay. Neither construction spoke to the nuances of Lee's experiences with sex work. I had for a long time harbored an idealized perspective—gazing up at a woman on the pole as a symbol rather than as a woman at work—which elided the realities of labor, class, and privilege. Flattening sex work to a rule-breaking act of empowerment was to indulge in a different kind of sexual fantasy.

I thought then of the journalist Melissa Gira Grant, who wrote in the book *Playing the Whore* that whore stigma applies to any woman—especially, though, if she is trans, queer, or a person of color—who steps outside the bounds of "appropriate" sexuality. The identification of such stigma, Grant argues, "offers us a way through it: to value difference, to develop solidarity between women in and out of the sex trade."[1] Listening to sex workers, advocating for decriminalization, challenging the bounds of appropriate sexuality—these were forms of solidarity. Pedestaling was not.

Any person openly existing on the taboo margins of sexuality is likely to become a figurative object to someone harboring conflicted or suppressed desires. It makes me think of a line that I once heard delivered on a porn set: "What would you do if *nothing* was holding you back?" It seemed corny at the time, but it continues to echo in my mind because those words tap into a core aspect of common sexual daydreams: being released from prohibition and shame.

I contemplated all of this as I hauled my carry-on overhead and slid it into an empty bin. Then, settling into my window seat, I thought of my mom, who had sometimes worried for me, because she knew too well how a woman could be punished for her sexuality, but who also told me, "Somewhere in you is the answer to what is right for you." What is right is not static: it means honoring the needs and desires of a shifting, growing self. None of us ever land anywhere always and forever (except in death, says my inner Wednesday Addams).

Marriage and motherhood are treated as final destinations, but I had older women friends now, a rotating cast of casual mom stand-ins, who told me about divorces rattling friend groups, spouses getting a terminal diagnosis, the shock of an empty nest. You could play it safe, hedge your bets—all for states that are only ever temporary. Just a few years earlier, I'd rushed to get engaged and then married, but now Christopher and I would occasionally look at each other, full of unwavering love and commitment, and say something along the lines of, "Why'd we get married, again?" The question wasn't why we were together, but why we decided to be together in such a traditional, predictable way, one that directly conflicted with some of our deepest-held political beliefs.

Sexual discovery is treated similarly, as though one must shed the outer layers, all external influences, to reach an authentic self: the whole nesting doll at the center. Never mind the impossibility of ever finding a core self completely untouched by the outside world. There are defining, vital moments of insight that speak to a core sexual identity, and then there are smaller, passing realizations: fascination, sensations, and hunger that fluctuate over the course of a lifetime.

Sometimes you fling open the door to a fantasy that's been knocking, only to see it flee down the block. In my electrified postpartum days, I suggested to Christopher that we play out that enduring deep-throating fantasy, which I understood on some level as an eroticization of real-world inequality. I tried to explain, as much to Christopher as to myself, just what it was that I wanted.

"It's like I want you to *do the patriarchy* to me," I told him irreverently. "Make me *choke* on your desire."

"Okay," he said, amused.

"But I want you to not *want* to do the patriarchy to me," I added.

"Okay," he said more cautiously.

"But I want you to be *good* at doing the patriarchy to me."

"Okaaayyy."

"But not *too* good."

Christopher "did the patriarchy to me," a couple of times. Then I watched bittersweetly as this longtime fantasy dissipated, like a stack of private pornographic images suddenly tossed into the wind. There had been a time when this departure would have felt a relief, a convenient realignment of the personal and political, but all that came to mind was, *Farewell, friend, maybe I'll see you around again.*

My work is frequently an impetus for Christopher and me to talk candidly about sex, which feels like knocking down the walls of conventional marital propriety. On one such occasion, these words spilled from my mouth: "My only regret is never having"—here I brought two spacious fists into the air—"*two dicks* at the same time." After he stopped laughing, Christopher said, "I mean, if you ever need another dick . . . we can talk about it." His tone was as playful as my impromptu miming of a dual hand job. On another occasion, he expressed regret that he hadn't experienced a rollicking twenties like I had. I started to remind him how hampered it had been, how not carefree. Then I said, "If you ever want to . . . we can talk about it."

There is a sense of possibility and mutual creation in our relationship, which feels more important than the specifics of where it takes us. You arrive and arrive and arrive again.

LOOKING BACK AT THE faking, the adversarial sex, and the drunken adventuring of my twenties, I wish better for that girl. Of course I do. I also know that at each step of the way, she was doing what worked for her at that moment, in that context. We can wish better for "our girls"—a world that values their desire, subjecthood, and pleasure—but that doesn't mean the social and political circumstances for that "better" are here. Sexual violence is pervasive, the state of sex education is abysmal, reproductive rights are under attack, the double standard is alive and well, and yawning pleasure disparities persist.

This is the enduring legacy of a stalled revolution, which liberated women to have sex in a world still mired in sexism and power imbalances. The traditional virgin-slut dichotomy has morphed into a continuum with greater possibility, as well as greater pressure, contradiction, and ambiguity. Now young women face additional neoliberal judgments around their perceived sexual agency and self-interest, appraisals that demand going through the motions of empowerment.

We should work to change the actual context of girls' lives, which means remembering what "empowerment" used to mean: a collective struggle, not an individual one. It requires changing rather than just individually enduring structural inequality. This doesn't mean discounting personal sexual narratives (says the woman writing a personal sexual narrative), but it does mean viewing these distinct journeys within a broader systemic context.

My single straight friends often have to make impossible calculations in anticipation of sexist stereotypes of the crazy, needy, desperate, slutty, prudish, bitchy, man-hungry, or biological-clock-watching woman. It's what I did—even, to a degree, with Christopher. How could you truly ask for what you wanted in that context? Heterosexual dating often feels like a game of not wanting too much. A single friend recently said to me, "You don't understand what it's like out here."

Inherent in the use of "out here" is a sense that I have found shelter in my marriage, and I agree. It's a reasonably safe place to express my desires and experience pleasure. I'm not worried about things like playing text message games or the absence of orgasm. I'm not worried about being sexually assaulted—by him, at least. I found a guy eager to give our baby my last name, an affront to a definitional aspect of patriarchy, but that doesn't mean I don't live in one. A relationship can feel like a safe haven and it can feel like a trap, but neither of these is freedom. After years of feminist cogitation, I ultimately found security in a foundational institution of women's protection and oppression: Marriage. *Monogamous, heterosexual, procreative marriage.*

Women's options are fundamentally constrained; their choices are not free. Until we change the context, young women will have to struggle to make sense of a world full of punishing contradiction, misdirection, and impossibility. They will have to find whatever compromises and solutions work for them. What is currently on offer in this partially changed world isn't sexual empowerment but rather survival. It's finding the best way to make do.

Too often, those who have safely reached the shores of adulthood look behind and blame young women for the choppy waters they now sail across, as though these women should be better navigators of their own oppression. Some shake their heads and cluck their tongues at "girls these days." This disapproval implicitly demands that girls try to enact the fantasy of a finished revolution. It asks them, as does so much of our culture, to perform.

WHEN I GOT BACK home from Las Vegas, trailing clouds of cigarette smoke and Axe body spray, Christopher was lying on the living room couch exhausted from several days of solo parenting. I checked the monitor, watching our baby take a few shallow breaths as he napped upstairs, before heading for the couch. It was the same brown leather one where Christopher and I first had sex and, more recently, where I went into labor. Now I liked to take some credit for its handsome patina. "It's well seasoned," I sometimes told guests who complimented it. I'd take a beat before continuing, "You're sitting right where I was when my water broke."

Curling up on Christopher, I told him about the opening shtick of *Magic Mike Live*, my tears, and my relief. Then, as the sun cast its dim winter light through the living room windows, I explained that yes, I wanted there to exist an equal world of sexual entertainment for women, an encyclopedic proliferation of pop culture, mainstream and pornographic, that took seriously the existence of women's desire, the potential of their gaze. "But," I told him, "even if I were to find a perfect representation in the commercialized realm, which I am unconvinced anyone ever does, it wouldn't speak to every other, or even most women." I wanted more than to have my desire acknowledged by an idealized piece of cultural ephemera.

I tried, poorly, to articulate this "more" to Christopher as we lay there on the couch with Hank, our wiry little mutt of a dog, who had wedged himself between our warm bodies. "I just want it to be you and me and my saggy boobs and unshaven legs," I said. Christopher gently shook my arm and said softly, "Yeah, babe." As in, of course, obviously. There were a couple of mutual droplets of tears, happy ones, because we already had all that, he was more than okay with it, and I was on the way there.

This was not about saggy boobs or body hair. It was about security, acceptance, and intimacy. It was about believing in my desires and desirability, my own feelings and lovability. It was about escaping the opposition of wanting and being wanted, and having a fuller, fluctuating experience of both. It was about the strength of vulnerability and mutuality, rather than the insistent, restricted recital of control. It was about admitting and lamenting the unevenness of the playing field.

As I went on about all this to Christopher, our dog jumped off the couch and began humping his favorite toy—his "lovah," we called it—a now-ragged stuffed tree log that rivaled his own body in size. He would hump that thing unrelentingly and unabashedly, no matter who was watching. Once, he humped it to the point of a painful hours-long erection and had to be taken to an animal hospital. His shamelessness was medically ill-advised but inspiring, nonetheless.

Speaking of shame, I had for years felt guilty about fantasies of eroticized power imbalances. These days, though, I marveled at the human mind's ingenuity, creativity, and resilience. I accepted what it sometimes takes to feel safe enough to want sex in the world in which we live. As the sex-positive feminist Lisa Palac has written of her submissive desires, "When you've got a lemon, make lemonade."[2] I not only felt great about making lemonade but also recognized the difference between genuinely wrestling for power in the bedroom and playfully pretending at the same with candor, communication, and reciprocal understanding.

Still, I sometimes wondered what my desires might look like if I wasn't such a product of our culture. This was the flip of the question asked by Sallie Tisdale in her memoir, *Talk Dirty to Me*: "Here I am, in the patriarchal, materialistic, sex-drenched, sex-phobic West—and who have I become, here?"[3] I loved that formulation for what it pointedly communicated about the development of a sexual self, and yet I could wail at the injustice of the setting, the "here."

But in my process of learning and then still further coming to believe that porn was performance, I'd had a concomitant realization: sex could be theater, too. This was a delightful fact, one I could roll around in my mind like a worn penny between fingertips. Personal fantasies, negotiated scenarios, dirty talk, porn—these were all forms of make-believe that could magically unlock pleasure. Where else do we get to so ecstatically, and sometimes collaboratively, pretend that things are other than they are?

In my sex life, with partners and on my own, this understanding had allowed me to escape into an illusory realm that provided safety and surrender, relief and rapture—and I wasn't done exploring the endless possible directions. "Sometimes," I told Christopher, lifting myself upright on the couch. Then I stopped, bashful about the words forming in my head, as though I was revealing my deepest, darkest, most perverted fantasy, the thing I wanted to role-play most of all. "Sometimes," I continued, "I want to step outside of our culture, or to pretend for a few moments that I can." Then I did; we did.

CHAPTER 12

Drive

I was the lone person on the beach at six forty-five a.m., with a blue-and-green-striped Tommy Bahama recliner, matching umbrella, netted bag of snorkeling gear, ziplock baggie of snacks, thermos of coffee, bottle of water, two books, one notebook, three pens, and two kinds of sunscreen. Parenthood has taught me a few things, including the virtues of packing all imaginable necessities for a toddler who at any moment might have a diaper blowout, demand a sippy cup of milk, or melt into a busy sidewalk screaming, "I want cracker! *Cracker!*" It's also taught me that time alone carries a preciousness that calls for packing as though you were yourself an ornery toddler, which means attempting to anticipate all manner of personal need, want, and flight of fancy.

This was our last day in Maui, on our first family vacation together. Christopher was back at our Airbnb with the baby, who at two years old was not much of a baby anymore. In the inescapably commercial language of parenthood, this was a "trade." I'd watched the baby the previous afternoon so that

Christopher could have time alone to go surfing. Now I got my couple of hours alone, immediately after the baby's six a.m. wake-up. Overhead, palm trees crackled like tropical static. A line of sun crept imperceptibly across the golden stretch of beach. Turquoise waves with blue-green undertones crashed and shushed, advancing and retreating.

I looked at those waves and I thought, inevitably, of my mom. Several years back, a group of us had come to Hawaii to scatter her ashes in the ocean. We had kayaked along the coast to a spot that comprised her favorite view on the island, and possibly anywhere in the world. The ashes, tossed by my dad into the air, exploded into a cloud, like the poof of a magician's wand, and fell to the water's surface, seemingly disappeared. Then I'd noticed the fog of ash passing under our kayaks in an unexpectedly coherent form, like a white marine mammal spinning below us, giving an ethereal show. I remember thinking of swimming after this mysterious shape, diving out of the kayak and following it into the dark depths. Instead, I'd sat there and silently begged it, "Come back, come back."

Now a couple came meandering down the beach, snapping me back to the present moment. They paused a dozen feet away and gazed down at their smartphone and digital camera, respectively. It seemed they were talking about camera settings and photo filters, the optimal way to capture the living postcard in front of them.

Then, out of the corner of my eye, I noticed a blip in the backdrop, like a broken pixel made real: just beyond the crashing of waves, a small rounded object had surfaced and then disappeared. As the couple continued fiddling and discussing, I kept watch. Suddenly, a rounded head with glistening brown patterning broke the surface—a sea turtle. It blinked its hooded black eyes, which were round and reflective like oversize marbles, before dipping back below. Just: "peekaboo," as my son would say.

Tears welled in my eyes. The timing begged me, against all reason and belief, to think of that turtle as a mystical maternal incarnation, a winking gift from the universe. More than that, though, I was touched by the juxtaposition of the oblivious couple and the breathtaking sea creature. These little moments— the ripple in the water, the breaking of the smooth facade—are waiting for us always, if we're looking and ready. For a long time, I hadn't been looking or ready. I had been adjusting the camera settings and photo filters on my own image, just as I'd been taught and expected to do.

Instead of holding back, instead of worrying what this couple would think about the woman sitting on the beach before seven a.m. crying at the sight of the ocean, I let the tears go. "You've gotten a lot better at crying," my dad has repeatedly told me, smilingly, in recent years. Tears do come easily these days, not because I'm sad, but because my emotions live closer to the surface, like that turtle, casually poking up its head. This is partly the result of having a kid, an externalized heart that renders me permanently exposed. It's also the product of living more fully in my own skin, instead of as an outside observer of it. When you stop watching, you start feeling.

For so long, I'd monitored myself according to both reigning cultural ideals and a range of feminist critique. Now when it came to sex, I felt an unfurling playing in fast-forward, like one of those corny nature-in-spring time-lapse videos. It would be just our two bodies—and then losing any sense of having separate ones. Other times, it would be the insistent *fact* of separateness that sank me deep into my own body. In either case, I would forget about having been taught in so many insidious ways how to have sex by a culture that valued appearance over experience. This wasn't a wholesale rejection of aesthetics or outside influence, but rather the fact of embodiment, an expansion of possible sensation.

The waves shifted from rolling barrels to vertical walls that collapsed with a resounding crash. The sound brought me back to that fifteen-year-old girl in denim cutoffs walking down a beachside path some thirty miles south of here because a boy had invited her to a party. That girl had followed a different boy into a cabana and later written in her journal, "He wasn't taking advantage of me, I did exactly what I wanted & got exactly what I wanted, same w/him." Recently, while rereading that journal, I recalled the part of that story that I wanted to forget.

Soon after getting together with Snow, my high school boyfriend, I'd accidentally left the journal in his car, where his friends promptly discovered it and began reading aloud from my much earlier Hawaii entry: cabana, 69, titty fucking, "he comes, yada yada yada." Afterward, Snow called me on the phone, voice vibrating with outrage, and he said: "I didn't think you were that kind of girl." I understood that being "that kind of girl" would mean losing him. So I said: "I didn't want to do all of those things, it didn't happen like I wrote it, you don't understand, I only made it seem like I liked it, I felt pressured, it was really intense, I was just trying to get through it, I wanted to get away."

I stopped writing in the journal after that, and I stopped trusting which story was true. Both versions were refracted through what I felt these boys wanted of me. I was fifteen years old and already losing my own perspective. All these years later, I have gotten it back: I was a girl living in a world where women's desire is narrowed to being desired, and where physical and reputational danger lurk behind every sexual encounter. I was a girl living in a world that had granted women new liberties alongside new burdens and existing limitations. Both stories were true; both stories were a lie.

Now I dug my bare toes, painted a questionable shade of "vacation" turquoise, into a mound of speckled sand. *This just does* not *have the right consistency for sandcastles*, I thought, remembering my son's earlier failed attempts. "Too crumbly." Then I took some sand, damp with morning dew, and rubbed it into my calves like a light exfoliant and felt the prickle of stubble that I had no plans of shearing back now that my beach days were nearly over. This was part of my ongoing negotiation between belonging and being, internal feelings and external reality.

Dusting the sand off my legs, I thought of the question I asked myself years back on that porn set: *Is the joke on me?* The answer seemed obvious now. The culture was the joke and I had found my own way to laugh at it. Mostly, I wanted it to change. I wanted more than individually making do. Another question came to mind, one I'd asked a long while ago and that now seemed rhetorical: *I had inherited the right to be sexual, to have sex, but on what terms, and to whose advantage?* I wiped my hands on a beach towel and reached for one of the books in my bag.

After reading a couple of chapters, I padded in flip-flops back to our white rental minivan. I scanned the radio and found my usual preference of indefensible pop music. Woman singer, auto-tune, chord progressions, disco beat. My hips slightly rocked against the seat. I felt the familiar rising, the fizzing over of champagne, and spun the volume knob to the right. I rolled down the windows, letting the heat intermingle with the AC, and bit my lip thinking of what Christopher and I might do during the baby's midday nap.

Then it hit me. "Huh," I said aloud. "*Huh.*" There was no dancing woman in my head. Where was the gyrating, hair-flipping me of my mind's eye? The disembodied, surveyed self who had appeared for so many years whenever I listened to music on my own now seemed to be gone. In fact, I realized with a startle, it had been many months since I'd seen her. Clearly, this wasn't a result of having forsaken the joys of indefensible pop music, although admittedly I sometimes traded raunchy lyrics for NPR these days, what with the toddler often in the backseat. Nor was this evidence of having rejected the pleasures of sexual theater or erotic make-believe, as my fantasies and sex life could attest.

As I turned the car onto the scenic, winding road up to the condo, I realized that she wasn't gone. She was part of me, just one facet of an expansive, borderless self. The dancing woman wasn't visible in my mind's eye because right now she was behind the wheel. I was driving the car.

Acknowledgments

Thank you, Christopher. You understood and believed in this book more than anyone else (including, at times, myself). Words cannot begin to express what your support, humor, compassion, intelligence, and acceptance have meant. Lucky me that with you, I don't have to find just the right words. To my bubbaloons, my mista: You give me endless joy. I knew I wanted to be a "rad mom," but I couldn't have imagined having such a rad kid.

Now I find myself writing these words: *I could not have written this book without my mom.* Of course, I did just that, but only because of what she had already given me. Dad, I am grateful for the loving example you set for me, as well as your consistent willingness to support me in telling the truth about my life—even when it involves talking about your porn subscription. Sorry!

To my extended family: You have continually challenged notions of "normal" and "acceptable" family conversation. Thank you especially to my aunts, Sue and Judy, for reading that long-ago

Elle essay and turning it into a positive point of (eek) family conversation. To Margie and Wini for the dinners, hugs, and invocations of my mom. Thank you to Chris and Melanie, and the broader clan, for showing me that it's not just Bay Area hippies who can hang with my subject matter.

Elissa, my "sister," thanks for: Badlands nights, "white bagels," Japantown photo booths, endless Gchats, *Step Up 3D*, Bi-Rite cheese, and knowing my taste in TikToks (pranks, dancing firefighters, baby animals). Thank you to all the friends who figured during the living and/or writing of this book, including Amanda, Anna L., Anna P., Brian, Daniel, Jake, Jill, Katherine, Lynn, Rebecca, all my beloved Sara(h)s, Snow, Stacey, and Susan. I love you all.

To my editor, Victoria Savanh: Thank you for getting and believing in this book right from the start, and for your ongoing support, enthusiasm, and clarity of vision. Thank you, also, to the supremely talented team at Penguin Random House. My agent, Jamie Carr, for being so tireless, patient, compassionate, trustworthy, and savvy.

Sarah Hepola, I'm grateful for your brilliance, empathy, generosity, and wit, as a friend and editor. Peggy Orenstein, all those emails, talks, and dog walks changed me and this book for the better. Brit Schulte: Your insights were utterly essential in taking the manuscript where it needed to go, and they were delivered with such striking nuance and compassion. Stassa Edwards, I love the way your brain works and will be forever grateful for what I've learned from your edits here and elsewhere.

Thank you: Susie Banikarim and Koa Beck for giving me the job that made this book possible. To Julianne Escobedo Shepherd and all my Jezebel colleagues: You are a deranged dream team unlike any other. Kelly Bourdet and Alex Koppelman for making me a better writer and reporter. A throwback h/t to some *Salon* folks: Kevin Berger, Irin Carmon, Mark Follman, Kate Harding, Ruth Henrich, Kerry Lauerman, Page Rockwell, Rebecca Traister, Joan Walsh, and Mary Elizabeth Williams. To Laurie Abraham for expertly shepherding several essays that helped inform this book. Susannah Breslin, the trailblazer: I couldn't have envisioned this book, this life, had it not been for you. Susie Bright for the eternal inspiration.

To every interviewee: Thank you for your trust, honesty, inspiration, and bravery. Over the years, innumerable people have influenced my thinking around sex work and porn, but to name just a few: Lux Alptraum, Lynn Comella, Jessica Drake, Melissa Gira Grant, Conner Habib, Maxine Holloway, Tina Horn, Kayden Kross, Lotus Lain, Jiz Lee, Lorelei Lee, Sinnamon Love, Maggie McNeill, Mireille Miller-Young, Mickey Mod, Jill Nagle, Toni Newman, Lisa Palac, Constance Penley, Siouxsie Q, Rooster, Gayle Rubin, Dylan Ryan, Celine Parreñas Shimizu, Annie Sprinkle, Mike Stabile, Margo St. James, Tristan Taormino, Sallie Tisdale, Courtney Trouble, Linda Williams, and Madison Young. I'm deeply obliged to everyone within the adult industry who has shared their trust, perspectives, and insights.

In lieu of the impossibility of acknowledging every feminist theorist whose work has meaningfully shaped my life and views, many of whom are already mentioned throughout these pages, I want to specifically thank all the thinkers behind the 1984 *Pleasure and Danger*, which is as relevant as ever. This book is also indebted to academics currently researching and theorizing around women's sexuality, desire, agency, and empowerment, including Laina Bay-Cheng, Lori Brotto, Meredith Chivers, Debby Herbenick, Sharon Lamb, and Deborah Tolman.

Finally, much gratitude to Hank for napping in my lap while I labored away at this book.

Notes

EPIGRAPH

1. Deborah Treisman, "Miranda July on the Wild Contradictions of Marriage," *New Yorker*, August 28, 2017, https://www.newyorker.com/books/this-week-in-fiction/fiction-this-week-miranda-july-2017-9-4.

PROLOGUE: "GIRLS THESE DAYS"

1. Deborah L. Tolman, Steph M. Anderson, and Kimberly Belmonte, "Mobilizing Metaphor: Considering Complexities, Contradictions, and Contexts in Adolescent Girls' and Young Women's Sexual Agency," *Sex Roles* 73, no. 7 (2015): 298–310, https://doi.org/10.1007/s11199-015-0510-0.

CHAPTER 1: PERFECT 10

1. Brittney Cooper, *Eloquent Rage: A Black Feminist Discovers Her Superpower* (New York: Picador, 2018), 177.
2. Deborah L. Tolman, *Dilemmas of Desire: Teenage Girls Talk About Sexuality* (Cambridge, MA: Harvard University Press, 2005), 178–88.
3. Laina Y. Bay-Cheng, "The Agency Line: A Neoliberal Metric for Appraising Young Women's Sexuality," *Sex Roles* 73 (2015): 279–91, https://doi.org/10.1007/s11199-015-0452-6.

CHAPTER 2: ADULT

1. Laura Mulvey, "Visual Pleasure and Narrative Cinema," *Screen* 16, no. 3 (1975): 6–18, https://doi.org/10.1093/screen/16.3.6.

2. bell hooks, "The Oppositional Gaze: Black Female Spectators," in *Black Looks: Race and Representation* (Boston: South End Press, 1992), 115–31.

3. Jill Nagle, ed., introduction to *Whores and Other Feminists* (New York: Routledge, 1997), 1–15.

4. Lib Copel, "Naughty Takes Off," *Washington Post*, November 30, 2003, https://www.washingtonpost.com/archive/lifestyle/2003/11/30/naughty-takes-off/0a0d69db-1a1d-4f81-b11c-abd08101793e/?utm_term=.2bc598acffca\.

5. Lorena Garcia, *Respect Yourself, Protect Yourself: Latina Girls and Sexual Identity* (New York and London: New York University Press, 2012), 5.

6. Patricia Hill Collins, *Black Feminist Thought: Knowledge, Consciousness, and the Politics of Empowerment* (New York: Routledge, 2008), 145.

7. Melissa Gira Grant, "Organized Labor's Newest Heroes: Strippers," *The Atlantic*, November 19, 2012, https://www.theatlantic.com/sexes/archive/2012/11/organized-labors-newest-heroes-strippers/265376; Jacqueline Frances, "Strip Club Management and Racist 'Preferences,'" Jacq the Stripper, August 17, 2017, http://www.jacqthestripper.com/blog/2017/8/17/strip-club-management-and-racist-preferences.

8. Judith Butler, "Imitation and Gender Insubordination," in *The Lesbian and Gay Studies Reader*, ed. Henry Abelove, Michele Aina Barale, and David M. Halperin (New York: Routledge, 1993), 307–20.

9. Judith Butler, "Performative Acts and Gender Constitution: An Essay in Phenomenology and Feminist Theory," *Theatre Journal* 40, no. 4 (1988): 519–31, https://doi.org/10.2307/3207893.

10. Michael J. Bader, *Arousal: The Secret Logic of Sexual Fantasies* (New York: St. Martin's Griffin, 2003), 17–49.

CHAPTER 3: CAUTIONARY

1. Tressie McMillan Cottom, *Thick: And Other Essays* (New York: New Press, 2019), 37–72.

2. N. Tatiana Masters et al., "Sexual Scripts Among Young Heterosexually Active Men and Women: Continuity and Change," *Journal of Sex Research* 50, no. 5 (2013): 409–20, doi.org/10.1080/00224499.2012.661102.

3. Erving Goffman, *The Presentation of Self in Everyday Life* (New York: Anchor, 1959).

4. Judith Butler, *Gender Trouble: Feminism and the Subversion of Identity* (New York and London: Routledge, 2007), 46.

5. Lisa Palac, *The Edge of the Bed: How Dirty Pictures Changed My Life* (New York: Little, Brown and Company, 1998), 34–35.

6. Sallie Tisdale, *Talk Dirty to Me: An Intimate Philosophy of Sex* (New York: Doubleday, 1994), 9.

7. Carole S. Vance, "Pleasure and Danger: Toward a Politics of Sexuality," in *Pleasure and Danger: Exploring Female Sexuality*, ed. Carole S. Vance (London: Pandora, 1984), 6–7.

8. Jessica Benjamin, "The Bonds of Love: Rational Violence and Erotic Domination," *Feminist Studies* 6, no. 1 (1980): 144–74, https://doi .org/10.2307/3177655.

9. Heather A. Rupp and Kim Wallen, "Sex Differences in Response to Visual Sexual Stimuli: A Review," *Archives of Sexual Behavior* 37, no. 2 (2008): 206–18, https://doi.org/10.1007/s10508-007-9217-9.

10. Ellen Laan et al., "Women's Sexual and Emotional Responses to Male- and Female-Produced Erotica," *Archives of Sexual Behavior* 23, no. 2 (1994): 153–69, https://doi.org/10.1007/BF01542096; Erick Janssen, Deanna Carpenter, and Cynthia A. Graham, "Selecting Films for Sex Research: Gender Differences in Erotic Film Preferences," *Archives of Sexual Behavior* 32 (2003): 243–51, https://doi.org/10.1023 /A:1023413617648.

11. Ann Fessler, *The Girls Who Went Away: The Hidden History of Women Who Surrendered Children for Adoption in the Decades Before Roe v. Wade* (New York: Penguin Books, 2007), 9.

12. Miz Cracker, "Beware the Bachelorette! A Report from the Straight Lady Invasion of Gay Bars," *Slate*, August 13, 2015, https://slate .com/human-interest/2015/08/should-straight-women-go-to-gay -bars-a-drag-queen-reports-on-the-lady-invasion.html.

CHAPTER 4: ROUGH

1. "2017 Year in Review," Pornhub, January 9, 2017, https://www.pornhub .com/insights/2017-year-in-review.

2. James K. Ambler et al., "Consensual BDSM Facilitates Role-Specific Altered States of Consciousness: A Preliminary Study," *Psychology of*

Consciousness: Theory, Research, and Practice 4, no. 1 (2017): 75–91, https://doi.org/10.1037/cns0000097.

3. Ellen M. Lee et al., "Altered States of Consciousness During an Extreme Ritual," *PLoS ONE* 11, no. 5 (2016): e0153126, https://doi.org/10.1371/journal.pone.0153126.

CHAPTER 5: WINNING

1. Vance, *Pleasure and Danger*, 1.

2. Sigmund Freud, "On the Universal Tendency to Debasement in the Sphere of Love," in *The Standard Edition of the Complete Psychological Works of Sigmund Freud*, ed. James Strachey (London: Hogarth, 1964), 179–90.

3. Melissa Gira Grant, *Playing the Whore: The Work of Sex Work* (London and New York: Verso, 2014), 76; Jill Nagle, ed., introduction to *Whores and Other Feminists* (New York: Routledge, 1997), 1–15.

4. Carol Leigh, "The Whore Stigma with Margo St. James and Gail Pheterson," YouTube video, 2:14, March 9, 2012, https://www.youtube.com/watch?v=PlXV370ipEI.

5. Melissa Gira Grant, "There Is No Such Thing as a Slut," Al Jazeera America, July 15, 2014, http://america.aljazeera.com/opinions/2014/7/slut-shaming-sexworkgenderclass.html.

6. Gira Grant, *Playing the Whore*, 77.

7. Paul D. Trapnell, Cindy M. Meston, and Boris B. Gorzalka, "Spectatoring and the Relationship Between Body Image and Sexual Experience: Self-Focus or Self-Valence?" *Journal of Sex Research* 34, no. 3 (1997): 267–78, https://doi.org/10.1080/00224499709551893.

CHAPTER 6: FAKING

1. Ellen Huet, "The Dark Side of the Orgasmic Meditation Company," *Bloomberg Businessweek*, June 21, 2018, https://www.bloomberg.com/news/features/2018-06-18/the-dark-side-of-onetaste-the-orgasmic-meditation-company.

2. Charlene L. Muehlenhard and Sheena K. Shippee, "Men's and Women's Reports of Pretending Orgasm," *Journal of Sex Research* 47, no. 6 (2010): 552–67, https://doi.org/10.1080/00224490903171794.

3. Debby Herbenick et al., "Women's Sexual Satisfaction, Communication, and Reasons for (No Longer) Faking Orgasm: Findings from a

U.S. Probability Sample," *Archives of Sexual Behavior* 48, no. 8 (2019): 2461–72, https://doi.org/10.1007/s10508-019-01493-0.

4. Breanne Fahs, *Performing Sex: The Making and Unmaking of Women's Erotic Lives* (Albany, NY: SUNY Press, 2011), 31–69.

5. Debby Herbenick et al., "An Event-Level Analysis of the Sexual Characteristics and Composition Among Adults Ages 18 to 59: Results from a National Probability Sample in the United States," *Journal of Sexual Medicine* 7, suppl. 5 (2010): 346–61, https://doi.org/10.1111/j.1743-6109.2010.02020.x.

6. David A. Frederick et al., "Differences in Orgasm Frequency Among Gay, Lesbian, Bisexual, and Heterosexual Men and Women in a U.S. National Sample," *Archives of Sexual Behavior* 47, no. 1 (2018): 273–88, https://doi.org/10.1007/s10508-017-0939-z.

7. Justin R. Garcia et al., "Orgasm Occurrence by Sexual Orientation in a Sample of U.S. Singles," *Journal of Sexual Medicine* 11, no. 11 (2014): 2645–52, https://doi.org/10.1111/jsm.12669.

8. Elizabeth A. Armstrong, Paula England, and Alison C. K. Fogarty, "Accounting for Women's Orgasm and Sexual Enjoyment in College Hookups and Relationships," *American Sociological Review* 77, no. 3 (2012): 435–62, https://doi.org/10.1177/0003122412445802.

9. Tolman, "Mobilizing Metaphor."

10. Bay-Cheng, "The Agency Line."

11. Jochen Peter and Patti M. Valkenburg, "Adolescents and Pornography: A Review of 20 Years of Research," *Journal of Sex Research* 53, no. 4–5 (2016): 509–31, https://doi.org/10.1080/00224499.2016.1143441.

12. Aleksandar Štulhofer, Azra Tafro, and Taylor Kohut, "The Dynamics of Adolescents' Pornography Use and Psychological Well-being: A Six-Wave Latent Growth and Latent Class Modeling Approach," *European Child & Adolescent Psychiatry* 28, no. 12 (2019): 1567–79, https://doi.org/10.1007/s00787-019-01318-4.

CHAPTER 7: JUST FRIENDS

1. Tisdale, *Talk Dirty to Me*, 8.

2. Sharon Lamb, "Porn as a Pathway to Empowerment? A Response to Peterson's Commentary," *Sex Roles* 62 (2010), 314–17, https://doi.org/10.1007/s11199-010-9756-8.

CHAPTER 8: HEARTBEATS

1. Tom Junod, "The Falling Man," Esquire.com, September 9, 2016, https://www.esquire.com/news-politics/a48031/the-falling-man -tom-junod/.

CHAPTER 9: PORN VALLEY

1. Crystal A. Jackson et al., "EXPOsing Men's Gender Role Attitudes as Porn Superfans," *Sociological Forum* 34, no. 2 (2019): 483–500, https://doi.org/10.1111/socf.12506.

CHAPTER 10: "MOMS"

1. Susan Sontag, *As Consciousness Is Harnessed to Flesh: Journals and Notebooks 1964–1980*, ed. David Rieff (New York: Farrar, Straus and Giroux, 2012), 21.

2. Esther Perel, *Mating in Captivity: Unlocking Erotic Intelligence* (New York: HarperCollins, 2007), 151.

CHAPTER 11: I WANT

1. Grant, *Playing the Whore*, 76.
2. Palac, *The Edge of the Bed*, 140.
3. Tisdale, *Talk Dirty to Me*, 16.